Reflecting on WWII, Manzanar, and the WRA

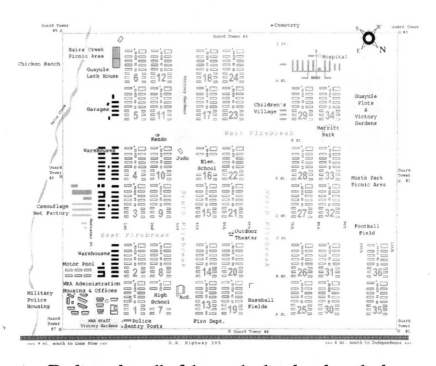

Dedicated to all of those who lived and worked
behind the fence in WWII Manzanar

Arthur L. Williams

Produced by:

FriesenPress
Suite 300 – 852 Fort Street
Victoria, BC, Canada V8W 1H8

www.friesenpress.com

Distributed to the trade by The Ingram Book Company

In REFLECTING ON WWII, MANZANAR, and the WRA, Art Williams has presented the reader with a view of WWII Manzanar history from a completely new perspective. As a Caucasian teenager living with his family in the Manzanar War Relocation Center, Williams has pulled from personal experience and exhaustive research to reveal in-depth the War Relocation Authority's (WRA) challenges in providing for the needs of 10,000 Japanese Americans unjustly incarcerated at Manzanar during World War II. Complementing his story are discussions on the government's role in their removal, and on Manzanar camp construction, as well as coverage of Owens Valley and WWII history and of the personal side of the men, women, and children who lived alongside the interned Japanese Americans. Anyone teaching west coast Asian studies should have a copy of this book in their library.

Richard Potashin, Manzanar Historian

TABLE OF CONTENTS

MANZANAR DESIGNATIONS

January 1972 - California Registered Historic Landmark No. 850

July 30, 1979 - National Register of Historic Places

February 1985 - National Historic Landmark

March 3, 1992 - National Historic Site

INTRODUCTION

After the bombing of Pearl Harbor by Japan in 1941, tens of thousands of people of Japanese descent were evacuated from the West Coast to US government assembly centers and relocation camps and interned there for the duration of WWII. Manzanar was the first of such camps and housed over 10,000 Japanese-American men, women, and children within a one-mile-square fenced area. Unbelievably, in the years since WWII, we have largely failed to teach our children about this scar in our history, although recently there has been a growing renewal of interest in this area. Most Americans have no idea that so many of our nation's residents were forced to live out the war in centers in some of the hottest, coldest, and driest places in our nation. Even fewer know that there was a non-Japanese-American workforce also living within these camps. Inside the same fenced boundary of Manzanar alone, along with their families, lived over 200 War Relocation Authority (WRA) staff members whose jobs were to ensure that the internees' basic needs were provided for and to see the camp ran as smoothly as possible. These people were teachers, doctors, nurses, and engineers, to name a few. In total, over four hundred Americans who were not evacuees lived inside the same fenced area. This book is an attempt to share the feelings and challenges of the employees who managed and directed the daily operations of these camps. This book not only highlights their existence, but also discusses the ups and downs of their daily lives as well as their reliance on a work force of thousands of interned Japanese Americans. As the teenage son of two WRA staff members, I was one of those living within the confines of the camp at Manzanar. In addition to my own experiences living in Manzanar, as well as of visiting the Tule Lake Internment Camp during its operation, I have spent over ten years accumulating information on this subject. This book was written out of my unwillingness to see the existence of so many from inside the camp, living and working alongside the Japanese Americans, lost to history.

This book focuses not on the story of the Japanese Americans who were interned in Manzanar, but on the staff members who lived their lives in and around Manzanar at the same time. For a complete historical picture of Manzanar, one must know that there were three distinct groups of people living in and around the camp: the evacuees, the WRA staff and their families, and the Military Police (MPs) in charge of guarding the camp. A focus on the civilian employees of the WRA allows for a new perspective of life within Manzanar. Besides the personal look at life within camp, this book also goes into great detail on the creation, both conceptual and physical, of the camp. Covering the camp from prehistory to site selection, to design, construction, operation, post WWII demolition, and to the Manzanar of today, brings yet another view of the camp. For historical reference, this book provides a look at the changes on the West Coast during WWII and discusses the forced evacuation of the Japanese Americans. It describes the diversities within the Japanese-American population and the price paid for throwing together groups of people with vastly dissimilar cultures and motivations into a small, confined space, and discusses some of the consequences of the government's actions during this process.

While doing research for a separate project, I noticed that, although lists have been compiled and published of the Japanese Americans that were forced to live in Manzanar, nowhere were the WRA employees and their families recorded. To this end, I have compiled a list of all the WRA staff and family members that I could find who lived at any time within the confines of Manzanar. This information will, most likely, be of interest only to descendants of these people, but I feel their time in camp was historically significant. I have also compiled employee lists for two additional groups of people—those of the Wartime Civil Control Administration (WCCA), who were the original startup employees and preceded the WRA in managing Manzanar's daily struggles, and of the US Army Military Police (MPs). These lists are not exhaustive and are constantly growing, but are far beyond those which, to my knowledge, have previously been recorded.

My hope for this book is threefold: that readers gain a broader perspective of all the lives behind Manzanar's fences, that they get a better feel for life in California during WWII, and that they acquire additional information about one of the most controversial events in our nation's history.

ACRONYMS

Due to the subject of this book, I use many acronyms throughout. Although I define each one as it first appears, I understand how difficult it might be to remember them all. To clarify things, I have included most of the acronyms below for reference.

Capt.	US Army Captain
CCC	Civilian Conservation Corp.
Col.	Colonel
EO	Executive Order
EPA	Environmental Protection Agency

FBI	Federal Bureau of Investigation
FDR	Franklin Delano Roosevelt
Gen.	General
IJN	Imperial Japanese Navy
INS	Immigration and Naturalization Service
JACL	Japanese American Citizens League
LADWP	Los Angeles Department of Water and Power
Lt.	Lieutenant
MAP	Manzanar Appointed Personnel
MP	US Army Military Police
MWRC	Manzanar War Relocation Center
NPS	National Park Service
OPA	Office of Price Administration
ONI	Office of Naval Intelligence
OVRC	Owens Valley Reception Center
PCH	Pacific Coast Highway
Pvt.	US Army Private
QMC	Quarter Master Corp.
Supt.	Superintendent
UCLA	University of California Los Angeles
UNRRA	United Nations Relief and Rehabilitation Agency
USO	United Service Organizations
V.E. Day	Victory in Europe, marking the end of WWII in Europe
VFW	Veterans of Foreign Wars
V.J. Day	Victory in Japan, marking the end of WWII with Japan
WASP	Women Air Force Service Pilots
WCCA	Wartime Civil Control Administration
WDC	Western Defense Command
WPA	Works Progress Administration
WRA	War Relocation Authority
WWII	World War Two
YMCA	Young Men's Christian Association
YWCA	Young Women's Christian Association

HISTORICAL DATES

October 14, 1940:
US Nationality Act of 1940 requires all resident aliens to register annually. 91,858 Japanese register.

December 7, 1941:
Japan bombs the US naval base and fleet in Pearl Harbor, Hawaii. US Navy loses most of its Pacific fleet. Four carriers, the Lexington, Enterprise, Hornet, and Yorktown, are not in Pearl Harbor and remain as our only defense force.

December 8, 1941:
At the same time they were attacking Pearl Harbor, Japan attacks Wake Island and invades Guam. Because both islands are west of the International Date Line, the attacks are dated December 8.

December 11, 1941:
The Western Defense Command (WDC) is established and the West Coast of the United States is declared a "theater of war."

December 20, 1941: Japanese sub I-17 shells tanker off Cape Mendocino.

December 23, 1941:
After a courageous battle in which two Japanese destroyers are sunk, Wake Island falls into Japanese hands.

December 29, 1941:
All enemy aliens in California, Oregon, Washington, Montana, Idaho, Utah, and Nevada ordered to surrender all contraband, including short wave radios, cameras, guns, and binoculars.

January 25, 1942:
Roberts Commission Report on Pearl Harbor blames Gen. Short and Adm. Kimmel for not taking precautions against the attack. The report also says that Japanese spies who were not attached to the Japanese Consular Corps were on the island of Oahu.

January 30, 1942:
California Congressional Delegation meets in Washington to urge the evacuation of enemy aliens from the West Coast.

February 2, 1942:
Registration of enemy aliens begins. FBI starts random search and seizure raids at the homes and businesses of Japanese aliens.

February 15, 1942:
First exodus of enemy aliens from restricted military zones.

February 16, 1942:
Department of Justice rounds up 1,266 alien Japanese along the West Coast.

February 19, 1942:
President Franklin D. Roosevelt signs Executive Order 9066 empowering the U.S. Army to designate areas from which "any or all persons may be excluded."

February 23, 1942:
Japanese submarine I-17 shells Ellwood Oil Facility north of Santa Barbara.

February 25, 1942:
"Battle of Los Angeles." Trigger-happy artillery batteries fire at suspected aircraft, killing three civilians with friendly fire. Thirty-thousand troops are assigned to defend the West Coast between Fort McArthur and Santa Barbara.

March 11, 1942:
The Wartime Civil Control Administration (WCCA) is established for the exclusion of certain civilians from the West Coast.

March 17, 1942:
Construction of Owens Valley Reception Center (OVRC) at Manzanar begins.

March 18, 1942:
Executive Order 9102 establishes the War Relocation Authority (WRA).

March 21, 1942:
First evacuees arrive at Manzanar.

March 25, 1942:
Fearing Japanese attack, school board plans to issue I.D. tags to all school children on the West Coast.

March 31, 1942:
San Francisco News reports that Joe DiMaggio's elderly Italian parents could be evacuated from San Francisco due to their enemy alien status.

April 18, 1942:
Jimmy Doolittle and 16 Mitchell B-25's take off from the USS Hornet and bomb Japan in retaliation for Pearl Harbor attack. The offensive boosts morale but inflicts little damage.

April 28, 1942:
The population of Manzanar reaches 7,101.

May 4-8, 1942:
Battle of the Coral Sea. US Navy loses the carrier Lexington, and the Yorktown sustains heavy damage. Japan loses one light carrier. A tactical victory for Japan.

June 1, 1942:
Administration of Manzanar transferred from the WCCA to the WRA. OVRC is renamed Manzanar War Relocation Center.

June 4, 1942:
Battle of Midway. Japan loses four carriers and the US Navy loses the Yorktown. The US Navy is down to two carriers in the Pacific. Japan has lost five. The Battle of Midway is a tactical victory for the US Navy. Japan is still undefeated on land and has removed all British, Dutch, and Americans from South Asia.

June 1942:
Children's Village Orphanage is established in Manzanar. Of the ten camps, Manzanar has the only orphanage, which eventually reaches a population of over 100.

August 7, 1942:
Completion of evacuation of all persons of Japanese ancestry from the West Coast. The first USA land based offensive in the Pacific takes place in the Solomon Islands, Guadalcanal.

September 9, 1942:
Japanese seaplane launched from submarine I-25 bombs Mt. Emily near Brookings, Oregon. Japan scores first aerial attack ever to American homeland.

September 14, 1942:
Manzanar Elementary School opens with 1,001 students in grades 1 through 6.

September 22, 1942:
Internee numbers peak at 10,046, more than doubling the total Inyo County population.

October 15, 1942:
Manzanar High School opens with 1,376 students in grades 7 through 12.

October 27, 1942:
Japan sinks USS Hornet in battle of Santa Cruz Islands. US down to one sole aircraft carrier.

November 15, 1942:
First evacuee released for "permanent relocation." First two volunteers for the army leave Manzanar for Camp Savage, Minnesota. There would ultimately be 17,000 Japanese Americans serving in the US Army during WWII.

November 1942:
Construction of last of eight Manzanar guard towers completed.

November 24, 1942:
Ralph P. Merritt becomes Project Director at Manzanar.

December 6, 1942:
Manzanar riot erupts. Military Police fire into a large crowd gathered at the Internal Security Police Station demanding the release of Harry Ueno, arrested for allegedly assaulting Fred Tayama. James Ito is killed and ten other internees wounded. One later dies.

February 10, 1943:
Loyalty questionnaire circulated to internees in all ten relocation camps. Those proclaiming loyalty to the US will be given the opportunity to relocate to an area other than the West Coast. The young men proclaiming loyalty to the US will become eligible for the draft. Those stating loyalty to Japan are soon relocated to the WRA camp at Tule Lake and become exempt from the draft. Approximately 500 of those claiming loyalty to Japan are to be transported to Mexico and return to Japan aboard a Swedish ship during the war. Over 5,000 are returned to Japan after the war.

July 31, 1943:
Tule Lake Relocation Center is designated a center for all disloyal internees.

October 9, 1943:
The first internees leave Manzanar for the Tule Lake Center.

January 20, 1944:
Selective Service Induction resumes for Japanese Americans.

February 19, 1944:
Cornerstone ceremony held to begin construction of high school auditorium/gym.

February 26, 1944:
The last of a total of 2,165 Manzanar internees claiming loyalty to Japan are relocated to the Tule Lake Center.

June 1944:
Manzanar Elementary School classrooms centrally located into one block—
Block 16.

November 1944:
First Japanese bomb-laden hydrogen balloon launched from Japan lands on
US soil.

December 18, 1944:
In a pair of rulings the US Supreme Court upholds the wartime relocation of
Japanese Americans, but states undeniably loyal Americans of Japanese ancestry
cannot continue to be detained.

January 2,1945:
The West Coast Exclusion Order is lifted.

February 1, 1945:
Seven mess halls close as Manzanar population drops.

February 14 to March 26, 1945:
Battle for Iwo Jima

May 8, 1945:
Victory in Europe (VE Day)

May 12, 1945:
President Franklin Delano Roosevelt dies. Harry S. Truman takes office.

May 29, 1945:
Manzanar school classes meet for the last time.

June 21, 1945: Battle for Okinawa ends.

July 30, 1945:
Japanese sub sinks US Indianapolis in Philippine Sea. Six hundred US sailors die.

August 1, 1945:
Ralph Merritt receives Administration Notice 289 requiring the scheduled relocation of all remaining internees.

August 6, 1945:
Atomic bomb dropped on city of Hiroshima.

August 14, 1945:
Emperor Hirohito announces Japan's surrender to the United States.

August 15, 1945:
Victory in Japan (VJ Day)

September 2, 1945:
Japan's surrender signed aboard the USS Missouri.

September 4, 1945:
The WDC revokes all restrictions against Japanese Americans.

November 21, 1945:
The last internee, a four year old boy, leaves Manzanar at 11:00 a.m.

June 30, 1946:
The War Relocation Authority is officially disbanded.

April 24, 1997:
City of Los Angeles transfers 814 acres, including 540 acres within Manzanar's original fenced camp area, to the National Park Service (NPS).

April 24, 2004:
NPS holds official grand opening of the Manzanar National Historic Site.

May 22, 2004:
Reunion for former WRA employees and their families held at Manzanar.

CHAPTER I
A BRIEF HISTORY OF THE OWENS VALLEY

Former Site of Manzanar War Relocation Center

SETTING

The site of Manzanar, with its personal history so intertwined with that of my own, rests approximately in the center of the Owens Valley, a long narrow valley in Inyo County, California, approximately twelve miles wide and 100 miles long—the deepest valley on the North American continent. The word "Inyo" is an Indian word said to mean, "The dwelling place of a great spirit."

The Sierra Nevada Mountains to the west and the Inyo White Mountains to the east were uplifted to heights of over 14,000 feet. Fully fourteen of the fifteen peaks in California reaching above 14,000 feet are in Inyo County and border Owens Valley. Mt. Whitney, the highest point in the lower forty-eight states, and Bad Water, the lowest point on the North American continent are both in Inyo County, about 100 miles apart. This region offers a vast array of geologic features such as lava flows, faulting and uplifting, metamorphosed ocean sediments to the east, and massive granite formations of the Sierra Nevada Mountains to the west. The location, formation, and human activities of this area have combined to create a landscape and climate that are at once stunning and yet harsh and unforgiving.

Many who lived in Manzanar retain vivid memories of not only the scorching summers, freezing winters, and choking dust storms, but also of the first beautiful winter snow on the mountaintops each year. Throughout the year, this area experiences temperatures from below freezing to significantly above 100°F. Due to the rain shadow effect, this high desert receives fewer than five inches of rainfall each year. It is also well known for its relentless winds which reach upwards of sixty miles per hour. All of these climatic elements combined to make the internment and the working and living conditions at Manzanar War Relocation Center even more challenging than they might have been in a more hospitable location.

EARLY HISTORY

The Manzanar War Relocation Center and its related stories occupy only a small, albeit powerful niche in an overall history of the Owens Valley. Long before WWII and for thousands of years, Owens Valley was inhabited by the descendants of native Shoshone and Paiute peoples. In 1833, Captain Joe Walker became the first recorded person of European descent to pass through the valley. Walker brought the second wagon train from the east through this valley in 1843. The Walker River and Walker Pass are named for him. Prospectors would follow approximately a decade later, and mining would begin in 1860. The miners were followed by cattle ranchers who provided beef for the mining camps.

California

In 1861, Samuel Addison Bishop and his wife drove 650 head of cattle from Fort Tejon to an area now named Bishop in honor of him. A war arose out of the conflict between the cattlemen and the Native Americans. At one point all non-natives were driven out of Owens Valley. In 1863, the US Cavalry was brought in, and after several battles, they succeeded in rounding up 908 Native Americans and forcing them 175 miles from Independence, in the Owens Valley, to Ft. Tejon. Only 850 successfully completed the arduous journey. In the end, the death toll from these conflicts exceeded 1,000 Native Americans along with untold prospectors, miners, cattlemen, and US Army cavalrymen. Following the removal of the Native Americans, settlers established farms in the valley's rich soil, and tree crops thrived. It was a new era in Owens Valley history.

For the next thirty years, Owens Valley read like a page out of the old west, complete with steamships, mines, gambling, prostitution, and rampant crime. In 1872, Owens Lake operated its first steamship, the Bessie Brady, followed by the Mollie Stevens five years later. Both ships hauled mining materials east to Keeler and on the return west, gold and silver. In 1878, Inyo County Sheriff Passmore was shot and killed in Lone Pine. The next year the new lawman, Sheriff Moore, was shot and killed in Independence. The Carson Colorado Narrow Gauge Railroad arrived from the north to move mining supplies and ore in 1883, and twenty-seven years later, the broad gauge arrived from the south, bringing supplies to build an aqueduct which would change the face of the valley forever.

At one time, the southern end of Owens Valley was dominated by Owens Lake, a huge body of water covering upwards of 108 square miles and spanning nearly the entire width of the valley. This desert lake, a product of volcanic action to the south, was fed by the Owens River and other nearby streams and was the lifeblood of a once thriving farming community. Sadly, the farming potential of the Owens Valley was never realized.

A PATTERN OF DECEIT

With agriculture continuing to develop in Owens Valley, helped along by the booming mining camps of Tonopah and Goldfield—ready markets for the valley's commodities—the outlook seemed bright for a prospering Owens Valley future. The promise of prosperity was further boosted with the help of a prominent agricultural developer from Southern California, George Chaffey, who had under the auspices of the Owens Valley Improvement Company, laid the groundwork for an agricultural subdivision complete with a town site, water system, and 20,000 fruit trees. Farms were prospering and local businesses were growing beyond anything the Owens Valley had previously experienced. On a per acre basis, farming within the area had the potential to equal that of the illustrious San Joaquin Valley. The recently created Federal Reclamation Service recognized the great potential for expanding Owens Valley agriculture by constructing a major irrigation project anchored by a storage reservoir in Long Valley and canals running down the east and west sides of the valley. At the behest of supervising engineer for the Reclamation Service, Joseph B. Lippincott, studies were initiated to explore the feasibility of such a project. Valley residents besieged Washington with petitions supporting the project. Glowing editorials streamed forth from local newspapers. However, not one square yard of concrete was ever poured or one irrigation gate ever installed. Reclamation's irrigation project never got beyond the planning stage, as in a gross example of conflict of interest, Lippincott was hired by the Los Angeles Water Department as a consultant to locate water for its own city. The city of Los Angeles at that time was growing rapidly, and along with its mushrooming population came an ever increasing need for water. The LA Water Department informed their new consultant that they wanted the water from the Owens Valley. It's true that money talks, and as such, Lippincott sided with the bigger city, agreeing that the needs of LA superseded those of Owens Valley agriculture. The city hired agents, most prominently, Fred Eaton, a former mayor of Los Angeles, to pose as ranchers and employees of the Reclamation Service with the intention of buying up the land in the southern half of the Owens Valley. In doing so, they became the new owners of the riparian (water) rights to the Owens River and most of the streams that fed into it. They misled the locals, telling them they were only interested in moving the "surplus" water to Los Angeles. In 1913, the city completed an aqueduct 233 miles long, including over forty miles of tunnels, which diverted the Owens River and many of the small streams feeding into the Owens Lake. With the completion of this new $24,600,000 aqueduct, the City of Los Angeles Department of Water and Power (LADWP) succeeded in diverting all the water from Owens Valley to the nearly complete demise of the local farms. The people from the valley who had staked their future on a federal irrigation project found themselves without water or hope. This loss of water also brought the downfall to the many businesses that had arisen to support the agricultural community, and that were supported by its dollars. As a final insult, Los Angeles would proceed to deliver all of *their* surplus water to farms in the San Fernando and Los Angeles basin. They also succeeded in persuading President Theodore Roosevelt to approve the expansion of the forest service boundary down to the Owens Valley floor, adding an additional 275 thousand acres to the forest, thus eliminating any future growth that might require additional water. Locals were justifiably outraged. In 1924, dynamiting of the aqueduct by irate valley inhabitants began and did not stop until 1927. During one year alone, the aqueduct was dynamited six times. To say the locals detested everything that Los Angeles represented would be an understatement. In the end, over five hundred farms and countless additional businesses were lost. With property prices dramatically depressed, Los Angeles bought up much of the valley—eventually owning 95% of all farmland and 85% of all town properties—eliminating any hope for a rebirth of this once burgeoning community. Farming in the area ceased and the entire small community of Manzanar disappeared completely with the removal of the last farmhouse in 1935. The only evidence of Manzanar's farming days became the slowly dying orchards and a few concrete flumes. The area which had once been productive farmland decayed into alkali flats, sand, and sage and would remain that way until WWII. Loss of the valley's water dealt a devastating blow to the local inhabitants and created a hatred for government officials which would resurface years later as Manzanar became home to over 10,000 unwilling new residents.

MY OWENS VALLEY LEGACY

My family's association with Manzanar began over a hundred years ago during the area's heyday as a farming community. My grandparents, Arthur Fredric and Leona Williams, father, Arthur Loren, and two aunts, Hazel and Dorothy, lived on a small apple farm in Manzanar thirty years before there was a war relocation center. At that time, Manzanar (Spanish for "apple orchard") was a small fruit growing community. The town consisted of a post office, school house, general store, blacksmith shop, and a town hall which was used for everything from church services, dances, and meetings, to funerals and fruit packing. At various dances and performances there, my grandfather could be heard playing his guitar or the community's piano while my father sang. Aunt Hazel Williams (McLeod), who lived to be almost 102, identified herself, the little girl directly under the horse's head, and my father, the boy right under the window on the back left, in the picture below which was taken in front of Manzanar's town hall.

Town of Manzanar 1916

My father and aunt in front of Manzanar Town Hall 1916

Music and dancing weren't the only pastimes in Manzanar's farming days. At the mouth of the nearby Georges Creek Canyon, local community members built a campsite which one might have called their private community retreat. At the camp were tables and two double beds elaborately crafted out of willows. My father told me his uncles had planted trout in Georges Creek. Families would load their wagon, hook up the team, pack up the kids, and travel the short distance to the site. Upon arriving, camp would be set up and stones would be arranged in the creek to

5

hold melons and milk in the cold water. When he was a young boy, my father had started going there with his father. He loved the camping and fishing and loved the area for its remoteness. Once he was deemed old enough, he took a horse and mule and packed up into the Sierras every year, staying alone and deer hunting for two weeks at a time. In turn, I remember going to Georges Creek as a boy in the 1930s. Sometime during the war, while we lived in the evacuee camp, the Georges Creek campsite was destroyed by campers for firewood. Many of us continued to go there and camp out, but it never had the same feeling. The thought of outsiders moving in on our "private" campsite was totally unacceptable. As for my father, as much as he loved the Georges Creek campsite, he never returned once "outsiders" started using the area. He shared a sentiment with many raised in the Owens Valley—that certain areas of this valley were special to the locals and should be off limits to anyone else.

In 1917, shortly after leaving the ranch, my grandfather, then only 47, passed away. My father, along with my aunts, and my grandmother would face difficult times without my grandfather. My grandfather had been the rock that had held the family together, providing security, income, and comfort. After grandfather passed away, my father and Hazel were forced to quit school to support their mother and younger sister Dorothy. Just when things looked as if they could not get worse, Aunt Dorothy, then six years old, passed away from diphtheria. Aunt Hazel never got over the loss of her father and little sister. To her and to my father, the years living on the Manzanar farm, before the grievous loss of their father and little sister, were their happiest. Dad and Aunt Hazel often spoke contentedly of when they were all living together on their family farm. There was frequent reminiscing about the artesian well on their property—the water table so high deep ditches had to be dug to drain the farmland. They also talked often about the numerous ponds brimming with migrating ducks and geese.

My cousin, Warren McLeod, and I on a family
camping trip to our grandparents' old farm - 1937

In my youth, I cannot remember taking a vacation that was not spent visiting the old apple farm.

Most vacations were spent camping out on its site—now the property of the City of Los Angeles. Each year we returned to see that a few more apple trees had been replaced with native vegetation. It was tough for the apple trees to survive without water. Yet, my father and Aunt Hazel never stopped loving the place. My mother went along on those trips, but neither she nor I shared or understood the feelings that my father and Aunt Hazel had for this desolate looking place. The two of them, on the other hand, seemed to be desperately trying to relive a time in their lives when they had enjoyed the security and love of their father and little Dorothy.

In 1938, while living in Southern California, my father leased a farm in Owens Valley. He saw this as his opportunity to recreate those happy years that he had enjoyed as a young boy. He equipped the 500 acres with livestock and farm equipment, and made a deal with a friend to farm it. The business arrangement and tough farming conditions met with failure. My mother, baby brother Tom, and I lived on the farm for one long, miserable year to farm, liquidate assets, and recover part of my father's investment. During this time my father continued to hold his job and live in Southern California. The ranch experience did not dampen my father's love for Owens Valley, but for me it intensified a growing contempt for the place. Living on the farm was really tough, and for a kid just eleven years old, I had to grow up fast. There was no longer any playing with other kids or going to the beach as I had enjoyed doing in Southern California. This farming was hard work. My lightest days were the ones in which I went to school. Weekends were filled with work from morning to night—planting, watering, weeding, harvesting, hauling, and selling. I learned that life on our farm was endless work from sun up to sun down and it only escalated during the summer months. The list of things that had to be done was endless. With the burning memory of my father's failed farming experience, my mother and I, who had never enjoyed spending each vacation camping out at the old Manzanar farm site, developed a loathing for Owens Valley.

When my mother, brother, and I finally moved away from the farm and returned to Redondo Beach, mother and I hoped it would be forever. We would have been happy never again setting foot in the Owens Valley. As fate would have it, after a couple of years of living my dream in a beach town, my father came upon another opportunity to return to Owens Valley. He applied for a position at the Owens Valley Reception Center (OVRC) with the Wartime Civil Control Administration (WCCA). I do not recall my mother's reaction, but as a young teenager, I was devastated, angry, and heartbroken. I was one month away from graduating from the eighth grade with my friends in Redondo, and I had had enough of Manzanar and the Owens Valley. I felt I was being ordered to return for a second term in hell. We did, though, go back to Manzanar, live inside the war relocation camp alongside the evacuees, and like them in some ways, learn to adjust. I discovered that the absence of the farm, with its endless list of chores, and the presence of other camp kids to hang out with—something I didn't have on the farm—made this Manzanar experience far less detestable than the last. After a year, I settled into life in the valley and found it was not so bad after all, but my time there would never rival my happiest years living at the beach.

When the Manzanar camp closed, everyone including evacuees, staff and their families, and the Military Police (MPs) left, scattered in all directions. There had been nearly a hundred staff children living in the camp, a number of whom had become close friends, yet for nearly five decades, I had not seen or heard from any of them since the camp's closure. As for the camp itself, all but one of the wooden structures was removed, leaving nothing resembling the camp that once existed—nothing to come back to. The camp we had once known had disappeared. Yet years later, as improbable as it may seem, and in spite of the great disappointment I felt having been forced to return to Manzanar so long ago, I now find I share my father's love for Owens Valley. The beauty I see in the valley, and its surrounding mountains, and my memories of long ago have finally brought me back—back to the valley, to locating my old friends, and ultimately to the creation of this book. These days I and my old friend and fellow Manzanar resident, Fred Causey, are able to do occasional docent work at Manzanar. Although Fred and I essentially lived the same life in camp, I cannot, as he does, state that my years in Manzanar were some of the best in my life, but time has certainly softened my image of the place.

Town of Independence, California - 1943

A TALE OF TWO TOWNS

There are two small towns on either side of Manzanar. At just six miles away, Independence, with a population during WWII of considerably less than a thousand, is the closest to Manzanar. Ten miles to the south of Manzanar is Lone Pine with a population of more than double that of Independence. The Inyo County seat, established in 1866, is in Independence. Before and during the war, Lone Pine's financial survival depended primarily upon nearby mining operations, tourism, and the movie industry. Due to its unique geology, consistently sunny days, and open expanses, this area was and still is something of a hotbed for movie locations. Over 400 movies have been filmed in the area to date. At times, two production companies could be filming out of Lone Pine simultaneously. It was big business for the community. Also, both small towns have relied for years on tourism and thru traffic between Los Angeles and Reno, Nevada. Lone Pine is the gateway to Mt. Whitney and to Death Valley as well as a common stopover spot after coming across the desert.

A look at Independence in the early 1940s would have told you how dependent this small town actually was on thru traffic. Despite its small size, Independence was dominated by five service stations, four auto mechanic shops, four cafes, two hotels, and a motel. Tourists who broke down on their way through could find a place to get their car repaired as well as a place to eat and a place to stay, but they had better have deep pockets, because there was little sympathy or respect shown for out-of-towners there—especially those from Los Angeles. I make this statement from firsthand experience as I worked in one of the Independence gas stations while going to high school. The owner/mechanic was my boss. He knew all the tricks of the trade and taught me many of them. I could write a book on how to clip tourists with car trouble in an isolated small town. I was always told to check the oil, because that was where he made big bucks. My boss would have me pour the oil into the engine quickly, not letting the oil can sit and drip dry, for he had a big drum in the back to collect the oil leftover in the cans after the quick fill. As viscous as oil is, this amounted to considerable oil over time. He would then have me use this oil for the oil changes I performed. In effect, he was selling the same oil twice. He would also drive to Los Angeles and buy a load of cheap retread tires to sell to the tourists passing through, feeling that, if there was a problem, it was highly unlikely the hapless customer would make the trip all the way back to complain. I do remember one instance when two fellows came in on their spare, bought one of the bosses retreads and happily drove off. In less than twenty minutes they were back. The sidewall had blown out and they wanted the tire replaced for free. Did they get it? Not from my boss. His standard answer was repeated at stations throughout town. "Don't you know there's a war on?" When it came to engine problems he was a creative genius at maximizing a profit. He taught me a lot about servicing and repairing cars and I have always appreciated it. After leaving Manzanar, I had lost track of him for over ten years when I happened upon him scratching out a living in the Mojave Desert. He had the only gas station or repair shop for miles in either direction. There he was with his ever present, positive attitude touting "location, location, location." It was the perfect place for a man of his talents. I always saw him as a survivor—a symbol of what it takes to survive in this ever changing environment where creature comforts are scarce.

Town of Lone Pine, California - 1943

Another character I remember is Frenchie. Whenever I closed up the gas station at night, I would go to the Pines Cafe. Frenchie was the chef and owner. One night I came in, prepared to order my usual breaded veal cutlets, only to notice that they were no longer on the menu. After I made something of a fuss, Frenchie came out of the kitchen and said, "Order the chicken fried steak."

"But I don't want a chicken fried steak. I want the veal. I eat the veal every time I'm in."

"Don't you know the difference between veal cutlets and chicken fried steak? You put white gravy on the veal, and brown gravy on the chicken fried steak. Order the chicken fried steak."

Confused, I stammered, "There must be more to it than the color of the gravy."

Frenchie's reply, "Not in the Pines Cafe."

Whatever Frenchie learned in France about cooking, he left there. He was another local who left propriety at the door in order to squeeze a living out of Independence. In this case, even the locals were subject to his corner cutting techniques.

One evening after locking up the Union Service Station, I went to the Pines Cafe for my usual. Frenchie came out of the kitchen and said, "Today is a special day. It is Bastille Day." He told us this was the day the people of France rose up against the king and won their freedom. Totally out of character, Frenchie started singing

"La Marseillaise" with passion. After he finished, he said, "We have lost it all to the Germans. They have taken our bread, cheese, wine, and women. We have lost everything." This was a reminder that we were not just losing the war in the Pacific but also in Europe.

In those days there seemed to be a number of single old men in town. Down by the cemetery and the creek, along with one old outhouse, were several shacks where these men lived. They enjoyed no retirement and existed by performing odd jobs for the town folks. Anybody with a troublesome tree would call on Mr. Johnson, who must have been in his seventies at the time. He would come with his axe and a file, cut the tree down, split it into fireplace sized sections and sell it. He, like most of the men of the makeshift village, worked until the day they died. Life was unforgiving.

CHAPTER II
ASIANS ON THE WEST COAST

THE CHINESE PAVE THE WAY

While WWII and the bombing of Pearl Harbor led many West Coast inhabitants to a fear of and an outright hatred towards Japanese, in truth the prejudices against Asians had a longstanding history in California, beginning with the discovery of gold there in 1848. From the moment James Marshall's discovery at Sutter's Mill became public knowledge, people the world over—including many Chinese—dropped what they were doing and headed to the goldfields of California in the hopes of striking it rich. Most didn't strike it rich. Farms, railroads, and mines in California were particularly hard hit by the loss of their workers. California's population in 1850 was a mere 92,597, but this number would swell to over 560,000 within twenty years. Soon after 1850, Chinese were brought in under contract by the thousands. Initially they were welcomed as they were considered hardworking, willing to do most any job, and accepting of little pay. Within eighteen years, there were 75,000 Chinese workers in California, and more were on the way. The Chinese, who built the railroad from west to east, are credited with laying track faster than the European workers who were building their section from east to west. In 1869 the Intercontinental Railroad was completed with the driving of the Golden Spike at Promontory Point, Utah. With this final hammer blow, approximately ten thousand Chinese were out of a job at a time when America was experiencing great job shortages throughout. Between 1868 and 1882, an additional 160,000 Chinese arrived to the West Coast, bringing the total Chinese West Coast population to 235,000. Many feared the Chinese were soon to become the majority race in California. This created the first, widespread anti-Asian sentiment in our country. Rioting drove many of the Chinese to urban areas for protection. The Chinese's reputation of working hard for little pay caused a problem for the local labor force, which the locals fought through their numerous unions. This battle was taken all the way to Congress which eventually shut down immigration from China by enacting the Chinese Exclusion Act of 1882. Through treaties with China and several immigration acts, Chinese immigration ceased until 1943.

ARRIVAL OF THE JAPANESE

The Chinese Exclusion Act opened the door for Japanese to enter the United States. In 1885 the Japanese government gave approval for their nationals to come here as laborers, and many took advantage of this opportunity. Unlike the Chinese, the immigrating Japanese were largely trained—often in trades such as landscaping and farming. Like the Chinese, they had a very strong work ethic, but their training and initial acceptance gave them an opportunity to displace a large number of Chinese. Since they had come from a primarily conservative culture, many saved and pooled their money to start businesses here, often turning to the thing they knew best—farming. It was not uncommon for Japanese nationals to rent and work farmland until they were able to buy it.

The vast majority of Japanese in the initial wave of immigrants were male laborers. By 1900, a mere fifteen years after the arrival of the first Japanese, there were 24,326 male and 985 female Japanese—a ratio of 24 to 1. With these heavily skewed numbers, Japanese men desiring a more permanent life in the US were in fierce competition for the few women available to them. The advent of the Japanese picture bride—not unlike the popular institution of internet dating for singles today—became the solution to this problem. In the hopes of finding a suitable wife, a Japanese man would exchange pictures and letters with women from his homeland, select a bride, bring her to America, marry, and start his family. Within the next twenty years, this country saw a tremendous increase in the Japanese population, particularly women, as the population rose to 87,817 men and 22,193 women, bringing the proportions to a more equitable 4 to 1.

With a rapid influx of most any immigrant group comes increased visibility, followed closely by discomfort, disdain and/or fear by those peoples previously established, and the Japanese were just the next in line. Soon they too were the victims of the same contempt that the Chinese had experienced not long before them. By 1906, all schoolchildren of Asian descent in San Francisco were segregated from the local schools. In 1907, an understanding between Japan and America, called the Gentlemen's Agreement, was developed in which Japan agreed to stop issuing passports to all Japanese laborers wanting to immigrate into the US. In exchange for this, President Theodore Roosevelt was to urge the city of San Francisco to stop its segregation of students of Japanese descent. Many Japanese would circumvent immigration controls by entering the US from Canada, Mexico, or Hawaii. America effectively stopped the flow of Japanese to its shores with the Immigration Act of 1924, barring any further immigration from Asia until the act was revised in 1952. In December of 1941, there were 160,000 Japanese in Hawaii and over 6,000 in Mexico. Additionally, laws existed preventing Japanese immigrants from attaining American citizenship, and in California, preventing any person without American citizenship from owning land. Meanwhile, with increasingly more children being born to recently established Japanese families, there came a generation of children with United States citizenship and the opportunity to become legal landowners regardless of the law. In spite of restrictions put in place by the American government, by 1940 landholdings of people of Japanese descent were significant. Fully ninety percent of the produce and a major portion of fresh flowers for the greater Los Angeles area were produced on farms owned or leased by families of Japanese origin. These entrepreneurs owned and or rented land, farmed, trucked, and sold their produce. In effect, they were nearly the entire produce market of Southern California. Land in Southern California was inexpensive compared to in Japan, so many a farm family worked diligently from grandparents to small children to save and reinvest in more land. In 1943, there were 94,000 Japanese Americans in California alone. The March 1943 issue of Reader's Digest reported that Japanese Americans in California held $200,000,000 in land values before their WWII confinement, with a gross annual agricultural production of $100,000,000 on land both owned and leased. Roy Sakioka, the first Japanese American to be listed in Forbes 500 after the war, was an extremely successful produce farmer in California who had been interned with his family in Manzanar. The highest producing potato farmer in the US during WWII was a Japanese American interned in another relocation center. Despite the barriers placed in front of them, through patience, hard work, and dedication, many of these determined immigrants and their descendants would continue to be successful and patriotic members of American society.

CHAPTER III
SOUTHERN CALIFORNIA
BEFORE THE WAR

THE GREAT DEPRESSION AND A SIMPLER TIME

Just before WWII struck, the United States was clawing its way out of a severe depression. The unemployment rate was staggering, people were literally starving, and President Franklin D. Roosevelt's New Deal had proven to not be the secret bullet which was promised to return our country to its feet. Being financially conservative in this economic climate was not optional—it was something all adults had to be. There were no unemployment checks, food stamps, or free medical care to sustain you through the hard times, and there were no credit cards to fall back on. This was a time of cash, but very little of that.

Before WWII, a two car family was a rarity. Generally a husband would take the sole family car to work while his wife stayed home cleaning, cooking, and caring for their children. It was often the wife's job to keep the family's costs down and her arsenal consisted of patches for pants' knees, hand-me-downs, and darning needles for holey socks. Rarely did families go out to dinner. In the 1930s, when I was in my preteens, my father took the family out for dinner less than once a year. Since women seldom had cars to drive, services came to her. The newspaper, milk, eggs, and butter were all delivered to the doorstep. The Helms man delivered bread and pastries; the Good Humor man brought ice cream; the iceman, who was disappearing with the advent of the electric refrigerator, was still seen delivering large chunks of ice for the true ice boxes. There was even a man who came through occasionally to sharpen knives and scissors. If there was a grocery store close by, it was usually a locally owned, family run operation, and a woman would get her exercise carrying groceries home—not at a fancy exercise club. Instead of trash pickup, each family had an incinerator in their backyard where they would burn their trash. The population was small, manufacturers used a lot less packaging, people bought far fewer things, plastics were not used for packaging yet, and the word "smog," although already coined, had yet to be heard by the general public, so nobody seemed to see burning all this rubbish as an unhealthy practice. Communication during this time was a telephone party line, one which neighbors shared with others who could, and often made a practice of, listening in on their neighbors' conversations.

The outskirts of downtown Los Angeles consisted of numerous small, satellite communities surrounded by large, open, rural areas. Water from Owens Valley actually gave Southern California a surplus for increased farming activities in these open areas. I remember seeing farms scattered around North Redondo, Culver City, Venice, Palos Verdes, Whittier, and the San Fernando Valley, to name just a few places. Quite a few of these were farmed by Japanese Americans. Roads were two lanes, traffic was light, and stop signs were few. There was no such thing as a freeway, nor was there a need for one. In the Los Angeles area, public transportation was accomplished by Pacific Electric Railway's "Red Car" system. The hub for the Red Cars was in downtown Los Angeles, and it reached out in all directions to the beaches and San Fernando Valley, as well as Orange, San Bernardino, and Riverside counties. It was inexpensive transportation, used but not excessively crowded. As young teens, my cousin Warren McLeod and I took the electric Red Car from Burbank to a department store in Los Angeles to ride up and down on the only escalator we had ever seen. People enjoyed truly simple pleasures in a time when entertainment required creativity instead of cash. As for the Red Car, it is ironic that today we are looking for ways to reduce or replace diesel and gasoline with a return to using electricity for transportation.

The major industry in Southern California at this time was oil production and refining which had been around since before 1900 and by 1923 was producing an unbelievable third of the world's supply. Other top industries were farming, aircraft manufacturing, and the motion picture industry. The movie industry before WWII employed over 30,000 people in Southern California. Beaches may have been popular during the summers there, but the movies were well attended all year long. Movies were inexpensive in a time when people had little if anything to spend on entertainment. A ten cent trip to the theater would get you a double feature, a newsreel, and a cartoon. In early 1942, the price was raised a penny to eleven cents. A penny in those days had real value. I do not remember ever seeing a person walk by a dropped penny without stooping to pick it up. We were all amazed and excited when the first colored movies arrived a couple of years before WWII. The first full length, color movie I remember seeing was the animated *Snow White and the Seven Dwarfs*. It was such a memorable experience that after more than seventy years I still remember my mother taking me to the Fox Theater in Redondo Beach to see it. After years of black and white ones, colored films were akin to magic. In 1939, two wonderful color movies, *Gone with the Wind* and *The Wizard of Oz*, came out. Besides movies, hamburgers and milk shakes each only cost a dime.

Movies were not the only form of entertainment for cash-strapped families in the prewar years. The big bands were huge hits—their music, mesmerizing. Every local soda fountain with a jukebox became a popular teenager hangout. Tommy and Jimmy Dorsey, Harry James, Benny Goodman, and Glenn Miller were in style as were the Jitterbug and bobby sox. For evening entertainment most families spent their time gathered around the radio to hear Lowell Thomas present the news and to listen to programs such as *Inner Sanctum, The Green Hornet, The Shadow, Red Skelton*, and *Amos and Andy*. Just as you might expect to see in a Norman Rockwell painting, I would lie on the carpet and get as close to the radio as possible. By today's standards, radio reception would have been considered terrible, but it was all we knew and we loved it. My favorite radio program was *The Lone Ranger*. At the end of each episode they always said the same, "Who was that masked stranger?" followed in the distance by, "Hi Ho Silver!" This still brings a lump to my throat. On Sunday mornings we bought from young boys pulling four-wheeled carts either the *LA Times* or *LA Examiner*. We eagerly anticipated reading the next sequence in the comic strips of "Katzenjammer Kids," "Prince Valiant," "Popeye," and "Lil Abner" to name a few. Life was simple prior to WWII, but with the impending war effort and population explosion, the US saw its small, rural communities growing outward while its open spaces were shrinking.

CHAPTER IV
AT WAR WITH JAPAN

BEFORE PEARL HARBOR—JAPAN'S FATEFUL DECISION

Since the beginning of human existence, the world has seen active expansionism for trade and raw materials. Japan, though, was late to industrialize, and when it did, it found it had on its small islands little raw industrial material to work with other than small deposits of coal and iron. In 1889, Japan sought to expand its empire. In 1904, Japan defeated Russia along its eastern border. During WWI, it fought on the side of the allies, only to see France and Britain reap rewards far in excess of what it itself gained. In 1931, the Japanese invaded Manchuria; in 1936 they joined the Axis Powers; a year later they invaded China. With their own eyes on trade with China, the USA and Britain began supplying China with materials to defend itself against Japanese occupation. Diplomatic negotiations were opened with Japan wanting the US and Britain to stop sending supplies to China, while the US and Britain insisting Japan withdraw her troops from there. Following unsuccessful negotiations with Japan, the USA began an embargo cutting off all sales of scrap iron and oil to this small country. With its military draining funds at five million dollars a day, Japan was nearly broke. Also, before the embargo, the US had been supplying 80% of Japan's oil, which had dwindled down to a two year inventory. Feeling pushed into a corner, Japan developed a master plan to cripple the US Navy, seize islands in the Pacific (Dutch West Indies and Malaysia) which had supplies of oil and rubber, and take China. It knew the American people were strongly opposed to war and figured if attacked, it would take them two years to prepare for it. By that time, Japan hoped to have the resources and land acquisitions necessary to negotiate peace—keeping the islands it needed the most and offering others in exchange for peace. It was a serious underestimate, for the United States geared up for war in months, not years.

In light of the fact that our Pacific Fleet was conveniently relocated to Pearl Harbor by FDR, and that powerful members of our government had more than a strong inkling that Japan was poised for attack, it seems extraordinary that the US was not on alert in the Pacific. Why had the Pacific Fleet been moved from San Diego to Hawaii? Why was nearly the entire fleet docked instead of on alert, or better, dispersed at sea? Why was all commercial ocean shipping routed into the South Pacific, leaving the northern route wide open for the Japanese fleet to slither through unobstructed? The US military knew that Japan's fleet of six carriers had left Japan and was on radio silence, and was fully aware of the tensions mounting between our two countries.

With the stage so overwhelmingly set for an American disaster, Japan's planes, secreted in on its six carriers, were able to damage or destroy all eight battleships of the Pacific Fleet along with three cruisers, four destroyers, and 320 aircraft. All four American aircraft carriers, the Lexington, Enterprise, Hornet, and Yorktown, which had mysteriously been ordered out of Pearl Harbor prior to the attack, were untouched, becoming our only remaining means of defense. After court marshals and numerous investigations, the answers as to how we could have been so poorly prepared prior to the attack at Pearl Harbor remain to this day.

AFTER PEARL HARBOR—LIFE DISRUPTED

With the December 7, 1941 attack on Pearl Harbor, Japan managed to effectively eliminate the US Navy's Pacific Fleet, killed 2,402 servicemen, and wounded over a thousand others. Inhabitants of the West Coast were terrified. Japan was quick to follow up its bombing attack by sending submarines to the West Coast. The successes experienced by these submarines brought to the American public a feeling that the war was not just out in the Pacific, but also here at home. On December 20, 1941, just thirteen days after the bombing of Pearl Harbor, a Japanese submarine identified as I-17 shelled a US tanker off of Cape Mendocino, California. The tanker crew survived and the ship washed ashore north of Crescent City. Three days later a Japanese submarine sank the oil tanker Montebello off the central California coast near Cambria. On Christmas Eve, 1941, submarine I-17 was scheduled to shell west coast cities, but increased US air patrols caused the plan to be scrapped. On February 23, 1942, I-17 surfaced, and just after 7:00 p.m., fired seventeen rounds from her deck gun at the Ellwood oil field storage facilities in Goleta, north of Santa Barbara. The shots were wild and there was little damage to oil field facilities. That night the Coast Guard had had the responsibility for patrolling the Ellwood beach, so seaman Jack C. Hart, armed with nothing more than an old WWI rifle and a guard dog, walked the beach as shells from the submarine flew overhead. Jack C. Hart has passed away, but his brother, William Hart, MD., recalled Jack relating the story of the attack to his family. Dr. Hart expressed to me how his brother felt on that dark night, that "...he was alone facing a Japanese invasion of the West Coast." This action by Japan struck fear in many living near the Pacific Coast and it brought home just how accessible our land really was to them. The shelling triggered a fear beyond that of being bombed, to one of actually being invaded.

Japan's submarine I-17 was commissioned on January 24, 1941, in the Yokosuka naval yard in Japan and was a giant among submarines. It carried a Yokosuka E14Y seaplane, seventeen torpedoes, and had a compliment of ninety-four officers and men. During the attack at Pearl Harbor, it was positioned north of Oahu to attack ships which might try to escape. Although it saw no action, the fact that this submarine was operating for two months that we know of off our coast and thousands of miles from Japan, could help explain why the Office of Naval Intelligence (ONI) and General DeWitt, guardian of the West Coast, suspected Japanese-American fishing boats of passing messages to and possibly refueling Japan's submarines. I find it not coincidental that the first Japanese Americans evacuated from the West Coast to Manzanar were fishermen and their families from Terminal Island in Los Angeles harbor and Bainbridge, Washington. The possibility of them assisting Japanese subs was just too much for Office of Naval Intelligence (ONI) to bear. After seeing no action at Pearl Harbor, I-17's mission was to proceed to the US's West Coast. Besides I-17, there were two other Japanese submarines, I-25 and I-26, operating off the coast from Canada to Oregon. On September 9, 1942, a seaplane was launched from I-25 to carry out the first aerial attack on the US mainland near Brookings, Oregon. There, two 180 pound incendiary bombs were dropped over Mt. Emily, causing little damage. This same submarine, earlier in June, shelled Fort Stevens near the mouth of the Columbia River, again inflicting no damage. Following this attack, I-25 was credited with sinking two tankers off the West Coast.

Later in the war, Japan launched huge, bomb-laden balloons with a sophisticated design that enabled them to sail over the Pacific and land or drop incendiary devices on American soil with the hopes of killing people and of starting fires in our forests. These balloons were thirty-three feet in diameter and filled with hydrogen. They each carried an antipersonnel bomb as well as incendiary devices. There were approximately 9,000 such balloons launched from Japanese soil over a six month period. They traveled 5,000 miles to North America—three days on the jet stream at over 30,000 feet in elevation. Our government initially kept the arrival of the balloons a secret so that the Japanese would not know they were successfully arriving over our soils, but following the death of a pregnant teacher and four young boys and a girl ages 11 to 14 who were killed by one of the bombs on May 5, 1945, the government felt informing the public of the dangers was more important than keeping up the ruse. I do not remember hearing of the people who had been killed by the balloon, but once the word of them was out they became a heated topic and had everybody looking to the sky for the next one to fall. Spotters were stationed throughout the Northwest to report any balloon sightings. Many people had trouble imagining that balloons of this magnitude could sail so quickly to a target so far away. Nonbelievers created interesting speculations as to the launch sites of the balloons, including Japanese submarines and even the Japanese internment camps. In total there were thirty such balloons shot down, 100 found during the war, and 150 found after the end of the war. They landed as far east as Michigan, south as Mexico, and north as Alaska. One was reported to have come down in Santa Monica, another in the ocean outside of San Pedro, and another in Saticoy, California, a mere four miles from where I live. Yet another was shot down over Santa Rosa by a P-38 fighter plane. The teacher killed by the one balloon to prove deadly was Elyse Mitchell of Oregon. A monument now stands at the site of the tragedy some seventy miles northeast of Klamath Falls and is now in the US National Register of Historic Places. Although these balloons were intended to take lives and start fires, with the exception of the incident in Oregon, little physical damage was caused. Their presence, though, did have a significant psychological effect on many, primarily those living in the northwest.

Author as a boy on Kohala fishing barge—1934

On Christmas day, just 18 days after the attack at Pearl Harbor, the U.S. Navy bombed a fishing barge, the Kohala, off Redondo Beach. I was living a block from the beach and had fished off of this very barge as a young boy. The day of the bombing, I remember hearing the explosion and witnessed the confusion of those living on our block. It was subsequently rumored the navy was trying to sink a Japanese submarine and hit the fishing barge accidentally. I traveled along the south beach and saw the Kohala in pieces on the beach, but no submarine. Even though this turned out to be our own bombing, the war was beginning to feel closer to home.

On February 24, 1942, just one night after submarine I-17 sent rounds sailing into Goleta, California, an event occurred that has been referred to as "The Battle of Los Angeles." What was believed to be an air attack by enemy planes flying over Santa Monica, Culver City, North Redondo, and Long Beach, California, was in fact, a harmless US weather balloon aimlessly drifting over the area. Our own military fired 1,440 rounds of antiaircraft ordnance in just over one hour. The fallout was like rain. Three civilians were killed by friendly fire and several others died of heart attacks. It was a sleepless night for over two million Americans. I was living in Redondo Beach at the time, not far from the shelling, but only faintly remember this incident. I do recall my father telling us to stay away from the windows. At several different times we had air raid alarms and blackouts. One in particular, I vividly remember. I came out of a movie theater one night to find air raid sirens blaring and search lights panning, giving the impression of an attack. There was panic everywhere. Everyone was running as fast as they could travel, myself included. I really thought our fears of invasion had been realized. Panicked people were asking each other if we were being attacked, but nobody had any answers. It was total confusion and hysteria. Block wardens were running wildly, making sure every house on their block had its lights out. With the lights out, it was difficult to find one's way, or to see oncoming cars. This one incident, I have never forgotten. Interestingly, as the war moved on and I would see newsreels of cities like London under attack, I always had this mental flash back to that night in Redondo Beach. I could see the civilians running and those same scared faces. The difference was, in London they were under attack and bombs were falling. Over the next several months, similar false alarms were sounded in the San Francisco Bay area. They experienced the same: blackouts, block wardens scurrying to check lights, search lights hunting for enemy aircraft, sirens, and panic in the streets.

America had enjoyed few successes in the beginning of the war, a fact that was felt with a growing sense of dread. The United States military could not rule out the possibility that Japan could, at any time, attack the West Coast. In May 1942, our code breakers deciphered a Japanese message relaying plans to do just that. The question is, was it correctly deciphered. Then, in June 1942, Japan took over a couple of Alaska's Aleutian Islands, again bringing the war closer to our own doorstep. People on the West Coast lived with the uncertainty of not knowing where Japan would strike next. The military initiated many precautions for just this reason. One such precaution was to move the 1942 Rose Bowl game off the West Coast— the only time in history such a move has occurred. Having a huge gathering of American citizens all in one location so close to the coast seemed like a dangerous risk at the time. Another safety measure taken was an elaborate effort to conceal airplane manufacturing plants by covering them with camouflage intricately decorated to look from the air like housing developments, complete with streets and parks. Actual cars, houses, and artificial trees were placed on top of the camouflage to give it a more accurate, three dimensional appearance. I twice visited my Uncle Elmer McLeod, chief test pilot at Lockheed, at his work—once before and once after the camouflage was added. The aerial photographs below show Lockheed's Burbank, California plant before and after the addition of its WWII camouflage.

Lockheed in peacetime

Lockheed under camouflage

In 1943, Lockheed employed over 90,000 people and it was this same year that the famous Skunk Works research and development program was founded, working on their first jet aircraft, the experimental XP 80 fighter. During 1944, Lockheed produced a total of 5,864 aircraft. At 9,924, more Lockheed P-38s were produced than any other single type of aircraft by that company. Along with their own airplanes, they would also produce 2,750 B-17s for Boeing. The Germans were shooting down the B-17s faster than Boeing could produce them.

In addition to concealing airplane manufacturing plants, the army also heightened its invasion readiness with numerous artillery installations at various points where they felt Japan might come ashore. Eventually, 30,000 army troops were stationed along the California coast from Palos Verdes to Santa Barbara. Shortly after the attack on Pearl Harbor, and while I was living in Redondo Beach, California, barbed wire was placed along the top of the South Beach bluff, and an army unit was moved in to man the artillery.

Remnant of WWII gun tub at the Ventura River

In the hills of Palos Verdes, Army Infantry units were training—something I witnessed from much closer than I ever intended. There was, at that time, a riding stable next to Redondo Beach in the Palos Verdes foothills. To get to the horse trails from the stable one had to pass through an infantry field training ground. On one particular occasion, the stable owner, knowing that I had previously owned a horse, put me on a particularly nervous steed which I less than affectionately nicknamed Screwball. The horse was a bit anxious when I got on, but settled down as we went along. As we passed through the training grounds on our way to the riding trails, a shot was fired from above by a soldier hiding close by in tall grass. Screwball went vertical, came back down beside the trail and we were off, racing down a steep slope over the diving, dodging forms of soldiers who had been hiding in the grass and bushes. As my frantic horse and I forced several more soldiers out of hiding, the opposing infantry unit in this mock battle took advantage by shooting even more rounds over their newly exposed adversaries, causing poor Screwball to escalate his terrified jumping and running. That ride ended my association with Screwball, the stable, and the infantry field training grounds, but proved to me that the army really was conducting training in our Palos Verdes Hills during the war.

A COMMON CAUSE

With our admittance into the war, people on the West Coast were scared. We felt we had been pushed into this war—something no one wanted. We knew we had to build up defenses here and push Japan back across the Pacific. There were great questions about our ability to win the war, because at that time, we were definitely losing. While giving a lecture recently at Manzanar, a Japanese American, Noby Miyasaki, had this to say, "Our family was stranded in Japan when my father heard of the attack at Pearl Harbor. My father said, 'This will be the end, for Japan cannot win.'" Interestingly, this sentiment seems to have been mirrored on both sides of the ocean—the same, yet reversed. We knew we had to win, but questioned whether we could, and if we could, how long it would take, as we were fighting a war on two fronts—one in Europe and one in Japan. There are few people left now who remember the West Coast's frustration that Washington D.C. was giving too little support to the war in the Pacific. We felt strongly that far more materials and men were going to the fight in Europe. In truth, by agreement between President FDR and Britain's Winston Churchill, Europe had been given the highest priority, and that side to the war did come to an end first.

The moment President Franklin Delano Roosevelt announced that this country was at war, our war machine, which had already been supplying Great Britain with food, fuel, and war materials, gained momentum, pulling our country together. It became awe inspiring to experience the only time I know of in our nation's history when everybody united for a single cause. The West Coast experienced a surge of pride, patriotism, and efficiency in a very short time. I feel, unless you personally lived on the West Coast during WWII, it would be impossible to convey the emotions shared by those of us who did. I lived a block from the ocean in Redondo Beach until May 1, 1942. The war in the Pacific felt very close. What was so amazing was just how fast the changes came and how they hit all of us—old and young alike. I began delivering the Redondo Beach Daily Breeze newspaper before the war, and right after the bombing of Pearl Harbor, we paperboys took pride in learning how to fold newspapers without using rubber bands. Rubber became one of many war materials not to be used frivolously. We collected paper, metal, and, although I still don't know why, string. Families would collect string and wind it into a ball.

All of this war effort on the West Coast called for a very large civilian work force. There was a shortage of men so high school kids, like myself, and senior citizens filled vacated jobs. One summer, at the age of sixteen, I worked two jobs for a total of sixteen hours of work each day, six days a week—for fifty cents per hour. It felt good, as a kid, to be able to contribute. People came to California from other states, creating a huge increase in the West Coast population. For the first time, a very noticeable increase in traffic was seen. During shift changes at the large aircraft factories, key streets leading to and from the factories became one-way-only so workers could get to work on time. Women, for the first time, left their homes by the thousands to fill jobs left by men who had joined the service and to fill positions in the accelerated war materials factories. It was estimated that over six million women went to work during the war. Two hundred thousand more women joined the military. Our nation discovered that women could do much more than wash, iron, cook, and sew. They filled a multitude of jobs previously considered impossible for women. They worked in the shipyards, aircraft factories, railroads, and more. No one ever thought women would or could run a bead with an electric arc welder. They did it well, and they did it ceaselessly. This was not the birthplace of the liberated woman, but it was definitely a huge step in them proving to themselves and to others that they could do much more than they had previously been given the opportunity to do. Many women would never return to a complete, stay-at-home, pre-WWII lifestyle. In spite of the iconic figure of the June Cleaver mom of the fifties, WWII had planted a seed.

Like governments all around the world, ours used propaganda to gain support for the war. We were reminded daily that men were dying for us and that it was our duty to support them from home, in any way we could. Posters, like this one, were displayed prominently.

What did *you* do today
. . . for Freedom?

Today, at the front, he died . . . Today, what did *you* do?
Next time you see a list of dead and wounded, ask yourself:
"What have *I* done today for freedom?
What can I do tomorrow that will save the lives of
men like this and help them win the war?"

WWII poster

They often contained slogans geared toward uniting the country into one war machine. Slogans such as "Loose lips sink ships" and "His life is in your hands" abounded and brought the desired result of making this a personal war with each and every one of us working against the enemy. As previously stated, movies were a common diversion from the everyday strains of work and the stress of living with the constant reminders of war. Movies always began with a newsreel covering the most recent developments of the war. Some of these newsreels were quite graphic. Remember, Japan had not signed the Geneva Convention, and as such, operated with no apparent rules on the proper treatment of prisoners or civilians. Many atrocities were clearly displayed in film and some were disturbingly graphic—at a time when the entertainment industry had yet to numb our senses with a constant barrage of bloody images. It was shocking and hit us close to home. If the newsreels were designed to build hatred for Japan and the Japanese it worked. Back here at home, one of the biggest risks to the safety of people of Japanese descent came from returning American veterans who had been fighting "Japs" overseas. It left the Japanese Americans on the West Coast in a difficult and dangerous situation, for they looked just like the enemy and were sometimes treated as such by their now angry, suspicious neighbors. Today we call this racial profiling, but during WWII there was no such term.

Where we had never lost a war up through WWII, it is difficult to recognize any war since as a clear victory. Unlike the wars in Vietnam, Iraq, or Afghanistan, in which a good percentage of the population questioned our need to participate, there was no doubt why we were in WWII and no question as to our need for a victory. There was tremendous support for WWII with the rallying cry from the people to defeat Germany, Italy, and Japan and then to bring our troops home. During WWII, our heroes were our servicemen—not the overpaid, ill-mannered athletes and actors that people too often admire today. Servicemen have never since been held in such high regard as during that time. Although service people returning from our most recent wars have garnered an improved level of respect, our treatment of those who returned from Vietnam was unconscionable—a large sector of the population taking out their anger for the government on the young men who had already suffered the most. During WWII, joining the armed forces was the honorable thing to do, and like many, I joined the Navy right out of high school. Although the shooting was over, there were still hundreds of thousands of troops overseas waiting to return home. After being overseas myself for a year, the Navy sent me to school in Philadelphia. The war had been over for more than two years, yet the honorable treatment for servicemen still prevailed. After finishing the school, I was allowed to go back to California on leave. When I arrived by train to Chicago, it was in the morning and the height of commuter time. I stepped off the train onto a very long platform packed with commuters. I thought I would never be able to carry my bulky seabag through that mass of people. I picked up the bag, slung it up onto my shoulder and started to inch forward when suddenly the crowd parted just as the Red Sea had done for Moses. The tightly packed crowd was making room for a returning serviceman. Thinking about it brings a lump to my throat all these years later. I wish there were some way I could share with you that feeling we all seemed to have for this country. It was more than pride and it goes beyond description. To understand the degree of loyalty that came out of WWII, you must remember that WWII was a war to defend OUR country, not a war for somebody else's freedom. The United States would eventually lose about 406,000 military to the war and that made WWII personal. It was not long into the war before almost everybody knew someone who had died fighting. People with a loved one in the service placed a small flag with a red star on it in their front window. If a person lost someone in the service, they put a gold star on their little flag. There were millions of flags in windows and hundreds of thousands were gold. Every week of the war, a casualty report was released and the numbers of dead were frightening. The price for freedom was escalating and we all knew it. In fact, some people felt that the casualties were actually higher than reported, questioning the motives of the government for releasing the numbers that they did.

The country and its people geared up in many other ways for the war. Defense factories were expanded and soon operating around the clock, seven days a week. On the West Coast, Henry Kaiser put in shipyards which turned out a liberty ship every day. Boeing, Douglas, Martin, North American, Lockheed, and Convair built dozens of airplanes every day. This country built the largest air force the world had ever known, consisting of an astronomical 80,000 combat aircraft. The skies over Southern California filled with planes being flown from the factories to overseas destinations. In the Midwest, the family passenger car production stopped and didn't start up again until the war was over. The factories were converted to make tanks, trucks, weapon carriers, and jeeps. When Willys, a manufacturer of small passenger cars could not keep up with the demand for jeeps, Ford stepped in and built them too. The military vehicles moved to the West Coast along with the troops for the fight in the Pacific. It was not uncommon to see military convoys traveling down Pacific Coast Highway (PCH) for hours on end headed to the port of Los Angeles and the war in the Pacific. United Service Organizations (USOs) sprang up in 1941 to entertain service personnel, attracting top notch entertainers who were devoted to helping the war effort in the way they knew best. Make no mistake— serving the troops' morale was nearly as important as serving their physical needs. In fact, some entertainers, including the world famous Al Jolson and Glenn Miller, gave with their lives. Of course you cannot mention the USO without mentioning Bob Hope, who made entertaining the troops his lifelong mission. Additional entertainment superstars did their service in other ways ranging from signing up for battle to serving food to the troops. The Hollywood Canteen became a famous place where movie stars served coffee and donuts to the servicemen and women. The megastar Clark Gable was above the maximum draft age of thirty-eight, yet he volunteered for the Army Air Force and flew missions over Germany. Jimmy Stewart did the same. John Payne was in the Air Force, and Tyrone Power was a pilot in the Marines who flew in the Pacific. Glenn Ford, Lee Marvin, George C. Scott, and John Russell all served in the Marines in the Pacific and were decorated for their combat experiences. Robert Ryan was in the Marines in Europe and was decorated for combat. Many movie stars who stayed home traveled the country in support of war bond drives.

WWII war bonds

Buying war bonds was not just a patriotic thing to do, but played a vital role in funding the war. The war was running up an enormous debt which was being funded from within the country, not from foreign countries, as we see happening today. Everyone, including many Japanese Americans held in camps, bought war bonds. The books came in various denominations and had a ten year maturity. The one pictured is a $5.00 book which I picked up at my local post office. I bought ten cent stamps from money earned selling newspapers in Redondo Beach and pasted the stamps in the book until it was full. There were also payroll deduction plans through most employers. Big name movie stars went on war bond drives across the country encouraging everyone to help fund the war. Besides purchasing war bonds,

Americans were also doing their part by conserving countless natural resources. Rationing hit everybody except those in Congress with coffee, meat, sugar, butter, gasoline, and shoes (one pair per person per year) being a few of the things that were restricted. It is rather interesting how the government rationed gasoline. A person would first register all the tires on his car and then he could apply for gasoline ration stamps. The government decided what amount of gasoline he would qualify for and would then issue him an A, B, or C sticker, with C qualifying for the most gasoline. Sliced bread disappeared by government orders to save on the metal used in slicing. Nucoa, (pronounced Nu-ko) margarine, a substitute for butter, came in a white block into which you hand mixed the yellow color to make it look like butter, but it did not help it to taste like butter. Few complained.

Not only were America's citizens working at a feverish pace, so too was the government. At a time when there were fewer lawyers, less government, and little gridlock in our nation's capital, progress was made on a scale unheard of today. Democrats and Republicans found common ground on many projects and worked together, knowing that there was no time to stall for party politics—no time for long, indecisive debates. Decisions might not have always been correct, but they were made and agreed upon quickly. When the government feared that Japan might invade Alaska, it approved a 1,400 mile long highway connecting Alaska to the USA and got it built in a remarkable nine months. Today, this same project would take years.

In Southern California, everywhere I looked I was reminded that we were in a war, from the airplanes in the sky, the military personnel on the streets, and the factories turning out war materials, to Hollywood turning out war movies, and radio and newspapers giving us battle locations and casualty reports. An entire nation of people learned the names and locations of islands they had never heard of before—the Gilberts, Solomon's, and Marshalls, Guam, Wake Island, Midway, Tarawa, Iwo Jima, and Okinawa. We lived and breathed this war. During my lifetime this country has fought in many battles and wars, yet none ever consumed me like WWII. I can't help but think everyone who lived on the West Coast during WWII shared this feeling.

CHAPTER V
SELECTING A SITE

WAR RELOCATION CENTERS

ASSEMBLY AND RELOCATION CENTERS

With fear of Japan, and hatred for all things Japanese growing in the country, it was not long before the American government ordered the evacuation of all persons of Japanese origin from the West Coast. Manzanar was selected to be the first site for housing Japanese-American men, women, and children to prohibit them from inhabiting the West Coast. Before discussing the selection of Manzanar as a camp site, it is necessary to understand the difference in the terms "assembly center" and "relocation center." Assembly centers were existing facilities the government used as initial evacuee collecting and holding sites until the more permanent relocation centers further away from the West Coast could be built. These assembly centers, for the most part, were fairgrounds, race tracks, and rodeo grounds—facilities designed and used for holding livestock. The evacuees were housed where animals had previously been or in new, very temporary housing built for the evacuees on these same sites. Most evacuees were then moved to their appointed relocation centers where they stayed for the duration of the war, although many qualified for relocation to the East where they could live free of barbed wire fencing and armed guards. All ten relocation centers, commonly called "camps," were not held to the same restrictive level. The four camps (Manzanar, Poston, Gila River, and Tule Lake) within the "exclusion area" in the West were far more restrictive. The evacuees in those four camps had to stay within the confines of the camp and could not wander outside without War Relocation Authority (WRA) authorization. Evacuees housed within one of the six camps (Topaz, Minidoka, Heart Mountain, Granada, Rohwer, and Jerome) outside of the exclusion area could shop in the nearby towns, participate in recreational activities with the local town teams, and work on the farms in the area. Of the ten camps, Manzanar in California and Poston in Arizona were the only two camps to be designated as both assembly centers and later, relocation centers.

ASSEMBLY CENTERS

Total number of evacuees that were processed through each assembly center.

Fresno	5,120	Puyallup	7,390
Manzanar	9,666	Sacramento	4,739
Marysville	2,451	Salinas	3,594
Mayer	243	Santa Anita	18,719
Merced	4,508	Stockton	4,271
Pinedale	4,792	Tanforan	7,816
Pomona	5,434	Tulare	4,978
Portland	3,676	Turlock	3,662
		Total	**91,059**

RELOCATION CENTERS

The maximum number of evacuees at one given time in each of the ten relocation centers.

Gila River	13,348	Minidoka	9,397
Granada	7,118	Poston	17,814

Gila River	13,348	Minidoka	9,397
Heart Mountain	10,767	Rohwer	8,475
Jerome	8,497	Topaz	8,130
Manzanar	10,046	Tule Lake	18,789
		Total	**112,381**

The selection of Manzanar as a location for housing evacuated Japanese Americans began with a man named Robert L. Brown. Brown was born in Pasadena, California, on March 11, 1908. He earned a degree in English and a general secondary (teaching credential) from the University of Southern California. His first job was teaching high school in Big Pine, California, which is located only thirty-four miles from Manzanar. Through his contacts in Owens Valley, he was offered the job of starting an Inyo-Mono Counties Publicity Bureau to promote tourism to those two counties which had been hard hit by the depression. His most effective tools in the promotion of tourism to Owens Valley were the newspapers. He worked hard to develop friendships and working relationships with several newspapermen in Los Angeles, one of whom was Manchester Boddy, owner of the Los Angeles Daily News. Boddy had become sympathetic to the plight of the valley and very helpful to Brown in using his paper to promote the valley.

In early 1942, after five years of promoting tourism to Owens Valley, Robert Brown got a call from Glenn Desmond, the Director of Public Relations with the Department of Water and Power (DWP) in Los Angeles. Desmond and Brown had been asked to attend a meeting in Los Angeles. The chairman of this meeting, none other than Manchester Boddy, informed those in attendance that he had received word from US Attorney General Biddle that the army was going to move all Japanese Americans away from the West Coast, and that it was to be done quickly. Boddy informed the group that he had suggested to Biddle they move the evacuees to the Owens Valley. He based his choice on the facts that the valley was isolated from the coast, was an area with a low population density, and being significantly hard hit by the depression, would benefit greatly from the infusion of money that such a camp would bring. Inquiring how many evacuees were expected to be housed there, Brown was told 100,000. Both he and Desmond responded that there was no possible way that the Owens Valley could handle that number of people. They were both directed to contact the Assist. Attorney General Tom Clark. Thomas Campbell Clark, born in Dallas, Texas in 1899, and with a law degree from the University of Texas, was the US Assistant Attorney General in 1942 and the civilian coordinator for the selection of Japanese-American camp sites and for the subsequent evacuation. He would go on to be appointed Attorney General by Harry Truman in 1945 and later to be appointed to the Supreme Court in 1949. He was also to write the majority opinion prohibiting the reading of the bible in public schools. In their first meeting, Clark agreed that bringing 100,000 additional people into Owens Valley was not a good idea. Clark revealed that there were other locations, including Death Valley and the upper Mojave Desert, also being considered for camp locations. During their second meeting, it was agreed that a local Owens Valley committee was needed to study and make recommendations for a camp. On the first such committee was Ralph Merritt who would go on to become chairman of the Owens Valley Coordinating Committee, and later, WRA Project Director for Manzanar. Others on the first committee were Roy Booth, head of the Forest Service for the Eastern Sierras, Spence Loudon, head of the Highway Division there, William Dehy, a well-respected Inyo County judge, and George Savage, editor of the Chalfant Press in Bishop. A short time after the first committee was formed; Tom Clark requested Brown and Savage meet with him in San Francisco. During that meeting, Clark informed Robert Brown that Brown was to take a job working for him. Brown replied that he wanted to think it over, but Clark informed him that it was a done deal—he had been hired the day before. Brown was now working for the Wartime Civil Control Administration (WCCA). He was entrusted with the tasks of assisting in the selection of a site for an Owens Valley relocation camp and of smoothing the way with the local communities for that camp.

Owens Valley Coordinating Committee from left: Wallace Howland (FBI), Rex Nicholson (WCCA), Col. McGill (US Army), Ralph Merritt (Chairman), Clayton Triggs (WCCA), Col. Kelton (US Army)

While Robert Brown was in San Francisco meeting with Tom Clark, the Corp of Engineers swooped into the Owens Valley making Brown's new job unnecessarily difficult before he even had a chance to get started. Without contacting the local committee or Brown, the Corp of Engineers released information that a relocation camp was to be built in the valley for 100,000 Japanese. For a number of reasons, the locals were terrified and outraged, leaving Brown with a major public relations nightmare. Later, the Corp of Engineers returned to the valley, but this time, they collaborated with the local committee in selecting a site. There were several locations within the Owens Valley under consideration, including Olancha, Bishop, and Manzanar. With the number of potential Japanese-American evacuees coming into the valley set at 10,000 instead of the previous, less realistic 100,000, the Corp of Engineers and the Owens Valley Coordinating Committee were able to agree on Manzanar as the most promising site. This decision was based on the accessibility to electricity and water, the low population density of the local community, and the availability of 7,500 acres of agricultural land.

A FRIGHTENED COMMUNITY RESPONDS

Independence and Lone Pine, the two small towns on either side of the proposed camp site, were still much like the old west—made up of a few bars, schools, and churches and populated by cattlemen, miners, and a sheriff. This was a very conservative area that didn't take well to strangers and called everybody from Los Angeles "flatlanders." For these close-knit people who had been railroaded to the point of bankruptcy over water rights in the not too distant past, anything the government forced upon them was met with hatred and suspicion. These sentiments were still prevalent when the government announced plans to build a camp for Japanese Americans at Manzanar. It was estimated that only about ten to twelve percent of the local residents from the Owens Valley had strong negative reactions towards having a relocation camp built in their backyards, but some of those became very outspoken opponents of the camp and anything that had to do with it. Ten thousand people, the number of Japanese Americans expected to be housed in the camp, outnumbered all the residents in the entire valley at that time. The population density of Inyo County, the county encompassing the valley, was just one person per square mile, where the camp was slated to house 10,000 evacuated Japanese Americans in one square mile. The thought that the government was proposing to bring in a number of evacuees greater than the entire existing population of the valley and crowd them onto one small square mile was mind boggling. In the minds of the locals, these were people the government considered to be of potential danger to the country's safety, otherwise, they would not have been forced to evacuate from the West Coast. Knowing nothing about Japanese Americans, the locals visualized them as dangerous and feared they would escape the camp—in numbers greater than themselves—and attack them in their very homes. County residents wanted assurances that the internees would not be able to escape. Not only were the Japanese Americans considered a potential danger, but also, if given Inyo County residency and allowed to vote, by their sheer numbers, they would control the outcome of every local election. This, the locals vehemently opposed.

To allay the fears of the valley populace required an ongoing commitment to honesty, information dissemination, and education about who the incoming Japanese Americans really were. Besides public relations work, actual physical measures were implemented to assure locals of their safety. To begin with, county residents were guaranteed that the camp's periphery would be patrolled twenty-four hours per day, 365 days of the year. After being built, the camp had eight tall guard towers added to increase the impression, if not the reality, of security. To eliminate the tensions surrounding the voting issue, the post office within the Manzanar camp became a branch of Los Angeles, not Inyo County. With this unusual concession made, any votes submitted by Japanese-American internees would be counted in a heavily populated county two hundred miles away, and not in the one in which the voters themselves resided.

Possibly the strongest negative reaction to a camp at Manzanar actually came from where you might least expect it—the distant Los Angeles basin. There were those who felt a camp at Manzanar was downright stupid. Why? Because the drinking water for over one million Southern California residents passed very close to the proposed camp site. What would prevent these Japanese suspected of spying and espionage from sabotaging the canal and contaminating or poisoning the LA-bound water? Why should LA County residents consider them trustworthy in Manzanar if they weren't considered so while residing on the West Coast? It was a strong argument, but both General DeWitt and the Assistant Attorney General Tom Clark insisted the camp be built at Manzanar and they won by force. General DeWitt declared that during wartime he could follow through with whatever he believed to be in the best interest of the military. He also gave assurances that there would be security at the camp continuously confining the evacuees.

As time went on, in many of the relocation centers that were built outside of California, Japanese Americans were not only allowed, but actually encouraged to leave their camps to shop in the local areas, thus infusing money into the local economies. Not so with those in California. The camps within that state continued throughout the war to have much greater security than in the other camps, although this security did slacken over time. Due to their irrational fear of Japanese Americans, the suspicious people of Independence, and to a lesser degree, Lone Pine, insisted on tighter security for Manzanar. The consequences for insisting on this heightened security included the perpetuation of their depressed economy, which might have been greatly improved by allowing an additional 10,000 shoppers to enter their towns. Had more locals recognized that these Japanese Americans were unarmed and themselves scared, were victims of the war, and were not looking for trouble, a more amicable relationship between the two could have ensued, to the benefit of both groups. Sadly, it was not to be. Locals not only prohibited internees from shopping in their stores, they complained loudly any time they saw a Japanese American outside the fenced camp. In fact, the fear and hatred in Independence reached such a pitch that a group of armed vigilantes formed to "protect" their small town. They made it very clear that they expected the US Army to keep all internees within the confines of the camp.

The man most responsible for the evacuation of Japanese Americans from the West Coast and later for the building of the camp at Manzanar was US Army

General John L. DeWitt. General DeWitt was born in Fort Sidney, Nebraska in 1880. At the age of only 18, he received an appointment as second lieutenant in the US Army Infantry, potentially due to the fact that his father was a general. He served in WWI, receiving a promotion in 1918 to full colonel. He was awarded the Distinguished Service Medal at the end of WWI. In July 1937, DeWitt became Commandant of the Army War College, and two years later was promoted to major general to assume command of the Fourth Army as well as the Western Defense Command with the responsibility of defending the West Coast from Alaska to the Mexican border.

On February 28, 1942, General DeWitt was in his headquarters at the presidio in San Francisco when he received approval from the War Department to build a camp at Manzanar. The camp had a construction budget amounting to $500 per person for a total of $5,000,000. General DeWitt immediately turned the design of the camp over to the Corp of Engineers in Los Angeles. The corp was told that the first evacuees would begin to arrive at Manzanar on March 21, 1942—less than a month hence. In just five days, the Corp of Engineers had completed a design for the camp, calling on their experience in designing camps for young, healthy service-men. Their standard design consisted of barracks laid out in rows, columns, and blocks with big firebreaks. Manzanar was not to stray from this basic pattern. From the outside looking in, Manzanar would look like any other military camp, but this one would be different in that it would be filled with families—families that would be forced to endure cold winters and hot summers in flimsily designed and rapidly constructed barracks.

CHAPTER VI
CONSTRUCTING THE MANZANAR CAMP

DEFINING MANZANAR

So what exactly was Manzanar? It has been labeled by various people at different times in our history an assembly center, a relocation center, an internment camp, a concentration camp, a prisoner of war camp, and a prison. Which is most true? That depends on your perception and personal experiences, for Manzanar fit many descriptions and even changed its function and appearance over time. To the Japanese Americans inside, it might legitimately have resembled a concentration camp or prison with its five-strand barbed wire exterior and eight guard towers. These citizens were not allowed to leave without government approval. Likewise, nobody was allowed to enter the camp without the same approval, making Manzanar restrictive from within and without. Some in Washington D.C. called it a concentration camp, at least before the world became aware of the horrors occurring within the concentration camps of the Nazi regime. Manzanar was most definitely not in the same category as those. Nor was it truly a prison like San Quentin, Folsom, or Alcatraz, for the level of freedom inside was far greater than that experienced by convicts within those prisons. As discussed earlier, its original designation was "assembly center" for as long as its primary purpose was merely to "assemble" people for later dispersal to the East. The head of the WRA and the Manzanar project director referred to Manzanar by its official title, "relocation center." They had both fought against the installation by the army of the eight guard towers as they specifically did not want Manzanar to look like a prison, but they lost that battle. Living inside the camp and looking out, the guard towers with their armed MPs, above all else, gave the camp a prison-like appearance, yet after December of 1943, the towers were unmanned throughout the day, and became completely unused from March 1944 until the camp's closure in November of 1945. In fact, even the barbed wire perimeter, without MPs to guard it, gave only the appearance of security. Staying in camp became more of an honor system with most Japanese Americans. While a few would sneak out to the Sierras for fishing—sometimes for days at a time—most choose to stay inside as there was really nowhere else to go.

Take away the outward appearances of Manzanar's barbed wire and guard towers and one would find something very much resembling any other government camp—military, Civilian Conservation Corp, or otherwise—except for the variety of ages and genders populating this camp. Underneath the exterior appearances, the people of Manzanar took part in many of the same activities one would in a normal American city, for within Manzanar's fences one could find schools, a hospital, parks, a dirt golf course, churches including three Buddhist temples, manufacturing plants, a post office, newspaper office, movie theater, bank, shops, social clubs, and more.

Evacuees and staff attending church

This facility though did much more than most government camps—it fed thousands of people from produce grown by its very residents in its own soil, and even had enough surplus to ship to other camps. Manzanar's Japanese-American farmers brought with them the skill, drive, and work ethic along with the desire to make Manzanar a better place for themselves and their families to live. When you see the site today it is impossible to feel the energy that was generated inside the camp with its hundreds of barracks and thousands of adults walking to work while their children hurried to school. The camp was a beehive of activity.

Those WRA employees or their family members that I personally knew, including my own parents, called Manzanar either "the camp" or simply "Manzanar," which is most likely why I call it those as well. Years ago I made the mistake of saying that I had spent part of the war living in an internment camp, only to have those I was talking with believe I must have been a prisoner of the Imperial Japanese. I was surprised to find that they had never heard of Manzanar or the plight of Japanese Americans in our country during WWII. I am happy to say that as time goes on, more people instead of fewer are aware of this event in our history. It is more difficult to repeat a mistake that has been memorialized.

DESIGN AND CONSTRUCTION

Knowledge of the construction process of the Manzanar War Relocation Center helps us to understand the challenges that the WRA faced in operating the camp and the evacuees' ordeal of living in it. Further, it gives us insight into the thinking and motives of the War Department.

The majority of the Manzanar facility consisted of thirty-six identical blocks or groups of barracks housing the evacuees and some staff members, an administration and staff area, a hospital and children's village, an auditorium, warehousing and additional working structures, plus a Military Police camp outside of the fenced boundary. Due to the critical housing shortage in the area in 1942, almost half of the WRA staff—nearly one hundred employees—and their families lived for a time in the same tarpaper barracks as the evacuees, with no kitchen or bathroom, using the community latrines, and eating at the block one mess hall. Many people are surprised to find that, indeed, there were WRA staff members living in the tarpaper barracks. This number would be drastically reduced, but never fully eliminated, as new staff housing was constructed.

From the very beginning of Manzanar camp's creation, there were serious mistakes. There was a dearth of time and money available for camp design and construction. The fault for this fell squarely on the shoulders of General DeWitt and Col. Karl R. Bendetsen, for they were in charge of the evacuation of Japanese Americans. It is believed they were both afraid Japan might try to invade the West Coast and they wanted all Japanese Americans out of that area as quickly as humanly possible. With time so limited, General DeWitt was to make only one visit to Manzanar during its construction stage. He was flown to the Manzanar airstrip, escorted by Military Police to the camp, given a tour of one barrack and one mess hall, and flown out. He was at Manzanar for less than two hours. During DeWitt's short visit, one of the evacuee chefs pointed out several serious shortcomings in the mess hall kitchens, but true to form, the chef's concerns were ignored and no upgrades or repairs resulted. Correcting obvious faults with the camp construction was not in the general's plans. General DeWitt and the War Department never intended to make Manzanar livable for a long period. The plan was to have the evacuees immediately removed from the West Coast, held in assembly centers, and then quickly relocated east of the Mississippi River. They had no intentions of housing Japanese Americans in these camps at government expense until the end of the war; therefore they weren't interested in building comfortable camps. The goal was to put roofs over the heads of the evacuees, but what kind of roof didn't matter. The following men were involved in the early supervision and control: Lt. Col. Edwin C. Kelton, contracting officer for the Corp of Engineers, and three Griffith Co. representatives: Supervising Engineer Leonard G. Hogue, J. Hopinstall, and C.E. Evans. When the War Relocation Authority (WRA) took over, they realized that it was going to be impossible for all the evacuees to move east on their own. Understanding that people would be housed in this camp for what could become years, the WRA accepted that the problem of overseeing repairs and upgrades to the camp to make it livable would be solely their own. Problems in design were to be expected as Manzanar was the first—the first site chosen, the first camp designed and built, and the first to receive evacuees. In June, after a review of the Manzanar camp construction, Colonel L. R. Groves from the Office of Engineers and Gen. DeWitt agreed on an improved construction standard for all future evacuee camps—not major improvements, but improvements nonetheless. All subsequent camps benefitted from the learning acquired in the building of Manzanar, and unlike Manzanar, all would be built and staffed before the arrival of the first evacuee. Had the Army Corp of Engineers and General DeWitt not learned anything else, this alone provided a tremendous improvement to the startup of the other camps.

Building barracks at Manzanar

CONSTRUCTION OF TARPAPER BUILDINGS

By March 6, the contract to build Manzanar Relocation Center was awarded to Griffith Co. The Contractor immediately started rounding up work crews and building materials so that on March 14, 1942, materials and a work force of 450 men showed up and work began, giving crews one week to prepare for the arrival of the first Japanese Americans. Given the timeframe, the objective was ridiculously unrealistic. The men doing the labor lived in tents, used slit trenches for toilets, and ate from a field kitchen. They were subjected to miserable living conditions—every bit as bad as or worse than what the evacuees faced. Since 20 by 100 feet was the common size for each of the 504 barracks, the contractor set up an assembly line-type construction. The crews soon totaled 600 men working six days each week, ten hours each day. The lack of time for planning and preparing resulted in a poorly designed camp slapped together by unskilled workers with low grade materials. Construction called for a minimalist design that provided no ceilings or interior wallboard, one-by-six-inch shiplap flooring on precast concrete blocks. There was no plumbing in the barracks—no toilets, showers, sinks, or running water for any purpose. Once construction got rolling, the contractor was completing two barracks per hour. All 764 wooden structures were completed within three months.

Inside an unimproved barrack

This photo shows what the interior of each barrack looked like once it was turned over by the Griffith Co. to the WRA. Looking up, one would see the A-frames and wooden roof, but no ceiling. Without a ceiling, and with wall partitions that didn't reach the roof, it was possible to climb over the short, interior wall into the apartment next door, and possible to hear every word spoken in the next apartment. Knots would pop out of the drying lumber leaving holes in the walls and floors. It was a common practice to collect lids from tin cans to nail over the holes to keep the dust out. The shiplap flooring had cracks you could see through to the sand and silt below, allowing dust to constantly come up between the floorboards. The lack of a ceiling meant heat in the winter escaped up through the roof and in the summer the black tarpaper roof transmitted the summer heat directly to the room below. These tarpaper barracks were a cooker in summer and an icebox in winter. The WRA quickly recognized that the floor and wall gaps were of great concern and tried to correct it by contracting outside work crews to lay down a floor covering. This failed when the local union would not allow its crews to enter the camp. Instead, a linoleum-like material called Mastipave was laid down by the evacuees themselves. This was a huge job requiring one million square feet of Mastipave to cover all the barracks' floors. Evacuees also installed wallboard to the existing walls and created ceilings. This treatment was required not just in the barracks, but also in the administration building, mess halls, and hospital, as all of those buildings were turned over to the WRA in similarly unfinished condition.

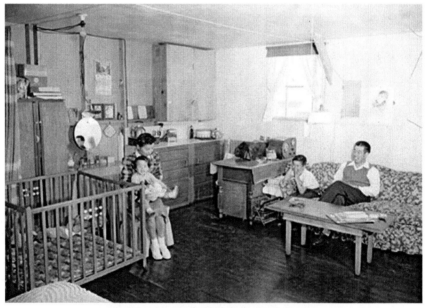

Barrack interior after improvements

All of these essential upgrades were completed by the evacuees before winter. Many evacuees, like Mr. and Mrs. Richard Izumo in the photo, took great pride in transforming their unfinished barrack into an eye appealing living space. To accomplish this transformation required the evacuees to pour their hearts and souls into making a home out of a shell, and required much of the materials to be provided by the WRA. For furnishings, the WRA would ship an evacuee's furniture from storage upon request. The sofa and baby crib in the photo are examples of such items. Other furnishings, such as the coffee table and cabinets in the photo, were manufactured by evacuees in camp.

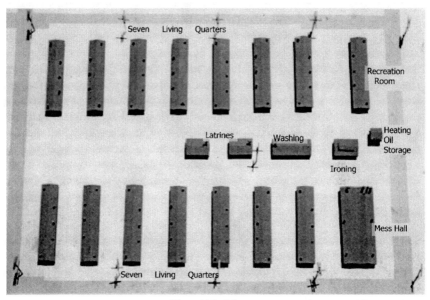

Typical block layout

TYPICAL BLOCK LAYOUT

Each of the identical thirty-six evacuee blocks was laid out as shown in the model above with fourteen barracks for living quarters—seven on each side. Each barrack measured 20 by 100 feet and was divided into four family living units measuring twenty by twenty-five feet (500 square feet), and equipped with nothing more than one drop cord light and an oil heater. Each block was to accommodate 280 people with each individual unit designed for an average of five family members. Some units were assigned to groups of bachelors. Initially, families larger than five persons still only had 500 square feet of living space, but in time, this would change. Each block also had its own mess hall (two 20-foot-by-100-foot barracks attached side by side to create a building of 40 by 100 feet each) and a recreation hall spaced further away from the apartment barracks to minimize disturbances. A laundry room, ironing room, women's restroom with showers, and men's restroom with showers each had concrete floors and were centrally located in the middle of each block. At the end of each block was an oil storage tank with heating oil and faucets for water.

Besides the previously mentioned poor building construction, the largest problem for families living in army-design barracks was the complete lack of privacy and standard amenities. Consider how often in a day you use water—to clean a spill, wash a child's face, brush your teeth, get a drink, use the toilet—the list goes on. These were family homes with people of all ages from newborn to developing teenagers to the elderly and they were living with no running water and no private bathrooms or bedrooms. Equally odious was that neither the community-block showers nor toilets were partitioned off from one another. This might have been acceptable for young men behind the lines in the military, but not for families. Both the evacuees and those WRA employees and their families who lived in the tarpaper barracks complained bitterly about it. It was embarrassing to everyone, but especially so for women and young girls. Most of the young girls and many of the women would wait until late at night to use the women's showers, hoping for a modicum of privacy. This minimum government housing was referred to by the Corp of Engineers as "temporary buildings of Regular Army Theater of Operations construction." Regardless of what name you put on it, it was not suitable for family living.

The relocation of evacuees out of the camp to locations east started on November 15, 1942, and gradually eased the overcrowded living conditions. Another significant reduction of evacuees at Manzanar occurred when those claiming loyalty to Japan were relocated to another camp at Tule Lake, California. They started leaving October 9, 1943, and by February 26, 1944, there was a reduction of 2,165 evacuees. From that time on, overcrowded living conditions were not an issue. The reduction of evacuees in camp offered the opportunity for the remaining families to move internal wall partitions and make living quarters larger.

BUILDING THE HOSPITAL

The original medical facility authorized by the army was as woefully inadequate as the other buildings described. In fact, it was very nearly overlooked completely. Originally, to care for the medical needs of 10,000 people, one 20-by-100-foot tarpaper barrack was set aside for providing medical care and a second as a ward with beds. A month later the army would allow additional barracks to be filled with beds for the sick. On March 21, 1942, the very first day of the first evacuee arrivals, the army quickly recognized they had fallen short of providing acceptable medical coverage, so approval was given to build a 250 bed hospital. Approval for this addition was granted uncharacteristically quickly as Japan was holding US prisoners and our government did not want word to leak out that this country was not offering excellent medical services to its resident Japanese. Griffith Co. got the contract to build the new hospital and completed it on July 22 of that year. It too had tarpaper on the outside, and like the barracks, was unfinished on the inside. The WRA would see to the laying of floor covering, installation of wallboard, and creation of ceilings. In a short time, this hospital would become the finest within 200 miles.

Those evacuees working in the hospital and their families were housed in nearby block 29, placing them close to the hospital for medical emergencies. Block 34 was used as a hostel for those not requiring a hospital bed, but in need of care. Setting aside this block relieved potential crowding at the hospital. As the Japanese-American doctors relocated to the East, they were replaced by Caucasian doctors, at which point, staff housing at the hospital was upgraded, and a new housing unit was added for the family of Dr. William Morse Little (head of the hospital) and three additional doctors.

...ONE DROP OF JAPANESE BLOOD

When the US Government ordered all Japanese Americans off the West Coast, the man in charge of implementing the move took the government literally. The orders were carried out to the letter, and along with the adults and families, astonishingly, all Japanese-American orphans, foster children, and adopted children, regardless of age, were rounded up, pulled from their homes, and sent to Manzanar. Their removal was arguably the most bizarre twist in the entire evacuation, for clearly these infants and children posed no threat to West Coast security. The orphans came from three institutions—the Shonien orphanage in Los Angeles, the Mary Knoll Home for Japanese Children in Los Angeles, and the Salvation Army Japanese Children's Home in San Francisco.

The orphans arrived completely unexpectedly, so a place had to be built for them in a hurry. Children's Village, completed in June 1942, became the finest tarpaper-covered buildings in camp. The village consisted of a building for the boys, another for the girls, and a third containing a mess hall, administration offices, and staff housing. These three buildings were each twenty-five by 150 feet and had double floors, double walls, double partitions, ceilings, and inside showers and toilet facilities, and even had a porch at each end. For convenience, Children's Village was located in the northwest area of the camp near the hospital.

Arthur L. Williams

Residents and staff of Manzanar's Children's Village

During the life of the Manzanar camp, there were over 100 orphans raised in Children's Village. Some of these orphans were only partially Japanese and some were as young as six months of age when they arrived. Because at one time marriages between Japanese descendants and Caucasians were illegal in California, and culturally frowned upon by American and Japanese societies alike, some biracial children were placed in orphanages to hide their existence. The arrest of some Japanese-American men by the FBI resulted in their wives turning their children in to an orphanage because they could not support them. These were just some of the numerous hardships and heartbreaks faced by Japanese Americans at the time. An employee from one of the orphanages in Southern California called Colonel Karl Bendetsen and asked if the evacuation of Japanese Americans applied to Japanese and partially Japanese orphans. The Colonel replied, "If they have one drop of Japanese blood, they go to the camp." These were harsh words that lay bare his coldness towards the entire Japanese race. There were additional ramifications of this decision. One of those evacuated was Mrs. Ethel Maruyama, a Caucasian woman who accompanied her Japanese-American husband and their two children to Manzanar. Mrs. Maruyama was one of a handful of interned Caucasians in a camp of 10,000 Japanese Americans, most disdainful of her interracial marriage. The societal pressure became so intense in camp that she applied to the army for a release for herself and her two children. It was granted in July 1942, by the regional director, and she was permitted by Major Goebel to leave Manzanar and return to her home in West Los Angeles which, by the way, was directly in the prohibited zone.

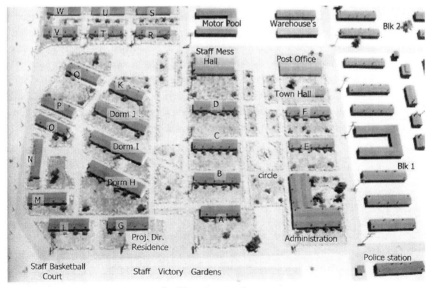

Staff housing area layout

STAFF AND ADMINISTRATION AREA

The WRA staff and administration area in Manzanar, which not only provided space for WRA administrative offices but also for employee housing, can be thought of as a camp within a camp. This area was located within the barbed-wire confines of Manzanar, in the southeast corner, with no barrier separating it from the majority of the camp which was occupied by the evacuees. Ultimately, with the combined total of WRA employees and their family members, the staff area housed over 400 people. It took a full year and a half for housing structures to reach their peak number of twenty-three units, providing housing for 183 WRA employees, ninety-two of whom had originally resided in blocks 1 and 7 of the tarpaper barracks. The WRA at Manzanar employed a maximum of 229 people at one time, leaving several staff members without upgraded staff housing. While some employees continued to live in tarpaper barracks for the duration of their stay, others chose to commute from Independence, Lone Pine, and as far away as Keeler and Cartago. Leealta Harris lived in a house trailer at the Manzanar airport, and yet another lived in the old Reward Mine mining shack which the Bright family operated in the Inyo Mountains. Clearly, housing was scarce in the area and people were willing to improvise.

The construction of the staff and administration section of the camp was completed in four phases. Phase I of these was completed by Griffith Co. under terms of the original contract to build the camp. This phase included the construction of the administration building, the police station, the staff mess hall, the town hall, a post office, and housing units A through F—each of the twenty-three staff housing units being identified by a letter (A through W). The remaining three phases of development were designed by the Farm Security Administration and constructed using staff supervision and evacuee craftsmanship. The design and construction of Phases II through IV were an improvement over those of Phase I and a tremendous improvement over those of the tarpaper barracks. Phases II through IV included the construction of housing units G and K through W, a laundry room, and the dormitories designated H, I, and J, as well as doctors' quarters at the hospital. These fifteen Phase II through IV staff housing units plus three dormitories totaled 38,280 square feet at a total cost of $110,633.

PHASE I

At the same time that they were constructing the thirty-six blocks of evacuee housing, the hospital, and the Military Police (MP) camp, the Griffith Co. held the contract to construct all the Phase I wooden structures within the staff area. Except for the tarpaper police station, Phase I buildings were covered with one-by-ten-inch wood drop siding, the interior walls and ceilings were covered with sheetrock, and the flooring consisted of tongue and groove timbers. The exceptions to this were the administration building, which was unfinished inside, and the jail which, by necessity, had a concrete slab floor to support a jail cell, and was tarpaper covered in the same manner as the thirty-six blocks of evacuee barracks.

Administration building

The L-shaped administration building was one of the very first buildings under construction. From the outside, it looked like a big improvement over the barracks. In truth, it only looked good on the outside. The interior was much like a tarpaper barrack with no ceiling and no wall covering, and with the same pervasive dust coming up through the floor. These conditions were soon corrected by the WRA while overseeing the same upgrades to the tarpaper barracks, mess halls, and hospital.

The Manzanar Post Office was a part of the Griffith Co.'s original contract and consisted of two 20-by-100-foot tarpaper barracks placed side by side. This was the only post office in the camp and was a branch of the Los Angeles Post Office. Since the postal service and the WRA were both government organizations, they made an agreement to have Robert Stengel, a postal employee, live in WRA housing. He lived in the camp until it closed, and then moved to Lone Pine just ten miles south of the camp where he continued working for the post office until his retirement.

The six original buildings constructed for staff housing, A through F, were delegated to be two family apartment buildings, two men's dormitories, and two women's dormitories. Phase I did little to relieve the housing shortage for it only provided accommodations for twenty-five out of the over 200 employees. Some employees moved into the evacuees' tarpaper barracks in the hopes that once the staff housing was completed they would be able to move into improved housing. A large number of employees signed on to work at Manzanar and had no idea what the living conditions were going to be like until they arrived. Upon discovering the conditions within the camp and finding there was nothing outside of the camp to rent, some prospective employees opted to back out of their Manzanar job before even starting.

What comes to mind for me when I see old pictures of the staff housing and administration area is how neat and tidy it was always kept by the Japanese-American gardeners that cared for it. The lawns were always closely cropped, the edges trimmed, the rocks bordering the walks kept freshly painted white, and there was not a piece of trash to be found anywhere. There have been numerous comments about how superior the staff area was to the evacuee housing areas. In fact, the evacuees referred to the staff area as "Beverly Hills." It may have seemed that way to the evacuees living in their tarpaper homes. Phase I housing units were better than the tarpaper barracks, but did not come close to the standard reached by the subsequent housing in Phases II through IV built by the evacuees. There was no question that with its green lawns and indoor plumbing, the staff area was a place of beauty and a superior place to live within the camp.

PHASE II THROUGH PHASE IV

The completion of Phase I spelled the end to the Griffith Co. contract. To complete the remainder of the camp, Project Director Ralph Merritt asked the evacuee craftsmen if they would agree to build the staff housing under WRA staff supervision. They not only agreed, but completed the job in eight months. With one exception, each Phase II through IV building was twenty by ninety-four feet and contained four housing units. Each end unit was a two bedroom apartment while each of the two interior apartments had a single bedroom. Besides the bedroom/s, each unit had a small living room, a kitchen, and bathroom with shower. Staff housing units K - W were very short on space. Where a standard, evacuee-inhabited tarpaper barrack consisted of four housing units within a space of 20 by 100 feet, the staff housing units K - W had the same four units in an area six feet shorter. Unlike the evacuees' barracks, each staff unit offered the convenience of a kitchen and bathroom, which was nice, but took a great amount away from an already tiny area. The two small interior apartments in each of these buildings provided some of the most cramped living quarters in the entire camp. There was no provision for cooling, but each unit did have an oil fired heater for the cold winters. Included in these building phases was a laundry room with a single tub—no washing machines—and clothes were dried outside on lines. The low humidity made the drying quick and easy but it required very strong pins to keep the wash on the lines in the Owens Valley wind. I seriously doubt there were many employees that did not leave a more spacious and nicer home than that which they moved into at Manzanar.

Evacuee-built staff housing unit

This is an example of one evacuee-built housing unit. I remember this particular staff building because it had two families in it with children my age. The Berrimans lived in unit L-1 on the left, and the Hayes family lived in L-4 on the far right. Mildred and Wilma Clydene Berriman and Bill and Lynne Hayes rode the bus with me to school every day, so I knew them especially well.

Project Director Ralph Merritt's housing unit

Housing structure G, which included Project Director Ralph Merritt's residence, was of the same construction and exterior dimensions as the other buildings, but had only two and not four apartments. Each of these two apartments contained the floor space of a two bedroom and single bedroom unit combined. By camp standards they were considered quite large and were by far the best accommodations in camp. The project director's apartment also had a beautiful rock wall and patio in front, constructed by skilled evacuee craftsmen. The rock wall is all that is now visible. There was only one other apartment to have a rock wall and that was unit D-5 which had been the project director's previous residence. One of the remarkable things about the project director's residence is that I do not recall anyone complaining about how upscale it was compared to all other housing in the camp.

When the project director moved from D-5, which had been built in Phase I, into his more spacious accommodation, G-1, I got to know unit D-5 with its enviable patio and stone walls quite well, for our family moved from Independence into that apartment and it became ours. Today, these two stone walls are the most prominently identifiable features in the entire staff area.

Site of apartment D-5 today

For more decades than I want to remember, I have gone back to the wall on every trip to Owens Valley. This is where I let my mind wander back to my youth in the camp—a time when I could see the white buildings, bright green lawns, freshly painted white rock borders, and the snapdragons my mother planted growing along our rock wall. Everything I remember seeing is gone with the exception of the wall. For me the wall evokes both feelings of tranquility and sadness. I suppose we all have a place we go back to—this wall has been, and still is, mine. It may not look like much, but I cannot go back to Manzanar without visiting this old friend. It evokes memories that have softened and improved with time. Now in my eighties, with my mother, father, brother, and most of the WRA employees who I knew gone, I sit there and think of my family and the kids I knew. When I lived in camp, I would go down to the river during the winter and shoot ducks. I always brought them home to pluck in this patio and I always heard the same thing—my mother telling me, "Don't let those feathers get away." My father, being a hunter, would either smile or laugh. When the wind was blowing, which was most of the time in Manzanar, it was impossible for those feathers not to get away. This wall holds fond memories of a difficult time that was, in retrospect, not all bad.

It was not until September of 1943, some fifteen months after the WRA employees arrived in Manzanar, when dormitories H, I, and J were completed to house sixty-nine bachelorettes, that some real relief was felt in the area of staff housing. Each of these three 24-by-140-foot units contained three single bedrooms, ten double occupancy rooms, two showers, two toilets, and a linen room. There were twenty-three WRA staff members, consisting mostly of female teachers and secretaries, in each of the three dormitories. I can only imagine the chaos in each of these buildings of twenty-three women all arising to go to work at the same time and sharing two bathrooms between them.

Residents of the newly constructed bachelorette dorms, from left to right: Nona Winchester (secretary), Edith Cox (teacher), unknown, Lena Harrison (teacher), Susan Shoaf (secretary), Martha Shoaf (teacher), Ione Bermaye (teacher), and Gretchen Ingalls (teacher)

The floors in the bachelorette dormitories were covered with a linoleum-type material which I vividly remember. This flooring came in rolls which the craftsmen rolled out and weighted down with bags of sand. On one occasion, for reasons I cannot comprehend, Rick Collins, the son of a WRA staff member, walked into a dorm with its freshly laid linoleum, picked up a sandbag and threw it down the hall. The linoleum began a rapid rewind, cracking as it rolled up, leaving sand all over the wooden floor for Rick to run and slide through. As a youngster, if there was trouble nearby, you could count on Rick to be a part of it.

The final housing buildings constructed with evacuee labor were built in this sequence: R, T, V, S, U, and then W. Though not surprising, it is noteworthy that there was quite a conflict in the manner in which staff housing was assigned. In the original phase I buildings, priority for housing assignments was based on job description—the employees with the most senior job titles received their units first. This created a flurry of concerns as the next phases of housing became available. Those employees who had arrived first to Manzanar, and had been waiting for over a year to move out of the tarpaper barracks with their communal toilets and showers, felt extremely slighted as other, more senior employees arrived and stepped immediately into new housing. The excitement of seeing housing go up and the anticipation of knowing you would be next to receive it, followed abruptly by the disappointment of finding the housing had gone to somebody new was just too much for some to take sitting down. They banded together and approached the project director with their concerns. It was the only time I can recall the employees gathering in number to face the project director. Surprisingly, he agreed with those who had endured the tarpaper barracks the longest and from that point on, assigned housing was based on earliest date of employment as opposed to job title.

THE AUDITORIUM

Manzanar auditorium

With approximately 2,700 Japanese-American students combined in the elementary and high schools, the University of California at Berkeley, the agency responsible for academic accreditation, required an auditorium be built on Manzanar's campus. The request was made to WRA Director Dillon Myer for an auditorium to be added, and he quickly approved it. Plans were prepared by the Farm Security

Administration, and the cornerstone for the new building was laid on February 19, 1944. The auditorium was built entirely by evacuee craftsmen supervised by the WRA staff, providing a shining example of how well the evacuees and staff could work together to accomplish an important task. Measuring 118 by 119 feet, the building was originally 14,140 square feet and cost $30,355. The materials used to build the auditorium were the best available at the time.

Construction of the auditorium was supervised by Oliver E. Sisler, construction and maintenance superintendent, with direct onsite supervision by Jewel W. Lawing, chief construction foreman. Lawing was hired specifically for his knowledge in large building construction. Also directly involved with supervision, and working for Lawing, was K. Kunishage. Millwork was provided by Jimmy Araki and his evacuee crew working from the camp carpenter shop. R. D. Feil, electrical engineer, and Malcolm Inman, electrical instructor, supervised evacuee electricians. Plumbing was installed by K. Bowker and the evacuee plumbing crews. Painting was carried out by J. Nakahama and the evacuee painting crews. When the auditorium was finished it was something to truly be proud of with its quality workmanship and materials. Sadly, the auditorium was only used by the Japanese-American schools for two semesters—one school year—from the fall of 1944 to the spring of 1945. It's unfortunate that this building could not have been completed earlier and enjoyed for the duration of the evacuees' stay. In this picture of the construction crew you will find fifty-nine Japanese-American craftsmen along with three WRA employees. All three staff members are standing in the back, middle of the photo with Oliver Sisler on the right and Arthur Sandridge (the tallest man) in the middle.

Construction Crew

The auditorium was the last building constructed at Manzanar, and is the only original wooden structure still standing of the over 700 structures built on the Manzanar War Relocation Center (MWRC) site. It is a survivor, yet it is not representative of the other wooden structures that once existed. The Manzanar auditorium picture on page 59 was taken after the National Park Service completed their restoration of the original building. It is now used as the National Park Service Interpretive Center, which along with the Eastern California Museum in Independence, contains a wealth of information regarding the history of Manzanar and the valley.

OUTSIDE THE FENCE—BUILDINGS OF THE MILITARY POLICE CAMP

The Griffith Co. contract included the construction of a Military Police (MP) camp outside of Manzanar's perimeter fencing. Although the Corp of Engineers stayed with the same building dimensions as those used in the evacuee camp, the materials used in building the MP Camp were the same as those used in the staff area, with its sheet rocked interiors, tongue-and-groove flooring, and complete absence of tarpaper. Exceptions to the standard construction were that the shower and latrine building had a concrete floor, and the motor repair building was simply a shed. The MP Camp was completed for occupancy during the summer of 1942. It was designed for a total military force of 200 men, fifty men per barrack, however, the actual maximum compliment was 135 men except for one brief period.

INFRASTRUCTURE

It wasn't just the buildings that suffered from the limited time available for planning and construction. There were major problems with the camp's infrastructure as well. The electrical system for the entire camp had only one main switch. Performing repairs downstream of the main required turning off all power to the entire camp or risking having newly trained evacuees work this high voltage system while hot—not a risk the WRA wanted to take. The WRA corrected this problem by installing a loop system. Equally problematic, the water reservoir had erroneously been located too low in elevation leaving the northwest area of the camp, including the hospital and several evacuee blocks, without adequate water pressure. WRA Fire Chief, Frank Hon recognized the error and had the issue corrected with the addition of a new water well. Camp design, or lack thereof, also called for all raw sewage to simply pour out onto the valley floor. This was corrected with the addition of a $150,000, modern sewage plant. These are but a few of the infrastructural problems inherited by the WRA when it took supervision of Manzanar over from the WCCA. For over a year, the WRA staff and the evacuees worked together to rectify most of the initial major design and construction flaws.

61

CHAPTER VII
THE EVACUEES

Just as no two individuals behave exactly the same, neither do the many individuals from any group of people. Members of the community of Japanese descendants at the time of the evacuation were no exception. In general, there were four major groups of people of Japanese heritage in the US at the time of the war. In many cases the individuals within these groups provided each other with a feeling of camaraderie and comfort during the evacuation. For others, the differences in their upbringings caused an inescapable friction that led to severe discourse. Packing thousands of socially and politically diverse people into such excessively tight, primitive quarters during wartime was a recipe for disaster and one which would express itself in violent ways.

ISSEI

The term "Issei" literally means "first generation" in Japanese. Issei, who represented approximately one-third of those interned in Manzanar, were born, raised, and educated in Japan. They often came to the United States while retaining their love for their native Japan. This is easy for me to understand, for I worked thirteen years overseas including an extremely pleasurable stay in England, yet there was never a foreign country to which I felt as bonded as the one in which I was raised and where my family lived. The Issei clung to Japanese traditions and mores such as a respect for age, family honor, and family leadership by the eldest male. By the time WWII struck, most had been in the US for over twenty-five years, was over the age of fifty, and spoke very limited English. With laws in place preventing immigrating Japanese from attaining citizenship, once their homeland Japan attacked, the Issei were automatically defined as "enemy aliens" by our government. Enemy alien refers to any non-citizen inhabitant of our country who is from a country with which we are at war. At no time does the term "enemy alien" indicate attitudes or actions of the individual with said label. The only Japanese residents who qualified for citizenship were those who served in the US military during WWI, or those born in the

USA. It was not until the Immigration and Nationality Act 1952, passed some seven years after the end of WWII, that Issei could finally acquire United States citizenship. Without internalizing the meaning of the term "enemy alien," those responsible for the defense of the West Coast might view 40,000 Japanese enemy aliens as a frightening number. To those that did not know better, it might seem as if there was a potential spy, saboteur, or Japan loyalist on every corner. What they should have seen was a potential shopkeeper, farmer, or family man instead. The Issei male was hard working and frugal, respected the law, and insisted his family follow suit. Had the Issei been almost anything except Asian, they might well have been highly respected in our society. As it was, every Issei "enemy alien" was automatically labelled a Japanese loyalist.

The Issei sent to Manzanar probably suffered the most through the evacuation process. They often suffered severe financial losses plus the loss of control of their families. Instead of their families eating at the same table where the Issei were previously in control, their kids were now eating with other kids in the mess hall and no longer looked to their Issei father for financial support or guidance. Where an Issei insisted everyone in the family work, the kids in the camp lost their incentive due to the meager wages, or often, a simple lack of job opportunities. The Issei himself, due to his foreign education, age, and poor English was unlikely to be accepted into a position of much authority. These jobs would go to a younger generation with US citizenship and a better grasp of the English language. This created another blow to his dignity and authoritative position. His life had been built around hard work, saving money, and building his financial security. He was now spending his life's savings and earning little to nothing. Robert Stengel, former postal employee stationed at Manzanar, told me he had never seen so many one-hundred-dollar-bills as he had while working at the Manzanar post office. These one-hundred-dollar-bills were not coming from a sixteen-dollar monthly check, but directly from savings. The Issei was now sitting around camp with nothing to do but spend his savings. He had time to think about his mistreatment, his financial losses, and the control he had lost over his family. He would exert his previously unquestioned authority and be ignored. In one incident, Issei men in Manzanar objected to the creation of a beauty shop by second generation girls. When the elder men were ignored, they took their frustration out by trying to burn down the building. Everything they had stood for and achieved in their working lifetimes was crumbling beneath them. Add to this the uncertainty of their future and that of their families they had always been entrusted with protecting and one can see how many Issei felt hopelessly emasculated at the hands of the US government.

NISEI

In Japanese, Nisei translates to "second generation." The Nisei represented the second generation of Japanese to live in America. They were the first generation of Japanese Americans to be born here, and therefore, the first to be eligible for

US citizenship. They were often the product of an Issei father and a picture-bride mother who had arrived between 1910 and 1920. Nisei represented over half of the Japanese-American community, even though they were still a very young group by the time of the war. In Manzanar no Nisei was over fifty-four years old. It is seldom mentioned that a full eighty-six percent of Nisei in Manzanar were twenty-five years old and younger. As a result of being born in America to Japanese parents, they were eligible for duel citizenship but less than 20 percent actually had dual citizenship, they virtually all spoke English, and they also spoke some Japanese. Through attending schools, they were often integrated into the American culture, were good students, well educated, and many had plans for professional careers that were interrupted by the war. A few had already emerged as fine doctors, dentists, and other professionals, such as Dr. Nakagi, a dentist in Manzanar who later opened a practice in Santa Barbara. He was outstanding, and after the war, was our family dentist for many years. The Nisei were a young group with young American ideals. The manner in which they dressed, their American interests, and the games and entertainment they enjoyed all went against the traditional Japanese Issei in camp. As a group, these young Nisei strongly supported the USA, despite the evacuation. As a result of their youth, their American education, and their strong English skills, they were given the better jobs by the WRA staff. Because of their outspoken, strong support of the US and the better jobs they filled, the Nisei were unpopular with large numbers of the older Japanese camp residents. There was a power struggle, with the Issei trying to hold on to what they had traditionally controlled, while the young Nisei were out to seize every advantage they could get from life. The Nisei were making huge strides towards integration into the American culture at the expense of the Issei who had no intentions of giving up their traditional control without a struggle.

SANSEI

Sansei translates to "third generation" and represented the children of the Nisei, their grandparents being the original Issei immigrants. For the most part, the Sansei were small children during the evacuation and, as such, did not factor prominently into the social/political conflicts of the time. The children were often the least affected by the evacuation, and as children tend to be, the most resilient.

KIBEI

Having briefly defined the first, second, and third generations of immigrants, one might think we had covered all the different groups affected by the evacuation, but there is still one more section of the evacuee population to consider. One could roll the complexities of the Issei and Nisei into one and still not touch on the issues faced by the Kibei. Like the Nisei, the Kibei were second generation inhabitants of the United States. The difference between the two is in their upbringing. Kibei were born in America, giving them US and the opportunity for Japanese citizenship, and were then sent to Japan, often at a very young age, to be educated. It was frequently the oldest child in the family who became Kibei, and there were a number of reasons that an Issei might send this child back to Japan to be educated. In some cases the children were sent back for economic reasons. The parents of a large, poor family often could not support all of their children and sent some back to be raised by grandparents or aunts and uncles. There were those Issei whose future in the USA was uncertain. Those that suspected they might return to Japan wanted their children schooled there so they could fit in with the Japanese culture, society, and educational system. A more common reason was cultural. The Issei's children were becoming Americanized and drifting away from the Japanese culture and an understanding of their Issei parents. To avoid this, children were sent back to Japan to learn the language and culture. A number of Kibei were not only educated in Japan, but had also served in the Japanese army, some growing to admire Japan's military government and its achievements. This is not difficult to understand, since Japan, with its very colorful and historic culture, had never lost a war and was spreading its empire across the Pacific. Understandably, their service in the military was paired with a strong dose of Japanese cultural indoctrination.

The concept of sending one's children home to be educated in one's own culture was conceived of with the best of intentions, but there were unexpected consequences for the children involved. The now-older Kibei who returned to the USA were not sure of where they belonged. Because of the war with Japan, they now had to decide where their future lay and where their loyalty should be placed. Although the Kibei could relate to their parents in a way that their siblings could not, through years of living in Japan, they lost the previously close associations they had with their younger Nisei brothers and sisters who had never been to Japan and were fluent in English—a language and culture now apart from their own. This cultural divide created complications within the family and the society they joined back in the USA. It created a young adult, poorly educated in American ways and weak in English, trying to find where he belonged. Another big problem for the Kibei was that the US government generalized that the Kibei's loyalties lay with the country in which they had been raised. This was unfortunate, for they were consequently labeled a security risk, possibly as a result of their recent contact with Japan's new military government. The government concluded that the nearly 18,000 Kibei on the West Coast were a greater security risk than even their parents who had been born in Japan. The Kibei were respected by the Issei for the recent connection they offered to their beloved homeland, but they were equally disliked in many cases by the Nisei. As long as they were in Japan they were considered too American; while in America, they were seen as Japanese. As for the WRA authority, they divided the Kibei into four categories based on certain risk factors: how long they had been in Japan, how much Japanese education they had received, how long they had been back in the United States, and whether they intended to stay in the states or return to Japan. Within the Kibei group could be found everything from a flag waving

American who would do anything to prove his loyalty to the US, to the person who hated everything about the US and couldn't wait to return to Japan. There was a mixture of attitudes and feelings about the US government and the evacuation. Generally, the Kibei withdrew from Nisei society and came to be regarded as a group apart—a minority within a minority. Their remoteness in terms of family, social, and economic life was often extreme. Kibei boys had difficulty in finding Nisei girls who would marry them. Kibei girls would marry other Kibei boys or Issei men. Kibei straddled two cultures in such a way as to make a fit improbable in either. Generally the loyalty expressed by the Kibei for the USA was in direct proportion to their proficiency in the English language, the amount of time they had been back in the USA, and the strength of their family ties. Those who arrived in 1940 and 1941, just in time for tensions to escalate between Japan and the US, and were struggling to learn English, tended to support Japan. The inconsistency within this Japanese-American sub-society is exemplified by the fact that there were a few Kibei relentless in causing a great deal of trouble for WRA staff and for other Japanese Americans alike, while other Kibei selflessly volunteered to serve the US army as translators in the Pacific interrogating captured Japanese military prisoners.

AMERICAN CITIZENS

One cannot forget that American citizenship ran throughout each of the groups named above. At the time, few Caucasian citizens or government officials acknowledged the prevalence of American citizens among the evacuees. Few Issei were citizens, but virtually all Nisei, Sansei, and Kibei were, some holding citizenship in Japan and the US. Because of this dual citizenship, their loyalties came into question as much as those of the Issei. At the time, the government estimated upwards of 40% of people of Japanese descent was loyal to Japan. Obviously, with "loyalty" being a state of mind, there was no way to know, but it appears the estimators had little knowledge of the population they were forming statistics about.

The point has been made numerous times that the United States locked up its own American citizens without a trial, in direct violation of their civil rights and of the Constitution. The government's position, which was defended in court several times, was that the country was at war and the West Coast was a war zone vital to the support of the war effort in the Pacific. That the Japanese residing there complicated the safety of the west coast. This explanation seems to have trumped any rights of the citizens within its borders.

CHAPTER VIII
THE EVACUATION

As a teenager living in the camp at Manzanar, I of course knew that all Japanese Americans had been moved off the West Coast, yet as strange as it may seem, I never questioned the necessity for such a move. I visualized the evacuees as Japanese and we were at war with Japan, and yet I never associated the people in camp nor the ones I had known in Redondo Beach with the enemy in the Pacific. It all seems so strange now. I saw firsthand the confinement of the old and young, the men and women. I could use my youth at the time as an excuse, but I know the question deserves more. When I look back nearly seventy years I think most of us were too focused on our own lives, our own problems, and rallying to the war effort to question our government. Simply put, as a teenager, I never questioned or doubted the government's decisions. During the war I never wondered how many evacuees were citizens of the USA. While in high school in Independence, I never heard a teacher express any reservations about the internment of the Japanese in the camp located only six miles away. Apparently they were as blind to the injustice as the rest of us, or too careful in their speech to allow their opinions to be publicly expressed. I never heard anyone ever voice outrage or even doubt about the government locking up United States citizens without a fair trial. Not until the Korean War do I personally remember questioning the actions of our government on anything. When I left Manzanar and Owens Valley, I forgot about what I had experienced in camp. It wasn't until nearly fifty years later, when I became involved with the Manzanar National Historic Site, my curiosity started building. The question I have asked myself since then is why I didn't see the injustice of a total evacuation. The truth is, as a teenager I did not make the connection between The Bill of Rights, citizenship, and Japanese Americans. I just never thought about it. It seems as though few else did either. In attempting to figure out how I had ignored such a social crime occurring all around me, I assembled information for my own knowledge, which I will share with you here. For a subject I vehemently wanted to avoid including in this book due to its controversial nature, I have spent much time working on the events and decisions behind the evacuation.

A CONTROVERSIAL HISTORY

It is doubtful there is a WWII West Coast issue more controversial than the mass removal of Japanese Americans from the West Coast, as directed by Executive Order 9066. Many prominent people, including then Secretary of War Henry Lewis Stimson, California Governor Culbert Olsen, and California Attorney General Earl Warren, argued at the time that a total evacuation was necessary. Two West Coast FBI offices endorsed the evacuation. Colonel Karl Bendetsen pushed it, and General John DeWitt, responsible for the defense of the West Coast, officially recommended it, while President Franklin Delano Roosevelt, along with Congress, approved it. One cannot understate how important public opinion—or in this case, public hysteria—is in the decision making by officials in government. At the time when the decision was made to evacuate all Japanese-Americans, it was widely supported. None of this, however, intimates that the evacuation was the proper course of action. Nearly seventy years after it occurred, emotions are still raw over the issue. Some wish to believe Japanese Americans were removed for their own protection; others believe they were removed to eliminate the potential for spying; still others think it was simple racial prejudice. I find most people have a very strong opinion about the evacuation, yet often their opinions are based on few facts. The following is not directed at changing your view, but merely providing details which reveal the complexity of this issue. After reading this section, ask yourself how you would have handled the defense and safety of the West Coast and its residents during WWII with the public hysteria that was prevalent during the time.

Before getting into the very complex and contentious issue of the evacuation of Japanese Americans, let's not forget these facts—the evacuation process to the vast majority of Japanese Americans and aliens was embarrassing, frightening, and a monumental hardship. It created health issues from which some died and financial losses from which others never recovered. It broke families apart geographically and emotionally. Being labeled a traitor in a country you have been loyal to, and made a home within, can be demoralizing. Being labelled a traitor in an area in which your physical appearance makes you look like the enemy can be terrifying. What is remarkable, despite the horrible treatment afforded them, the vast majority of the interned Japanese Americans stayed loyal to this country. After the war, when given the option to return to Japan, nearly all chose to stay in America.

It was, of course, not just Japanese Americans who suffered during the war. It is necessary to remember that countless other families were torn apart as a result of the war. Approximately 406,000 Americans lost their lives. Men lost their jobs when they were drafted. Women and children were forced to live with relatives—praying they would see their husbands and fathers again. The war was a horrible time that brought tremendous suffering. One distinction remains—once the war was over, the soldiers that returned came home to a hero's welcome. The Japanese Americans that returned to their homes had to rebuild their lives amid contemptuous, suspicious neighbors. In many ways, the war lasted much longer for them.

JAPAN SWEEPS ACROSS THE PACIFIC

The United States was now in a war with little fleet left to protect its West Coast or to push Japan back across the Pacific. Japan's shocking victory at Pearl Harbor was quickly described by the US government as an unprovoked, sneak attack. Though it might have been a sneak attack, that it was unprovoked is debatable. On the first day of the war in the Pacific, Japan bombed Pearl Harbor and attacked Wake Island and Guam. In one week they followed the first day's action with attacks against Malaya, Thailand, Burma, the Philippines and the Gilbert Islands. Japan was sweeping across the Pacific and there was nothing stopping them on land or at sea. It was not long before the British lost Singapore with 135,000 British troops experiencing a humiliating surrender. Japan was sinking the mighty British as well as the Unites States fleets. Hong Kong fell on Christmas Day. A real shock came when Japan bombed Darwin, Australia. Australia quickly looked to the USA for support. Our West Coast was the jumping off spot to the war in the Pacific. Every major port on the West Coast was shipping military supplies and men to fight Japan in the Pacific and support Australia. It would be nearly impossible to fight a war across the Pacific without these ports of disembarkation. There was no question Japan was a world power. They had been building a strong military for some time while the United States had been focused on trying to recover from a devastating depression and had downgraded its military since WWI. Japan was moving across the Pacific, taking island after island. If it were to take the war to the West Coast and seal off our seaports, it could conceivably take the entire Pacific including Australia. Japan was showing its awesome strength while the USA was showing its lack of preparedness. With all of this devastation appearing on newsreels and radio programs as well as in the newspapers, nobody could avoid knowing how dire things appeared. We had no idea where Japan would attack next, and there were scared people on the West Coast as a result. Soon after the attack, the Los Angeles Times and the San Francisco Examiner carried articles calling for the complete removal of all Japanese from the West Coast. The California Congressional Delegation, supported by California Governor Culbert Olsen and State Attorney General Earl Warren, wrote to President Franklin Delano Roosevelt echoing the Examiner's call. With the west coast press, nearly all high ranking government officials, and now the American public crying for the removal of Japanese aliens and Japanese Americans from the West Coast, it was a fait accompli. As the Pacific was falling into the hands of Japan, the President was faced with the decision of how to handle Japanese nationals as well as Japanese Americans on the West Coast. It was brought to the President's attention that when Japan invaded the Philippines, the local Japanese lined the streets, cheering the invading Japanese Army. This was likely a factor in the president's rush to evacuate all 120,000 Japanese descendants off the western seaboard. What if they too were to show the same support should their native Japan succeed in invading the West Coast? If they proved to be loyal to Japan, their vast farming operations in the West could feed an invading army. The question of their loyalty was impossible to answer. How does one tell a loyal person from a disloyal one? The proposal to interrogate every one was made, but the government was not comfortable with the effectiveness of interrogations to determine loyalty. Besides which, with the possibility of a Japanese invasion, no matter how remote, there was insufficient time to carry out interrogations of 120,000 people. On February 19, 1942, President Franklin D. Roosevelt signed Executive Order 9066, empowering the US Army to designate areas from which "any or all persons may be excluded," leading to the evacuation of all persons of Japanese descent from the West Coast of the United States. Would the outcome have been different had the newspapers focused instead on reporting about the countless, young, Japanese-American men who were in uniform, fighting for the United States, or on how many California residents of Japanese ancestry were actually US citizens? Regardless of public opinion, the army was deeply concerned with the large Japanese-American and alien population on the West Coast and with the possibility that any number of people could have been spies. Had Japan invaded our West Coast, the potential disaster would have been made even greater had a spy network been in place to direct the attacks. This was not a chance the US Army was willing to take.

SUSPICIOUS AND SUBVERSIVE ACTIVITIES

On December 29, 1941, all enemy aliens in California, Oregon, Washington, Idaho, Montana, Utah, and Nevada were ordered to surrender all contraband which included short wave radios, guns, cameras, and binoculars. The United States was in a war and it was critical for this country to remove the opportunity for espionage and sabotage. Never underestimate the potential damage caused by unchecked spying, for the cost can be enormous in lives and material. Keep in mind, the West Coast was humming with activity. Not only did its ports ship nearly all the war materials and military personnel to the Pacific, but it was very active in producing those materials and training the personnel. It was vital to the US war effort that information regarding the materials and personnel did not get into enemy hands.

By 1942, the FBI was performing spot raids and gathering evidence of Japanese-American activities. According to the government's *Final Report: Japanese Evacuation from the West Coast 1942, Office of the Commanding General*, it stated one raid in Monterey recovered 60,000 rounds of ammunition and many rifles. The number of Japanese organizations on the West Coast sounded alarming, with some 124 separate Japanese organizations along the Pacific Coast engaged in varying degrees of Japanese activities. Research and coordination of information had made possible the identification of more than 100 parent fascistic or militaristic organizations in Japan which had some relationship, either direct or indirect, with Japanese organizations or individuals in the United States. There was evidence that organizations were sending money to support Japan's military. According to this report, there were also at this time, large numbers of Japanese Americans participating in Shinto, Emperor Worship ceremonies—a tradition misunderstood and therefore alarming to the US government. In addition, there were over 10,000 members in the Heimusha Kai, an organization formed in San Francisco in 1937 that passed the following resolution, "We, the members of the Japanese Reserve Army Corps in America are resolved to do our best in support of the Japanese campaign in China and to set up an Army Relief Department for our mother country." This was a sampling of what General DeWitt weighed before deciding upon a total evacuation. In summary, the report states, "The Commanding General, charged as he was with the mission of providing for the defense of the West Coast, had to take into account these and other military considerations. He concluded the Japanese constituted a potentially dangerous element from the viewpoint of military security—that military necessity required their immediate evacuation to the interior."

According to David D. Lowman, Former Special Assistant to the Director, National Security Agency, Japan typically used Japanese locals to gather and deliver information to their consulates through a well-coordinated cell system where the information was coded and sent to Tokyo. Their consulates were the central coordinators both to and from Tokyo. There is considerable information available on pre-WWII Japanese spying activities through sources such as declassified FBI reports and David Lowman's own book, *Magic*. In his book he reports code breakers uncovered evidence of the Japanese government establishing a network of cells for spying and possible espionage through their west coast consulates. United States code breakers intercepted messages sent to Tokyo of naval ship locations, aircraft plant production, and more. Despite the claims in *Magic* and in the book *The Japanning of America*, by Lillian Baker, I was not successful in finding a single case of a Japanese American actually being convicted of spying. Information I did find in a declassified FBI report (9145-CI-JC) reveals Lt. Commander Itaru Tachibana, believed to be Japan's chief undercover spy on the West Coast, was arrested by the FBI on June 7, 1941, after he was caught trying to recruit ex-US naval officers for spying. Bail was set at $50,000 and the Japanese Consul in Los Angeles immediately posted bail to quickly get him out of the country. A search of his room in the Olympic Hotel in Los Angeles, revealed a book with names and plans for spying activities on the West Coast. Tachibana, though, was an officer in the Japanese Imperial Navy—not a Japanese American.

Lt. Commander Tachibana's career didn't end with his departure from American soil. In the Japanese attack on Wake Island at the same time Pearl Harbor was being bombarded, our military put up a tremendous battle before surrendering on December 23, 1941. Lt. Commander Tachibana had by this time been placed second in command of Japan's invading forces on Wake Island. He served under Rear Admiral Shigematsu Sakaibara. Whether it came to US prisoners or innocent civilians, it was not unknown for Japan's forces to rape, torture, and murder, and Sakaibara and Tachibana took their motherland's practices to heart. During Japan's occupation of Wake Island, one of the appalling things the admiral did was to order the execution of ninety-eight American civilians before a firing squad. When the admiral shipped off civilian construction workers to Japan, they beheaded five in front of the others to assure good behavior. Similar acts of barbarism were heard, read about, and seen in the newsreels, fanning the flames of the already widespread hatred for Japan and Japanese. At the end of the war, after Japan unconditionally surrendered and Wake Island was handed back to the USA, Sakaibara and Tachibana were tried for war crimes and sentenced to death. The admiral was indeed executed, but Tachibana's sentence was reduced to life imprisonment.

Three days after the attack on Pearl Harbor, Secretary of the Navy Frank Knox traveled to Hawaii. Upon his return he reported that Japanese spying had contributed to the success of the attack. In fact, Takeo Yoshikawa, an Imperial Japanese Navy (IJN) master spy stationed in Hawaii, had been regularly reporting to Tokyo the details of the US Naval ships in Pearl Harbor. His reports were the key to the Japanese success. According to the May 1997 issue of *World War II* magazine, Yoshikawa went on to spend time in an Arizona internment camp before being traded for American diplomats being held in Japan. While in the camp, his identity was kept secret even from the other internees there. In a later interview, Yoshikawa reported that he could not trust the Japanese-Americans interned in Hawaii as he found them to be loyal to the United States. In fact he was right. Soon after the attack, many Japanese in Hawaii went on to join the US army, volunteering to lay down their lives in support of their adopted country.

Immediately after December 7, 1941, all Japanese consulates in the USA were closed. This action eliminated the potential for spies in the US to send communications to Japan through a Japanese Consulate. All Japanese diplomats were moved to our finest resorts, Greenbrier and Homestead, to sit out the war as our guests.

According to the book *Magic*, US intelligence discovered that, shortly after closing all enemy alien consulates, Japan and Spain had worked out a cooperative arrangement to spy on the USA and transmit the information to Japan through a Spanish consulate. The door was closed on their plan when all Japanese descendants were evacuated from the West Coast. There is evidence Japan used spying before WWII for both military and industrial information. Japan had a reputation for copying others' industrial ideas. They had set up spy networks in Latin America, Mexico, Canada, Hawaii, and The United States. Some of those suspected of spying in these Latin American countries and Hawaii were rounded up and sent to the USA to be placed in the immigration naturalization internment camps. The Japanese naval intelligence in Tokyo was operating through the Japanese consulate in Hawaii. A great deal of information was transmitted to Tokyo through their agent Takeo Yoshikawa, a Japanese naval reserve ensign. One specific question from Tokyo was, "What day of the week has the most ships in Pearl Harbor?" Yoshikawa responded, "Weekends," hence the bombing on Sunday. On the military channel they presented a filmed interview with Takeo Yoshikawa in which he explained exactly how he got the information that was transmitted to Japan. Remember, like Tachibana, he was a member of the Imperial Japanese Navy and not a Japanese American.

In the spring of 1941, the FBI and the Office of Naval Intelligence (ONI) broke into the Japanese Consulate in Los Angeles well before Pearl Harbor and the arrest of Tachibana. The break-in was made possible due to the skills of a convicted safe cracker borrowed from prison. All documents in the consulate were microfilmed and returned to the safe from which they had been taken that night. Yes, we were spying. On December 10, from information taken from the consulate safe, 450 Japanese Americans were arrested by the FBI on suspicion of spying. By February 18, 1942, there were 2,209 Japanese aliens apprehended. This should have dealt a crushing blow to any possible subversive activity on the West Coast. The most knowledgeable person on enemy spy capabilities at the time had to be J. Edgar Hoover, Director of the FBI. He felt the Japanese spy network had been broken and any future spying would be minimal to none. He did express a deep concern with the large Japanese-American population on the West Coast should Japan invade. Nevertheless, he did not support a total evacuation. His four field offices on the West Coast were split on the subject, with both Seattle and San Diego strongly in support of a total evacuation, while Los Angeles and San Francisco were not. Hoover stated he felt a total evacuation was more politically driven than anything else. In his view, there was not enough evidence to support taking such drastic actions.

I'm not sure that the answer to whether there were Japanese alien or Japanese-American spies within our borders is as easy as many would want to believe. As humans we like to group things and people. It makes life easier to think that, "All [blank] are [blank]." Real life is seldom so neat. It is true that no Japanese American was ever convicted of spying, and many are quick to point that out. Those arrested on suspicion of spying were not Japanese-Americans. They were Issei— Japanese aliens—and were therefore not given a court trial. There might have been spies among them that were simply never tried and convicted. They were detained and later returned to their families in one of the ten relocation camps. The goal of the government was to detain anybody suspicious—including all Issei community leaders—and separate them from any opportunity for spying before it happened. Interestingly, the Kibei—those born in America and educated in Japan—were considered more of a threat than the Issei, for the Kibei were younger and con-sidered more impressionable and impassioned. Also, they had been living in Japan more recently and had been exposed to the Japanese military doctrine. In fact, after WWII, the Japanese government revealed that over 1,600 Japanese-American Kibei had served in the pre-WWII Japanese military. Were there potential spies of Japanese descent living in America that might have altered the course of WWII history had they not been incarcerated in a relocation center? Possibly. Did the potential for such spying justify a total evacuation of all Japanese-Americans in direct conflict with their Constitutional rights? Those in command at the time had to wrestle with that very decision.

Once Executive Order 9066 was initiated, the push to get evacuees off the coast and to get relocation centers thrown together was begun. In his book, *The President is Calling*, the first director of the War Relocation Authority, Milton Eisenhower, described his meeting with President Franklin Delano Roosevelt as follows, "Milton, your war job, starting immediately, is to set up the War Relocation

Authority to move the Japanese off the Pacific Coast. I have signed an executive order which will give you full authority to do what is essential.'The president looked up at me again and said, 'And Milton, the greatest possible speed is imperative.'"

From that moment the rush was on, explaining the lack of time necessary to implement sound procedures and to build a well thought out camp. Eisenhower, who shared the views of the president at the time continued, "When the Japanese attacked Pearl Harbor, our West Coast became a potential combat zone. Living in that zone were more than 100,000 persons of Japanese ancestry: two-thirds of them American citizens: one-third aliens...The uncertainty of what would happen among these people in case of a Japanese invasion, still remained. That is why the commanding General of the Western Defense Command determined that all Japanese within the coastal areas should move inland."

This quote by Milton Eisenhower summed up the top military concerns for the safety of the West Coast. The US military thought it more than a coincidence that so many Japanese Americans were living and or working next to an incredible number of military facilities. This was of tremendous concern to the Military. They could see no other way to protect these facilities other than to move the Japanese Americans out of the areas. In 1943, just one year after the evacuation, Milton Eisenhower, while no longer head of the WRA, wrote a letter to FDR (FDR-53, April 1943) stating a deep concern for the young Nisei confined to a camp. He apparently recognized the injustice of what was occurring.

ASSIMILATION AND ISOLATION

In a speech in 1907, Theodore Roosevelt had this to say about immigration and the true meaning of being American:

In the first place, we should insist that if the immigrant who comes here in good faith becomes an American and assimilates himself to us, he shall be treated on an exact equality with everyone else, for it is an outrage to discriminate against any such man because of creed, or birthplace, or origin. But this is predicated upon the person's becoming in every facet an American, and nothing but an American. There can be no divided allegiance here. Any man who says he is an American, but something else also, isn't an American at all. We have room for but one flag, the American flag. We have room for but one language here, and that is the English language. And we have room for but one sole loyalty and that is a loyalty to the American people.

Just as the first generation of immigrants from any country, the Issei from Japan were poorly equipped to satisfy this standard for becoming American. Most didn't speak English, making it difficult to seek employment or perform even the simplest daily task such as shopping, riding a bus, selling wares, etc. In a society more accepting of them they might have struggled through with a smile, learning English along the way. Unfortunately, as previously mentioned, Asians in general were by this time greeted with indifference at best, outright hostility at worst. They discovered quickly that it was simply more feasible to live in Japanese neighborhoods where shop owners, doctors, and all other people they needed to do business with spoke their language. Many ethnic groups do a better job of assimilating by the second generation as the children of the immigrants have gone to school in the United States and grown up to be fluent in English. Although the same situation applied to the Nisei, there is still one major difference between them and ethnic Germans or Italians. Because people of Japanese descent are easily identified from Caucasians, even second and third generation Japanese Americans found it difficult to blend and assimilate. Prohibited from marrying Caucasians, and is some cities from attending school with them, Japanese immigrants and their children were not given the opportunity to fulfill Roosevelt's ideal of becoming American. How does a group of people effectively integrate into a society into which they have been prohibited from participating fully? Most Japanese worked and lived near each other like a single unit. They held tightly to their culture, traditions, and language. In California alone there were 248 private schools for Japanese-American children. The schools brought in special teachers from Japan who brought with them their language, religion, culture, philosophies, and military virtues through teaching Japan's martial arts. Along with the fishermen, these teachers would be some of the first Japanese arrested by the FBI. The Japanese-American subculture had its own newspapers, clubs, unions, gangs, and societies. Many of the leaders of these groups were also included in the first wave the FBI arrested. Most of them worked and lived within their own circle of Japanese friends and family, and married other Japanese—by choice or lack of legal alternatives. The fact that there were few interracial marriages between Japanese and Caucasians made it that much easier for Japanese and their Japanese-American descendants to be rounded up and evacuated.

STEPS TO TOTAL EVACUATION

Just four days after the Japanese bombed Pearl Harbor, the United States, on December 11, created the Western Defense Command and with it, the west coast of the United States was declared a "Theater of War." The National Command Authority defines a "Theater of War" as "The area of air, land, and water that is or may become, directly involved in the conduct of the war." The West Coast certainly fit.

Once the decision was made to evacuate all Japanese Americans from the West Coast, implementation became the next order of business. In a memo dated January 5, 1942, referring to the evacuation, General John DeWitt stated the Army had no wish to assume any aspect of civil control if there were any other means by which the necessary security measures could be taken through normal civilian channels. The Justice Department (FBI) stated they were not equipped for handling an evacuation of such size and wanted no part of it, further they could not support an evacuation of citizens and felt it would have to be conducted by the military on a basis of wartime necessity. With this, the responsibility fell squarely back onto the military.

Following the coast's designation as a Theater of War, one of the very first actions taken by Gen. DeWitt was the establishment of alien exclusion zones. There were over one hundred such zones widely scattered throughout the coastal areas which included refineries, dams, harbors, power generating plants, war production plants, and military facilities. It was deemed imperative that all enemy aliens be removed from these areas to prevent potential spying and sabotage. Along with a number of German and Italian aliens, a substantial number of people of Japanese descent lived and owned property within these restricted areas. The zones covered a large area and were widely scattered, making it nearly impossible to keep all aliens out. Nonetheless, on January 30, 1942, an informal group composed of Washington state congressmen, justice and war department personnel, and representatives of the California Congressional Delegation unanimously approved a program to evacuate all enemy alien and dual citizens from these critical areas. General DeWitt first implemented a program of voluntary evacuation in which enemy aliens were encouraged to move themselves. This was, as one might expect, a hopeless maneuver. For evacuees to voluntarily sell their properties and possessions at a huge loss, often to move to an unfamiliar town with an unknown level of hostility was asking too much. About 8,000 Japanese Americans and Japanese aliens, including approximately 4,000 university students, did relocate far to the East, but others were too old and feeble, or didn't have the finances to do so, some because their bank accounts had been seized by the government. Thousands of residents of Japanese descent moved just east of the original exclusion zone only to have the government spew out more restrictive zonal designations forcing yet another move farther east.

With the lack of success experienced by voluntary evacuation, the army moved soon after to a forced evacuation from what they deemed the most critical areas—the Military Area No. 1 zones which lay along the westernmost edge of Washington, Oregon, and California, and the southernmost edge of Arizona. Soon after Military Area No. 1 was labeled the line of demarcation for evacuation, the decision was made to extend the area to Military Area No. 2 which encompassed all areas of the affected states not included in Area No.1. At this point, the government contacted states farther east in the hopes they would voluntarily accept the evacuees. As was expected, the other states were less than thrilled at the prospect of taking in people deemed "dangerous." Their argument was that if the designated immigrants were posing a threat to dams, power plants, and other high risk infrastructure in the Western States, they would be just as dangerous farther into the interior of the country. Colorado was the only state publicly willing to take on the evacuees as a part of their war effort, although a few hundred other Japanese-Americans relocated to Utah and Idaho.

Along with the confusing zonal changes came changes in exactly who was to be evacuated—originally all enemy aliens whether Japanese, German, or Italian. After extensive discussion about the loyalty of Italian Americans—in which, significantly, the first witness called was Italian-American Mayor Rossi of San Francisco—and an odd focus on Joe DiMaggio's Italian-immigrant parents, Italian aliens were deemed to be of lower risk and were hence excluded from the orders. With some exceptions, German and Italian Americans had assimilated into American culture prior to WWII. There were over one million German aliens—many, refugees who had fled Hitler. In addition, there were millions of Caucasians with some German ancestry complicating a total German evacuation. The size and complexity of the German and Italian presence in America made a total incarceration impossible, yet they possessed a greater threat to national security than did the Japanese. In the first three months of 1942, German submarines sank over 100 ships off the East and Gulf Coasts while Japan sank fewer than five. Some in government claimed German espionage figured into the success of the sinking of so many US ships.

With the resounding failure of voluntary evacuation and of the possibility of sending 120,000 evacuees directly to other states, the government moved to mass evacuation into assembly centers followed by relocation centers from where it was hoped the evacuees could be relocated farther east. The forced evacuation carried out by the army moved from one area of the affected states to the next with those deposed being given extremely short notice to liquidate their assets and pack what little they could carry. The executive order required government agencies to attempt to protect the belongings and economic interests of the evacuees, but this was largely unsuccessful.

EVACUATION FOR THE SAFETY OF THE EVACUEES

The newspapers, radio, and movie reels in the theaters were showing the brutality of the Japanese in the Pacific. It was constant and it was gruesome, resulting in widespread, bitter hatred for Japan. Unfortunately, there were those who did not make the distinction between the Japanese moving across the Pacific and Japanese Americans, some of whom had lived in the US their entire lives, and the press made no effort to support the latter. It is known that Filipinos murdered a Japanese American in Stockton, California; there is little doubt that it was a hate crime, for the invading Japanese Army in the Philippines did terrible things to the Filipinos. Within our borders, Japanese-American merchants and shop owners experienced harassment, defacement of their properties, and worse. Because of this, one often hears that the evacuation was implemented to protect Japanese Americans and aliens from impending violence, however, it is extremely doubtful that the true impetus for the evacuation was as altruistic as protecting the evacuees. There are countless minutes from government meetings and officials offering proof to the contrary—such quotes as those by the very men in charge of the evacuation. Revealingly, General DeWitt stated, "A Jap's a Jap, whether citizen or alien." Colonel Karl Bendetsen had his own thoughts on paying to feed and house Japanese aliens and Japanese-American evacuees in camps. He felt the army shouldn't deplete its resources for this purpose because the army's job, "is to kill Japanese not save Japanese." These do not sound like the sentiments of people concerned with the safety of the Japanese Americans. In addition, the initial plan of sending evacuees farther into the interior of the United States to live in an unfamiliar place surrounded by the general public does not indicate a concern to remove them from public harm as much as to remove them from west coast facilities deemed sensitive. In hindsight, some government officials noted that many evacuees were safer within the camps away from the hostilities of the general public on the West Coast, but I can find no evidence to indicate that this was a concern leading to the evacuation. It is too bad, because this certainly would have made the entire episode more palatable.

ADDITIONAL EVACUATIONS

As an aside, it is noteworthy that the Japanese-Americans were not the only ones to suffer through evacuation during WWII. Between 1942 and 1945, there were 10,905 people of German descent and 3,278 people of Italian descent arrested and placed in internment camps as well. As little known as the Japanese internment is, that of the German and Italian-Americans has been even less publicized. In some cases, entire families of German and Italian descent were rounded up and given no trial. They sat out the war in camps until as late as August 1948—three years after the end of the war and well after all Japanese-American internment camps had been closed. Also, unlike the Japanese Americans, they were never given the opportunity to voluntarily relocate to "safer" areas. For more information on the German-American and alien evacuation and their treatment during WWII, read *Undue Process* by Arnold Krammer.

Another less publicized side of evacuations during WWII is that the United States was not the only country evacuating enemy aliens. Because Canada also feared Japan might invade their western shores, they evacuated Japanese Canadians from British Columbia or incarcerated them there. There were 22,096 people of Japanese descent in British Columbia at the time. On February 27, 1942, the Canadian government ordered a massive evacuation regardless of citizenship. Eleven hundred Japanese-Canadian fishing boats were confiscated and sold, and the money used to build their internment camps. Men occupied one camp and women and children another. The losses experienced by Japanese Canadians due to the evacuation were estimated at over four hundred million dollars. The government made an initial offer to settle for twelve million dollars, but the offer was rejected. The same year the U.S. settled for $20,000 per person Canada settled for $21,000 per person. It might be added, the Canadian Japanese men were put on work gangs and separated from their families. It was much worse to be Japanese in Canada then in the USA. Mexico removed all of its Japanese residents from Lower California, and the British sent all Japanese from Singapore to their colony in India. Some Japanese living in South America were sent to internment camps in the USA. Interestingly, Hawaii, which was home to 160,000 Japanese descendants, did not resort to total confinement. They were an essential part of the island's work force, representing 40% of the population. There were some Japanese in Hawaii arrested and incarcerated on suspicion of being involved in spying, but the remainder were allowed to move freely throughout the territory.

CHAPTER IX
EMPLOYEES OF MANZANAR
– WCCA AND WRA

WARTIME CIVIL CONTROL ADMINISTRATION – WCCA

Upon creation of the WWII assembly centers, the Wartime Civil Control Administration (WCCA) was established to organize the basic operations within each camp. Its job entailed little more than receiving, housing, and feeding the evacuees. Existing for a mere ten weeks, and under the control of the War Department, the WCCA was to be a very short lived organization. After this brief, initial period, control of camp operations shifted to another organization, the War Relocation Authority (WRA), which was created by Executive Order 9012, and eventually operated under the Department of the Interior. Interestingly, Manzanar today is once again under the Department of the Interior and its National Park Service.

The WCCA was established on March 11, 1942, under the command of General DeWitt, with Colonel Karl Bendetsen and his staff making the day to day decisions. The WCCA staff was primarily pulled from the Works Project Administration (WPA)—its objective, to remove all Japanese Americans from the West Coast as quickly as possible. The WCCA was never intended to be anything more than a short term organization, just as Manzanar itself was intended to be a short term site, existing just long enough to serve as a collecting point until all Japanese Americans could be relocated east of the Mississippi River. This would prove to be a poorly conceived plan, impossible to carry out.

The responsibility for selecting employees for the WCCA at Manzanar landed on two WPA employees in Southern California, Russell Amory, who was head of the WPA for all of Southern California, and his assistant, Roy Burton. These two men made up a personnel roster for Manzanar from a list of WPA supervisors employed in Southern California. Additional employees were hired through advertisements run in Southern California, bringing the total WCCA employee count at Manzanar to fifty-five. This was only twenty-five percent of the number the WRA would employ once they got running. The WCCA staff at Manzanar were civilians working for the army who were about to face the biggest challenge of their lives.

Because moving such a variety of people, including old and sick adults as well as young children and babies, had never been undertaken before, and because of the haste with which the sweeping evacuation occurred, there were bound to be numerous mistakes made throughout the process. Unimaginably, the WCCA staff arrived at Manzanar at the same time as the first evacuees, leaving them literally no time to plan, schedule, learn their new jobs, or organize services. It is hard to imagine that this was the plan, but it was a harbinger of things to come. Another major problem created by those calling the shots from San Francisco was that the evacuees were arriving in large numbers faster than the contractor could build the necessary housing, latrines, and mess halls. On March 21, the same day the WCCA employees arrived, eighty-four evacuees arrived to help handle the evacuees to follow. Two days later, on March 23, the evacuee population reached 710, and only ten days after that, the population had grown to 3,286. Someone of authority was in a great hurry to get the Japanese Americans off the West Coast but was deeply out of touch with onsite construction. That "someone" was none other than Colonel Karl Bendetsen. As the WCCA was a brand new organization, there were no existing procedures or policies for staff to follow regarding anything they would need to do. The War Department had their staff on the Manzanar site on an excruciatingly tight budget and all procedural approvals had to come from Colonel Bendetsen's office in San Francisco, several days away. The initial WCCA staff members who came from the Work Project Administration (WPA) were selected because they had built work camps, organized work programs, carried out construction projects, and had experience in supervision. They were not the problem; it was Bendetsen and his San Francisco staff that hindered progress in the camps. Despite this job being different from anything they had done before, most WCCA employees used their supervisory skills creatively and adapted to the demands of the new job. Each day brought new challenges requiring creative thinking. The WCCA staff was charged with setting up virtually an entire city. It was necessary to be proactive with plans and reduce the need to be reactive to crises. Many evacuees were frightened and worried, others mad, and some were all three. Many spoke no English, making it impossible for the WCCA staff to communicate with them without an interpreter. Making matters worse, before coming to Manzanar, many evacuees had been given false or misleading information from Colonel Bendetsen about what they would find upon their arrival at camp. The WCCA staff was on the front lines when the evacuees expectations were dashed by the reality of the unfinished, poorly built, and ill-equipped camp that greeted them upon their arrival. They were to live and work face to face with the disappointed evacuees, but without the authority to rectify the many issues created at WCCA's San Francisco headquarters. Immeasurable credit goes to the overworked and unassisted WCCA employees in Manzanar for their ability to work with the evacuees, for without the cooperation and hard work of the evacuees, people would have gone hungry and had no place to sleep, and instead of being a huge mistake, it would have been a monumental disaster.

WCCA ACCOMPLISHMENTS AND SHORTCOMINGS

The WCCA employees at Manzanar were the first to recognize the value of the professional evacuees in carrying out the task of getting arriving evacuees settled into the camp, and later in their unparalleled contribution to the day-to-day operations of the camp. The implementation of having evacuees work alongside the WCCA staff began with Manzanar. This strategy would be replicated in all the subsequent assembly and relocation camps. Each of the blocks of barracks within Manzanar had a Japanese block manager whose job it was to solve problems as they arose within his own block. Problems were also discussed at weekly block managers' meetings. The acceptance of alien-Japanese Issei as block managers was begun by the WCCA at Manzanar, as was the policy of evacuees practicing self-government. All of these innovative WCCA programs were positive moves and a boost to evacuee morale.

The magnitude of the number of arriving evacuees combined with the building contractor's inability to stay ahead of this large number of arrivals, made for disaster. The WCCA got blamed for overcrowded accommodations, splitting up families, separating husbands and wives, and worst of all, putting married women with bachelors. The camp experienced a major uproar. The positive aspect was that each person had a roof over his head and three meals per day. An additional problem that was blamed on the WCCA was the shortage of latrines. Again, this was simply a result of too many evacuees—too little time to build. The entire process was not unlike the legendary Lucille Ball episode in which she is working on the brisk candy assembly line trying fruitlessly to keep up. The difference is, in the Manzanar version it was not at all humorous. The evacuee arrivals were pouring in way too fast for the WCCA staff and the volunteer evacuee work force to accommodate. It is vital to note that a major reason the evacuees ever got fed and assigned a place to sleep was due to the way in which the first evacuees to arrive at Manzanar jumped in to help settle in those that followed. This early group of evacuees consisted of doctors, nurses, cooks, interpreters, and more. They rolled up their sleeves, worked with the WCCA employees, and brought the camp to a functioning state, even though the pay they were promised never arrived as long as the WCCA was in charge. This was a major issue with the evacuees and the blame could be traced right back to the WCCA in San Francisco. General DeWitt and Colonel Bendetsen insisted that no evacuee would be paid more than the lowest paid army recruit. Paying a professional surgeon a buck private's salary is insulting and hard to imagine. The evacuee pay scale took months to work out while the evacuees continued working. The pay scale issue would not be finalized until the WCCA had been replaced by the WRA. In short, the indecisiveness of the army's top brass caused serious morale problems and financial hardships for those evacuees who were the most essential to the functioning of the camp. The evacuees had a legitimate gripe that they took to the local WCCA staff. Unfortunately, there was little the staff could do, for the gridlock was not a local issue.

There were many problems inherited by the WCCA, but none worse than the oversight by the Corp of Engineers in not building an onsite hospital. Immediately the problem was recognized and the WCCA, along with evacuee Los Angeles physician and surgeon, Dr. James Goto, set up several tarpaper barracks as a clinic. They established a ten bed ward, an isolation ward, an outpatient clinic, and a children's ward. Overflow patients were forced to wait on cots outside in the weather. Remember there was no running water inside the barracks, and no bathroom facilities. Portable outhouses were erected outside of the makeshift hospital, but the water problem remained.

Hospital outhouses

In short, the hospital situation was a disaster. Not only was there a need to treat the sick, but also to evaluate all incoming evacuees for possible contagious diseases. Within a ten week period, three Japanese-American doctors not only saw those that were sick upon arrival, but also examined and inoculated nearly 10,000 new arrivals. This was a staggering work load. Within that ten week period, one of the WCCA employees suffered a burst appendix, and Dr. Goto was able to successfully operate in a thrown together, tarpaper-barrack operating room. I remember my father coming home from work saying he had passed by the window of one of the tarpaper barracks and had seen an operation in progress. He went on to say, "There is no damn privacy in this camp. You can't even be operated on in private." He was appalled at what was going on in camp at that time. In one tragedy, a mother and her twins died during labor. It makes me wonder if these three deaths could have been prevented had a fully equipped hospital been available, or had the evacuation never taken place. Conditions that were rough later on were downright dreadful in the early stages of occupation.

Another evacuee, Frank Chuman, who was the head administrator for the Manzanar hospital, had this to say about the hospital conditions, "The Manzanar hospital started on March 21, 1942, as a half room clinic for minor ailments and compulsory inoculations for all the evacuees. We were at building 1, apartment 1 at the entrance to the center. One half of the apartment of twenty by twenty-five feet was for the clinic, consisting of a sterilizer, some chairs, and table with a lamp. The remainder of the same room had a sheet dividing the sleeping quarters of Dr. Goto and myself on steel cots with straw ticking." Chuman's job included the nearly impossible task of acquiring medical items for women and children through an army supply which only carried supplies for men. "What was in short supply were provisions, medical supplies, equipment, clothing, urinals suitable for use by women, both young and old, small children, and the elderly. The most headaches were those such as perineal pads [Kotex], diapers, female urinals which are of course different from male urinals, sheets, special surgical instruments for pregnant women who needed special forceps, Pabulum for babies, etc., which in ordinary life seem inconsequential but are monumental problems in wartime when supplies are scarce and ordering these items is difficult through government red tape through army procurement channels." Medical supplies were sent to Manzanar from the Fort Mason medical depot in San Francisco.

Besides the holdup with the hospital, the contractor was behind schedule with the water system. It was incomplete and in May, traces of E. coli (intestinal bacteria) were detected in the water at the same time that the camp was hit with a high incidence of dysentery. In the springtime, sheep were herded upstream to the west of Manzanar, and it was suspected bacteria from their feces might have polluted the camp's water supply. On the heels of this misery came an outbreak of measles—a result of close confinement. The WCCA staff along with local health inspectors was working on the problem, but it was not solved by June 1 when the WRA took over. The public health department also noted there was insufficient hot water in the mess halls during peak dish washing periods—another potential cause for the spread of diseases. The WCCA ordered additional equipment to solve these problems, but they too were slow in arriving.

Another major hurdle to overcome was in feeding thousands of people with the budget restraints put upon the camp. Since the WCCA was a branch of the army, General DeWitt set the evacuees' food costs to the army's allotment of $0.50 per day per soldier. Calling on the farming expertise of many of the evacuees, the WCCA was able to supplement the camp food supply to a major degree. John Harrison, superintendent with the WPA, was hired to set up and supervise the farming activities at Manzanar. He admitted the Japanese Americans knew far more than he did about growing crops and his job turned out to be to simply stay out of their way and let them handle things. He also set up a think tank of bright, young, college educated, Japanese Americans to create jobs within the camp for the evacuees. They came up with a plan for a chicken farm, hog farm, clothes making, and more. Despite only having one tractor, which often ran twenty-four hours a day, the farming program became extremely successful. The evacuees' farming skills along with the chicken and hog farms' operation brought costs in well below the $0.50 per person per day set by the army. During the life of the camp there were 28,790,221 meals served at a cost of $3,384,749.02. The average cost came out to $0.35 per person per day. This was only possible through the skill and efforts of the evacuee farmers. They were fantastic.

The WCCA was brought in to Manzanar to do a nearly impossible job. What they were able to accomplish, in many ways, was astonishing. What they were not able to handle in the short time the organization existed, was staggering. As the WCCA was dismantled and the WRA took over, structures were still not completed, there was no sewer system, students had missed an entire semester of school, people were receiving their medical treatment out of tarpaper buildings with no bathrooms or running water, no recreational equipment existed other than that brought by the evacuees themselves, and housing was overcrowded and poorly built. At the same time, farming was in full swing, everybody had a roof over their head, and ample food was being provided. The camp was just beginning to take shape, leaving a tremendous amount of work for the WRA and the evacuees to accomplish.

Many people wishing to report Manzanar in its worst possible light and equate it with a true prisoner of war camp tell the absolute truth about the conditions that existed in the first few months of the camp's existence. During this period there was near total chaos as a flood of evacuees arrived at the same time as those that were supposed to be organizing their arrival. Fortunately for those living there though, this picture is only partially accurate, for these severe conditions were extremely temporary. Once all the evacuees were settled and the WRA took over, the camp began to transform into a much more habitable place. With the determination and drive of the evacuees and the WRA employees, not only were improvements made in the basic living conditions such as food, housing, and sanitation, but parks and picnic areas were built, gardens planted, an outdoor theater added, a golf course and baseball diamond were created, and much more. Within the first three months that the WRA operated the camp, evacuees planted over 450,000 square feet of lawn, not only giving the camp a more habitable appearance, but also cutting down considerably on the ubiquitous dust.

Beautiful evacuee-created garden

Did the camp become an enviable place in which to live? No, it was still an internment camp with all the inherent problems that come with a forced habitation, but for many, it did become a safe, habitable place in which to live out the war.

Assist. Project Director Bob Brown, Project Dir. Ralph Merritt, unidentified man in back, WRA Director Dillon Myer, and Assist. Project Dir. Ned Campbell

THE WAR RELOCATION AUTHORITY – WRA

*After you have read about the WRA, if you are interested in learning more about the individual employee, turn to Appendix #3. They are listed there with what could be found some sixty years after the camp closure.

On March 18, 1942, the WRA was established and later, on February 16, 1944, fell under the Department of the Interior, which has the reputation of being the catch-all for government agencies that don't fit anywhere else. The WRA had administrative responsibility for all aspects of the ten WRA Japanese-American camps' day to day operations. Along with running the camps, the WRA was directed to relocate from them as many evacuees as possible to east of the Mississippi River in an effort to return them to a more normal lifestyle. The WRA got off to a very difficult start, but did overcome obstacles, correct mistakes, and make improvements, making life for the evacuees in the camps better over time. Of course, these improvements were a joint effort between the staff and thousands of evacuees. The WRA received heavy criticism from Washington D.C. and the army for being soft on Japanese Americans and was accused of running a social club. In truth, the WRA employees came to appreciate the Japanese Americans as individuals: men, women and children, not as the enemy. The WRA employees lived and worked in the camp, growing to understand more about the Japanese American and the complexity of the community behind the fence than any of those in Washington or in the military. Many would leave the camp after the war with feelings of camaraderie towards the evacuees. I know my parents did and often talked about how much they missed individuals they had worked closely with during the war. The army objected consistently to the WRA's handling of internal security and made a strong effort to take over, but the WRA resisted the army and Congress to maintain control within the fenced camp. The onsite WRA leaders recognized that army control inside the camp would be another blow to an already damaged evacuee morale. There was no denying from the outside the camp looked like a prison, but the WRA management did not want the inside of the camp to be a prison. That is why they resisted a security take-over, and that is one of the reasons they had their own staff and families living and working inside the camp alongside of the evacuees.

Where the main focus of the WCCA was towards organizing temporary housing for the evacuees, the WRA was looking to build a stable community with improved living conditions. The WRA, like the WCCA, recognized it was going to take thousands to fill the essential jobs necessary in this camp of 10,000 evacuees, and that a work force of that magnitude would be impossible to hire during the wartime labor shortage. The obvious answer was to have the evacuees fill the jobs themselves, and if the evacuees were going to do nearly all the work in the camp, the WRA believed, as had the WCCA before them, the evacuees should be permitted to govern themselves. These principles would be the foundation for the WRA at Manzanar and all the camps to follow. It would be the WRA staff's job to train, direct, and provide minimal supervision for the tasks at hand. In addition, it would be the job of the WRA to plan, budget, and direct, as well as serve on committees within the camp, and to answer to the higher authority outside the camp. Lastly befell upon the WRA the responsibility of keeping the local communities informed of the goings on inside the camp and of helping to reduce their fears—often this was no small task. Over time, many locals learned to accept the camp's existence in their valley, as their fears waned. For others, fear, anger, and prejudice would never fade away.

The first WRA Project Director, Roy Nash, was accused of not keeping the local communities informed about concerns within the camp. Nash was understandably reluctant to report that the camp was spreading raw sewage onto the valley floor, or that the evacuees were experiencing a near epidemic of dysentery and measles. Instead, he would keep quiet and focus on solving problems within the camp. What he should have done was enlist the help of Robert Brown who had years of experience working with the locals and who could have reported the truth while still maintaining the best possible relationship with the communities.

PERSONNEL ISSUES

From its very inception, the WRA was in trouble. Roy Nash began the transition from WCCA to WRA by offering only a few of the hard working WCCA employees their jobs in the newly formed WRA organization. A limited number of supervisory and managerial assignments were maintained by the people who had begun with the WCCA. As stated, a good part of the WCCA employees had been handpicked from a select list of supervisors working for the WPA. These were people with years of successful experience who agreed to uproot themselves and their families to come to Manzanar and were laid off abruptly after just a couple of months of employment. When the WRA took over, its offsite, upper management brought in civil service to develop pay scales for its onsite employees and to evaluate the WCCA employees for consideration in keeping their jobs during the move. Civil Service began by lowering many of the salaries previously received. Please refer to Appendix #4 for WRA salaries. Among the confounding decisions made was the one to pay a school teacher with a college degree less than a file clerk. Civil Service also proclaimed that many of the local hires failed to meet the minimum job requirements. As a result, a number of local WCCA employees were fired before replacements could be found, leaving holes in the organization and creating an enraged local population. The lightly populated communities were already suffering from a depressed local economy. These new job losses were felt deeply. The dismissals stirred up the local communities and made the WRA very unpopular before they could even get started. The WRA was accused of playing politics in their hiring practices. Many of the fired workers were angry with the WRA and refused to cooperate during the shift to the new organization. In retaliation, key former WCCA employees took all records at the time of their departure. The WRA came in with no knowledge of what had been attempted, what had or had not worked, what the evacuees had been promised, which evacuees were performing their duties well, and which needed further training or direction. In short, the WRA was off to a very poor start.

FILLING VACANCIES

Once the experienced and trusted former WCCA employees were laid off, the job of filling these vacancies became paramount. This would prove to be a difficult proposition for now the jobs were compensated with salaries that Civil Service had dropped below that of comparable jobs on the West Coast. Adding to the pay issue was the fact that these were temporary jobs in a remote location with horrid climate and no overtime pay. The positives, though, included the wonderful local hunting, fishing, and hiking opportunities, that the camp could often employ both husband and wife, that living expenses in camp—for those that chose to live onsite—were extremely low, and that those in fear of a West Coast invasion from Japan could relocate farther from the "action," assuming they had no fear of the 10,000 Japanese Americans they would be living with.

To fill the vacancies created during the turnover, the WRA turned first to the Bureau of Indian Affairs (BIA). This was no great surprise, as then Project Director Roy Nash had come from that agency. Several BIA employees accepted positions. The next step in recruiting was to advertise across the country. Pay scales in the southern and central regions of the country were lower than those on the coast and this strategy did lead to some success. Many compassionate individuals took employment feeling they could alleviate some of the suffering of the evacuees. Several people who were training at the Ross Aeronautical School, a civilian pilot training program at the Manzanar airport right across the road from the camp, took jobs at Manzanar while training to be pilots. Nearly all of those who worked for the WRA during their flight training moved on to pursue advanced training elsewhere, including two WRA female employees, Nona Highfill and Sara C. Shoaf, who had completed thirty-five hours of flying time at Ross and then volunteered for the Women's Air Force (WAF).

There were community members from Owens Valley who did meet the Civil Service requirements and filled positions. Most either ended up in the motor pool or as craftsmen. Finally, advertising job openings by word of mouth with friends on the West Coast met with mediocre success.

As if recruiting and keeping a staff were not difficult enough, no male hired was exempt from the draft if he passed the physical and was under thirty-eight years of age. Wilbur F. Lutzow in internal security—married with two children—was drafted away from his employment. Also drafted was Ray Buzzetti, Placement Officer, a college graduate and family man. Robert Throckmorton, Project Attorney, left for a commission in the navy, and Kenneth Horton, Chief of Internal Security, reported to the Army Intelligence Bureau. These were just a few of the male WRA employees lost to various branches of the service. Occasionally a female employee, for example Marian H. Smith who left for the Women's Army Air Force Service Pilots (WASP), was also lost to the war.

In 1942 the WRA recruited 209 new employees including twenty rehires out of a total fifty five from the WCCA and twenty more from other government agencies such as the Bureau of Indian Affairs. Keep in mind that at its peak the WRA staff only reached 229, over half of whom worked in the Manzanar school system. The total WRA staff represented a very small proportion of the total camp work force. The evacuees in the work force numbered in the thousands. Before Manzanar, Japanese Americans were primarily farmers, gardeners, and fishermen, some shop owners, and a smaller percentage were college graduates primarily working in the medical profession. Some of their most valued possessions brought to Manzanar were their work ethics, intelligence, and recognition for the value of an education. The challenge of the WRA staff was to take these values and the skill sets the evacuees possessed, and direct them to training programs that would fit the needs of the camp. When the WRA staff arrived, one of their first orders of business was to start up training programs in nearly every department including education, medical, firefighting, police training, clerical, and the crafts to name a few. The ability of the staff and the evacuee to work together in these training programs figured prominently in the success of meeting the needs of the evacuees throughout their time in camp. Consider for a moment a city in which virtually every job is vacant and those hired to fill the vacancies must all be trained at once. It is an overwhelming challenge, and exactly what the WRA staff faced when they reported to work.

Adding to the management issues at hand, many of these new WRA employees had never worked around Japanese Americans, and certainly not around such a large population of people who had been relocated against their will in this manner. It is understandable that many had reservations about how to win over those Japanese Americans they would be directing and training in their new endeavors. As for the evacuees, some no doubt harbored bitterness over working under WRA authority, but I believe most held the same aspirations about improving the camp environment as the WRA staff held, and put their feelings aside for the benefit of the Manzanar camp residents. There was another monumental change sweeping the country. Women, as previously mentioned, were entering the work place in huge numbers. Many were well educated, hard working, smart, and efficient. They were moving up in organizations as was happening within the WRA at Manzanar. My dad had spent his working life in a man's world—the marines and law enforcement. When Lucy Adams replaced Ned Campbell as assistant project director, my father and John Gilkey began reporting to a woman for the first time. Knowing my dad as I knew him, I would have expected him to come home and say we were to pack our bags as we were moving on. Just the opposite happened. In spite of her gender, Lucy Adams had all the qualities he admired in a boss. They got along great. Refer to Lucy Adams in Appendix #3 to see why.

PRIORITIZING

The WRA started out with a newly hired staff to carry out a very heavy workload. Given the countless, high priority projects to be done, there was a dire need to get organized and structure improvement programs quickly. One of the first orders of business was to get compensation for the Japanese Americans who had been working for several months under the WCCA and had yet to be paid. Within his first month in office, project director Roy Nash issued scrip to be used in camp. This was an effective, stopgap measure while cash payments were gridlocked offsite. With the change from the fifty-five employees under the WCCA to the over 200 with the WRA, enlarging the administration building moved its way up to the top of the priority list. Additional office space was desperately needed. With the plethora of evacuee complaints about the housing situation, WRA staff considered this to be a top priority as well. The oft mentioned upgrades to the barrack interiors were also begun immediately. Within a short time, staff was able to limit a single room of twenty by twenty-five feet to no more than six people. Everywhere the staff turned, there was another situation that required immediate attention, and the education issue was no exception. The camp had just three months to get a school system in place which would meet California State standards. The first elementary school classes began September 9, 1942, and the high school followed with classes beginning on October 15, 1942. Early on, thirty-eight students with learning impairments requiring special accommodations were identified, and Miss Eleanor Thomas was hired to conduct special classes in one of the new hospital wards.

Mrs. Helen A. Hill with her Manzanar Elementary School class

Constructing the 250 bed hospital was another of the high priority projects. The building was completed only one month after the WRA took over, but now required the addition of staff and medical equipment. A sanitation department was immediately established to ensure a healthy working and living environment in camp. The infrastructure upgrades, particularly the electrical, water, and sewer systems, were yet another priority, as was landscaping to address the issue of the dust. A recreation department was established, as were departments for screening and assisting evacuees for relocation, and a judicial committee consisting of three WRA staff members and three evacuees. This latter committee was advisory in nature with all final decisions coming from the project director.

Even the problems that were deemed a lower priority might have seemed horrific if the higher priority concerns hadn't existed. The hot water shortfall in the mess hall kitchens was not just an annoyance, but a true health concern. An additional eighty gallon hot water heater was needed immediately for each kitchen. The kitchen stoves in the mess halls were all coal fired, burning through 250 lbs. of coal per stove per day for a camp total of 4.5 tons per day. Further, the coal stoves were dirty and more labor intensive than oil, and with coal stoves it was necessary for the chefs to arrive hours ahead of their food prep time to prepare them for cooking. For good reasons, these labor intensive stoves had to be replaced with oil fired stoves. For the number of evacuees in camp there should have been thirty-six mess halls yet only twenty were operational at the time the WRA took command. Due to the number of people each mess hall was required to serve, most mess halls were still serving dinner at 11:00 p.m. People stood in line for hours just for a meal. There were shortages of equipment and serving sets in the mess halls. The army commissary was out of touch with the Japanese-American diet, sending large shipments of cottage cheese and buttermilk when the Japanese-American diet was rice based. There were still more problems surfacing each day, it seemed. Evacuee mess hall workers handling food had not been checked for syphilis or typhoid. The Corp of Engineers had grossly under designed the electrical system and it overloaded daily. There was insufficient water pressure because the water storage reservoir had not been built at an elevation necessary to provide adequate pressure. There were forty buildings used for warehousing with a substantial amount of supplies and materials within each, but unbelievably, no warehouse inventory system in place. The WCCA had had a card for each item, but similar items were not necessarily stored in the same warehouse nor were any item identified with a warehouse building number. To find anything required a time consuming job of hunt and peck. This is only a sampling of the problems that existed at the time Project Director Roy Nash arrived and the WRA took over. Between the unkept promises made by the army, lack of pay for work accomplished during the control of the WCCA, horrible camp conditions, and the very confinement itself, evacuees' morale experienced a rapid decline. These newly arrived internees had every reason to consider themselves prisoners of war.

One of the more surprising and challenging tasks laid out before the WRA onsite management was to persuade their higher authority to withdraw directives that were recognized locally as deleterious to the successful functioning of the camp. An example of this is when Washington dictated that, in a camp election, only Japanese Americans with US citizenship could vote. Early on, the WRA had recognized the necessity to foster Japanese-American leadership, placing internees into positions of responsibility, and allowing them to have a charter, hold elections, and participate on a commission with both WRA management and evacuee participation. Representatives of the local WRA administration acknowledged the Japanese' respect for age and allowed older Japanese, many of whom could not speak English, to hold the important positions of block manager. The WRA management in Washington D.C., though, was oblivious to the importance of the Issei in Japanese-American society. In what appears to be a largely punitive move, the offsite WRA management determined that block managers could be drawn only from those evacuees who held US citizenship. Then, after a meeting with a particularly volatile, anti-administration agenda was held in Japanese, Roy Nash mandated that all block managers' meetings must be held in English, a language spoken poorly, if at all by most Issei. These anti-Japanese alien regulations were devastating, effectively eliminated the native born Issei—previously the family and community leaders—from participating in any decision making. This was more than just an issue of honor and status within the Japanese-American camp community. Imagine both the father and mother of any family being denied the right to make decisions within their family and community, and those decision making powers being handed down to the children. This is a demoralizing and dangerous situation with potentially unpredictable results.

WORKING TOGETHER

I cannot speak for all WRA employees, but early on, discussions between my father and mother carried out around our dinner table showed how they perceived living in the camp and working with the evacuees as an adventure—something very different from any living and working condition they had ever experienced. Other than Harry Ueno, who was a particular thorn in my father's side and will be discussed in later chapters, I do not ever remember them complaining about any of the evacuees individually. Both of my parents marveled at how well the Japanese Americans worked together and how polite they were. I remember my father relating to us how he had watched a heating stove being moved. He commented that every one of the Japanese Americans, who could physically do so, got a hand on the stove to help lift and move it. He admired how hard they worked and how well they worked together. He went on to say that if a group of Caucasians had to move a similar item, there would be two or three straining a gut while the rest watched, pointed, and gave orders.

My mother was very happy working with her kitchen staff at the hospital. She used to brag about them and could find humor when there were misunderstandings due to language or cultural differences. She constantly commented on how hard they worked to please her. She enjoyed her coworkers at the hospital so much that I have to feel the evacuees liked her too. My father had very strong likes and dislikes—there was no gray area for him. If he liked you, you couldn't do anything wrong, but if he didn't like you, nothing you did was going to please him. The Japanese Americans in internal security, for the most part could do no wrong, while the members of the gangs and mobs skulking around camp were never going to find themselves on my dad's good side. Dad wanted these trouble makers out of camp as quickly as possible. He also was something of a perfectionist, so anybody not carrying his load, whether evacuee or staff, would find himself on Dad's bad side. Almost anybody who served in the military, especially the marines, earned his respect, including Japanese-Americans who were visiting while on leave.

Dietitian Mary Williams (my mother) with hospital kitchen personnel

When dealing with people, nothing is one hundred percent. No group of individuals is made of members that are completely alike, and the WRA staff was no exception. Staff members had differences and some did not get along well. Some did their own jobs running their own departments, but were reluctant to help another department. The chief of community services and the employment officer were the first to openly denounce each other in a staff meeting. The chief engineer, never too sympathetic with the evacuees, was the subject of a number of written attacks by the superintendent of schools, the chief of the agricultural section, and the community services management. A rift developed between the relocation officer and his chief, the head of the employment department. In another clash, it appears that Robert Brown and Ralph Merritt, longtime friends, were excessively critical of Roy Nash. There is a question as to why Robert Brown did not do more to help the

WRA and Nash in calming down the local communities, for Brown had the connections and the expertise to do so. It appeared that Brown wanted to see Nash fail to see his friend, Ralph Merritt, installed as project director. Even though Nash made mistakes, he undeniably had sympathy for the evacuees and was instrumental in correcting many poor conditions within the camp. Unfortunately his compassion for the evacuees led to some snap decisions that turned out poorly and were embarrassing to reverse. One such decision was to proclaim to the evacuees that they were free to enjoy the Sierra Mountains, lakes, and streams while in Manzanar. This announcement was met with rousing ire within the local communities which responded by fervently reminding the army that the Japanese Americans were supposed to be restricted to within the camp's boundaries. On another occasion, Nash took Japanese-American Dr. Goto and his wife to lunch in Lone Pine, again provoking the wrath of the locals. In response to the pressures put upon Nash, he was replaced as project director by Ralph Merritt in November 1942. Through his outstanding character and goodwill, Merritt became an exemplary leader in Manzanar.

John Gilkey, Arthur Williams (my father), and Willard
Schmidt in front of the police department

* * *

Merritt was born on a cattle ranch in Rio Vista, California along the Sacramento River. His father, originally from the eastern side of the Sierras, was a judge in Berkeley. Ralph graduated from UC Berkeley School of Agriculture in 1907. Following a long association with his university, Merritt served as president of the California Rice Growers Association and the Sun Maid Raisin Growers Association. He was heavily vested in Sun Maid and made a fortune there. In 1924 Merritt visited the Orient to open markets for Sun Maid Raisins in China and Japan. He is credited with placing the rising sun on the Sun Maid box to further promote raisin sales to Japan. Through the collapse of the Sun Maid Raisin Association in 1928, Merritt lost his fortune. In a horrible stroke of luck, just as he went broke, he also developed polio. He retreated to Eastern California to recover his health, for he had friends and relatives there. In time he became involved with farming and mining in the area. Ralph Merritt became well connected to the leaders in the Eastern Sierras. In 1937, he helped found Inyo-Mono Associates, a regional chamber of commerce dedicated to promoting tourism in the Owens Valley and Eastern Sierra. He became chairman of a committee working to improve relations with the City of Los Angeles when he was enlisted to serve on yet another committee—one to help sell the proposed Manzanar War Relocation Center to the local residents.

Project Director, Ralph Merritt

With a lengthy career in business, politics, and agricultural development, Merritt did much more than sell the camp to a suspicious local population. On November 1, 1942, Ralph Merritt filled the position of project director, guiding the development and operation of the camp until the camp was closed. His business relations with Japan and love of Japanese people and their culture made him an ideal candidate to manage the camp.

Many internees were touched by Ralph Merritt's philosophy of respect and compassion for those within the camp. He was recognized for his understanding, humanitarianism, and reasonable policies in running the camp. Early on he was a strong advocate for segregation but met resistance from authority, namely Dillon Myer, in Washington D.C. Merritt tried to stop the army from imposing a loyalty questionnaire upon evacuees. He further strongly objected to the army installing guard towers around the perimeter of the camp, saying the last thing he wanted was for Manzanar to look like a prison. His home was in the camp and he recognized the value of having his staff and their families live within the confines as well. This was Merritt's way of providing the staff with an opportunity to develop a positive relationship with the evacuees and soften the prison atmosphere of the camp. He felt strongly that Manzanar should be a relocation area, not a permanent home for the evacuees, and that they would be happier relocating to the East than living in the camp.

Ralph Merritt was no amateur when it came to politics and dealing with people and governments. He possessed skill in negotiation and had the look and demeanor of authority. Outside the camp he was recognized as a man who had roots in Owens Valley. This served him well when dealing with those in the valley who voiced opposition to the camp and the Japanese Americans in it. He was also adept at dealing with the Los Angeles Department of Water and Power (LADWP) who owned the land and supplied water and electricity to the camp, and who originally viewed Merritt as a local bumpkin farmer they could push around. To the benefit of the camp and all its residents, the LADWP was mistaken.

In later years, through his connections to the Japanese Americans, Ralph Merritt, was instrumental in establishing a Japanese-American Research Project at UCLA. He donated a sizable portion of his papers to the university.

Having lived a varied and interesting life of compassion and diplomacy, Ralph Merritt passed away on April 3, 1963, and was buried in Los Angeles County, California. He truly was the right man for the job of project director at Manzanar, and both staff and evacuees were fortunate to have lived and worked under him.

* * *

Having never worked as a government employee, I had no idea just how mismanaged and senseless things could be in government-run operations until I read the "WRA Manzanar Personnel Management Section" final report, dated March

1946. Keep in mind this was just one of many departments being hammered by Washington D.C. directives. One of the things the final report had to say, "The history of the Personnel Section from June 1942 to July 1944 is a record of the slow transition under Washington directives. When this section reached full staffing and efficient operation, Washington directives gradually dismembered the section, with corresponding reduction in efficiency." At one point in the constant confusion coming out of Washington, two key staff members quit at the same time. Directives were coming from the head of the WRA, Civil Service Commission, War Manpower Commission, and General Accounting Office. It is amazing the WRA at Manzanar could keep any employees or get anything done. It is no wonder the evacuees thought some of the WRA staff were totally muddled. The discord and administrative bungling were noted by the evacuees and used in evacuee circles to point out the ineffectiveness of federal management. Slowly the confusion was reduced as every department, staff member, and evacuee became better organized and improved their job performance and were able to fight back against some of these directives. There were also fewer troublemakers creating discord and distracting the staff from their normal routine. In spite of the improvements, frequent government changes and contradictions never fully ceased.

Assistant Project directors Edwin Hooper, Robert Brown, and
Lucy Adams with camp attorney Robert Throckmorton

The departments within Manzanar's boundary that became the most efficient were those that put a heavy emphasis on training and those that experienced the least government intervention.

The hospital was one such well-run department, first under Dr. James Goto, followed by Dr. William Morse Little.

Left: Dr. James Goto
Right: Dr. Paul Maier, Dr. Wilford Hanaoka, Dr. Morse Little

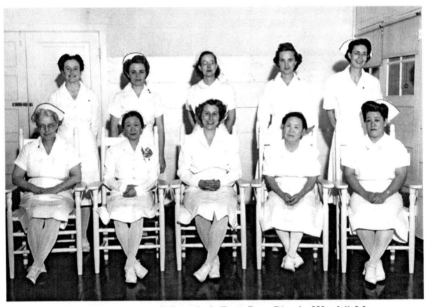

Manzanar nursing staff. From Left, Front Row: Blanche Woodall, M.
Akite, Josephine Hawes, Takahashi, unidentified. Back Row: Irene Gavigan,
Christine Little, Lucille Carney, C. Merritt, Dagmar Quarnstrom.

The makeshift school system, begun in tarpaper barracks with no textbooks or desks, turned out to be another such department. In the beginning, it faced great difficulty in attracting teachers. In time the education system made significant improvements and achieved high scholastic ratings, allowing its students to be accepted at fine institutions of higher education.

The teaching staff at Manzanar came from many different places, but most were recruited out of Southern California and many were right out of college. There were numerous young Japanese Americans emotionally crushed by the evacuation, who while attending school in Manzanar, were reminded by their teachers that they had incredible value. In many cases this positive influence gave them hope. There were Japanese Americans, who years later, recognized the persuasive power of their camp teachers and acknowledged just how much of a difference these teachers had made in their lives. In February 2005, a select group of teachers were honored at the Century Plaza Hotel in Los Angeles by the Japanese American Museum in Little Tokyo.

School teachers were not the only people in camp in charge of training. Almost every department there had a staff member training one or more Japanese Americans in some skill, trade, or procedure. As an example, there was only one union member carpenter in Manzanar, yet a carpenter shop staffed with evacuees was in full operation building furniture, and with WRA staff supervision, this group of eager, new carpenters built all phase II through IV buildings in the staff area as well as the auditorium. Don't get the impressions that the evacuees came to camp with no marketable skills, because that would be misguided. There were several fields in which the evacuees needed no training, and actually, taught the WRA staff. Agriculture and landscaping were two of these fields. There were also many highly skilled professional people interned at Manzanar, including doctors, surgeons, and nurses. Many people entered Manzanar, promptly rolled up their sleeves, filled job openings, and made an immediate difference.

EVACUEE WORK PERFORMANCE

As mentioned, many evacuees showed outstanding work performance while interned at Manzanar, most certainly for the benefit of their fellow man and not for the nominal pay they received, which ranged from a measly sixteen to nineteen dollars per month. Sandwiched between this minimal pay and the fact that the evacuees were forced to be in camp in the first place, one can understand why not everybody putting in their time at work was an exemplary employee. In the personnel management's final report there was a section addressing the alarming number of evacuees that were cutting short their eight hour work day. Some were coming to work late, others were taking a couple of hours for lunch and still others were leaving work an hour or more before closing time. This was a constant problem that the WRA tried to correct with only moderate success.

What is surprising, is that around 45% of the evacuation population in Manzanar was employed by the WRA. In April 1943, there were 9,170 evacuees in camp and a full 4,267 were employed. In December 1944, after segregation and relocations, the camp population dropped to 5,549 with 2,248 of those working. This represents a drop from 47% to 41% of the population providing services within the camp. To

complicate matters, in many cases the lost workers were the more skilled professionals who, because of their job qualifications, were successful in evacuating to the
East. This created a very real problem in maintaining services within the camp, as
virtually every department was hit with the loss of skilled workers. The department
hardest hit was the hospital, as experienced Japanese-American doctors and nurses
moved east where they could work for real world wages. The last year of Manzanar's
occupation saw the greatest challenges in procuring adequate help for all the necessary services provided within camp. By the next to last month, Manzanar housed
only 1,122 evacuees and a full 700 of them were working.

The beauty of The Sierras – Manzanar 1943

THINGS COME TOGETHER—CAMP LIFE 1944-1945

The miserable conditions in camp during its startup and for some time to follow
made a terrible situation even more loathsome. By 1944, the WRA and the evacuees working together were able to make a bad situation considerably more tolerable.

By the final two years of camp, the evacuees that were actively engaged in creating
conflict (and some unfortunate others) had been removed to the Tule Lake Camp.
Security at Manzanar was reduced to a single MP at the main gate, the guard towers
were empty, and the camp was at half its design capacity leaving empty barracks and

eliminating the earlier overcrowded conditions. For some large families, partitions were moved to create larger apartments. By that time, all apartment interiors had been upgraded with floor covering, wallboard, and ceilings, also providing a bit more insulation and privacy, although bathrooms and running water were never included in the improvements. A sanitation department had greatly improved health conditions, there was a 250 bed hospital staffed and operational, and the crowded mess hall conditions were eliminated, allowing meals to be served within normal eating hours. According to one of the original camp menus, a typical days' meals for the evacuees consisted of the following: Breakfast - stewed, dried fruit, farina with hot milk, French toast with syrup, cocoa, and milk. Lunch - baked macaroni and cheese, steamed rice, tsukemono (literally "pickled things," tsukemono is a dish of pickled vegetables served with practically every traditional Japanese meal), boiled fresh vegetables, head lettuce salad, an orange, bread, and tea. Dinner - beef sukiyaki, steamed rice, tsukemono, potato salad, spice cake, and tea. These meals were a great improvement over those offered at the camp's outset.

Dr. Genevieve W. Carter

Thanks to the tireless work of Dr. Genevieve W. Carter, Superintendent of Education, an extensive education system emerged where there had previously been none. There was a special school for handicapped children, a nursery school, a kindergarten, an elementary, a junior, and a senior high school which was headed by Rollin Fox, and a junior college. In adult education headed by Dr. W. Melvin

Strong, there were over 2,000 students learning thirty-four different subjects. Business classes were noticeably popular. As to the quality of the education offered, some of the Japanese Americans said it was terrible while others said it was very good. None ever said the tarpaper school buildings were wonderful. The minimum that can be said about the education the Japanese American received, was that it met the California standards of the time. The University of California at Berkeley, after inspection of the Manzanar schools said, "Any graduate with the grades will be accepted at our university." As within most schools, the quality of education received by each student was directly related to the effort that student put into it. I'm often asked if the school had a language department and if they taught Japanese. There was a language department headed by Mr. Harold Rogers. He could speak twenty languages including Japanese, but he did not teach it at Manzanar. After the war, he moved to Japan to teach. There he met and married a Japanese woman and raised a family. He never returned to the USA.

Along with the regular school system in camp, educational opportunities included beauty classes, Red Cross home nursing classes, bible classes, numerous vocational training courses, and dance classes featuring folk, rumba, and ballet.

As well as a variety of educational opportunities, the WRA tried very hard to provide a well-rounded mix of recreational ones. For sports, the camp offered ping pong, golf via a nine hole dirt course, baseball, basketball, football, tennis, martial arts, and more. There was a model airplane club, YMCA, YWCA, and a USO for returning Japanese Americans on leave serving in the US Army. Since there were no MPs in the towers and many internees loved to fish, the west side of the camp leading to the Sierras was a tempting, low risk escape route some would take for a day or more of fishing. Owned, managed, and run by the evacuees, was a commissary. Other internees edited, printed, and delivered a newspaper. Over 2,500 Sears catalogs were available from which to order items not available in camp. In addition, within camp one could find movies, barber and beauty shops, a shoe and a watch repair, a Bank of America, a library, and a post office. Places to worship were available for Protestant, Catholic and Buddhist followers. At one time it was estimated over 3,000 Protestant evacuees were in camp. Each department in this "tarpaper city behind a barbed wire fence" was now better staffed with both WRA and evacuee employees. Two years of organizing, training, and upgrading had paid off despite the gradual attrition of some very talented evacuees that left through the relocation process. Throughout the last several months of the camp's existence, Manzanar's WRA experienced serious personnel shortages. Including those evacuees who had successfully evacuated east, both Japanese-American and WRA personnel were beginning to leave to start new lives in anticipation of post WWII.

By 1945 camp began to take on a far less bleak appearance

For those who lived in camp during its last two years, there was a great increase in entertainment and educational activities, making camp much more comfortable. I know in my case that it took nearly two years before Southern California was only in the shadows of my mind. I had found a new life that was quite tolerable. I had new school and camp friends with whom I found recreational pursuits outside the camp that earlier we had not known were available. In the camp, I cannot help but think the Japanese-American kids found something new that they too could enjoy. For the Issei, I cannot think that the additional educational or recreational activities improved their lives much, for their limited English skills and advanced age must have made it difficult to join in. I can only imagine that they had the hardest time accepting the disarray into which their lives had fallen. Strangely, the roughest hour for many Japanese-American young adults in camp was to come as they left camp. They would be returning to a West Coast filled with still angry citizens through and with whom they had to find employment to support themselves, and they had to compete with returning war heroes for that employment. It was to be a new and frightening experience.

WRA MANZANAR STAFF BENEFITS

WWII was not the time for hauling in big salaries and huge benefits, and retiring in your fifties. None of the over 200 WRA employees were represented by a union, for unions representing government employees would come to California much later, accompanied by arguably outlandish salary and benefit increases. Local companies paid approximately $0.50 per hour or $4.00 per day for menial labor outside the camp. In camp, the Project Director was paid $6,500 per year while an elementary school teacher would receive the lowest possible in-camp salary of $1,620 per year. Expenses were, of course, lower as well: a postage stamp cost a penny, haircuts were twenty-five cents, gasoline would set a person back eighteen cents a gallon, and a hospital stay would cost fifteen dollars per day. It was a different time.

In 1942, the tax base was twenty-five percent, but the federal government forgave seventy-five percent of that. In 1943, the tax law was changed and there was nothing forgiven. The WRA payroll department withheld twenty percent of each WRA employee's salary to cover his or her taxes. All employees' salaries were graded on an annual basis and paid twice per month. Deductions were taken from the employee's salary for rent, meals taken at the staff mess hall, taxes, and war bonds, if the employee had signed up to buy them, as many did. All salaries, staff and evacuee alike, were frozen. The only way for a person to receive higher pay was to take a job with a higher salary or to have the job itself reevaluated, hoping it qualified for higher pay. As for rent, housing in the tarpaper barracks was rent free for both the evacuee and the staff. It would have taken tremendous nerve to charge to live in them. Once upgraded housing became available, rent was charged as follows: shared space in a dormitory was offered at $20 per month, single bedroom apartments cost $25 per month, and two bedroom apartments ran $35 per month. The rental fee included electricity, water, heating oil, and trash. The only evaporative coolers were the two installed in the project director's quarters. He left the one in D-5 when he moved into his upgraded quarters in G-1&2. There were no other air conditioning units in the staff area, in spite of reports to the contrary.

Initially the staff ate their meals in the block 1 mess hall. It offered the same menu as all the other mess halls in camp serving a Japanese and or American cuisine. Evacuees, of course, didn't pay to eat, but the staff paid $0.20 per meal. This rate changed with the construction of the new staff mess hall in which only American style meals were served and were charged at a rate of $1.00 per day for three meals, or $0.35 per meal. Breakfast, lunch, and dinner were charged at the same rate. The food budget for a typical family of four averaged approximately $50.00 per month at the time, so these meals were not considered cheap. This is one of the reasons, besides the fact that my mother was a fantastic cook, that our family ate nearly all our meals, with one exception, in our apartment. During school I ate all my break-fasts in the staff mess hall. A typical staff breakfast would be cereal (hot or cold), eggs, toast, orange juice, and milk. Pancakes were available upon request. I remember their breakfasts were the best I ever ate. I was not similarly impressed with the lunches and dinners. They were fine, but not as good as my mother prepared.

When we first moved into our camp apartment we ate in the mess hall, but soon we were eating in our apartment, where my parents hired evacuee Esther Ando to prepare the meals. My mother had been a stay at home mom from the time I was born. Now for the first time, both my mother and father were employed outside of the home, and they had a few things to work out concerning family duties. I was only a young teenager, but I could feel the tension in the air at this new arrangement. For families unaccustomed to being served, having someone prepare dinner and serve you in your home can be discomforting. The conversation at the dinner table was restricted in Esther's presence. We found ourselves, for the first time, eating in silence. It was such a strange feeling having someone stand there while we ate, that neither my mother nor father could handle it. Esther was also nervous for she had probably never been employed in this type of position before. The new routine quickly changed to Esther helping during the day and leaving once my mother arrived home, at which point my mother would prepare dinner. Like many a working mom today, my mother adjusted to not only working through the day, but also cooking our meals afterward. Esther assisted my parents with their transition to a two working-parent family by taking care of my younger brother Tom and doing the cleaning and laundry. It was a huge help to my mother without adding the discomfort of having someone "serve" us.

For those eating at the staff mess hall, there were precise procedures to follow. Each employee signed in at the front door and gave his mess hall "number" for his meal before eating. The cost of that meal was then deducted from the employee's salary for the pay period. It was necessary to have a "Meal Identification Card" issued by the administration in order to eat in the staff mess hall.

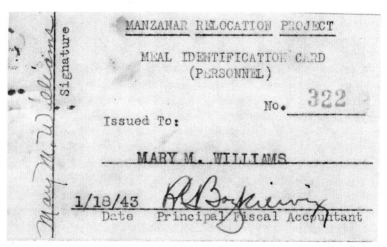

Mess hall pass

For those employees and their family members living within the camp, approval for the pass was given automatically, and the card was valid for as long as the person issued it lived or worked in the camp. Ranson Boczkiewicz, the WRA Manzanar principal accountant, issued and signed all meal identification cards. There were no Japanese-style meals served in the staff mess hall, but the evacuees complained that meals were better there than in their own mess halls. In fact, they were. The evacuee complaints about the food coming out of their mess halls was probably, in part, due to the meals being unlike those their own mothers had prepared. No institution can compete with a home cooked meal. Of course another issue added to the dissatisfaction—some internees, raised on Japanese food, considered the camp food unfamiliarly American, while others considered it "too Japanese."

With a staff as large as the one at Manzanar, medical issues arose upon occasion. Those WRA employees and their families living in the camp could only use the Manzanar Hospital for emergency treatment. Pregnancies were recognized as an emergency, allowing several WRA mothers to give birth at the Manzanar hospital. All the staff members and their families who arrived in the early stages of the camp were given shots when they arrived, just as the evacuees were, but all additional, non-emergency care had to be provided by offsite doctors. A few of the unscheduled visitors to the camp hospital included Bud Gilkey when he had his appendix removed, and me when I was placed in the hospital isolation ward with the measles. One night, a B-24 Liberator bomber overshot the Manzanar airstrip and the air force personnel injured were treated in the camp hospital by Japanese-American doctors. My Uncle Elmer "Mac" McLeod, chief test pilot for Lockheed broke his leg while on vacation near the camp, and the leg was set by one of the doctors in the hospital. Lockheed sent a plane to pick up McLeod at the Manzanar airport and fly him to Burbank. McLeod had a very interesting career in aviation, having taught Amelia Earhart to fly the Lockheed Electra 10-E that she was flying when she disappeared in the Pacific. Uncle Mac was only the second pilot to fly the P-38 Lightning.

One of the benefits to tolerating the conditions of WRA employment was the opportunity to save money. Even at the lowest possible rate of pay, a person who lived within the confines of the camp could still save money during their time at Manzanar. Let's use the example of a single elementary school teacher living in a dormitory and eating all of her meals in the staff mess hall. She would have earned the smallest possible salary offered to WRA employees in camp—$1,620 per year. All meals in the staff mess hall would cost one dollar each day or $365 per year. Rent would cost $20 per month or $240 per year, with all utilities included. After annual costs of $605 for room and board, that employee would have earned an additional $1,015 for the year. There was very little to spend money on around Manzanar, with most people entertaining themselves virtually for free, therefore even at the lowest possible salary, a frugal WRA employee could build their nest egg. For families in which both spouses worked, of which there were several, the opportunity to build a reserve was even greater. For some WRA employees, Manzanar provided the first time in their lives in which they had money left over after daily expenses. With the country slowly emerging from a depression, people had learned through necessity to live frugally, making this a financially profitable time for WRA staff.

CHAPTER X
LIFE IN CAMP

FIRST IMPRESSIONS

My father started with the WCCA in early April 1942. He was one of the fortunate few to arrive early enough to find a rental house in Independence, to avoid having to live in a tarpaper barrack with his family. It is strange that after all these years I still remember riding in the family's 1941 Ford up Highway 395 past the camp to our rental home in Independence. It was around May 1, 1942, and the camp was still under construction. I had camped out with my family in that same place on the old family ranch site many times, so I knew what it had looked like, but what I saw this time was a total shock. There were hundreds of tarpaper barracks neatly laid out in rows to the south of where hundreds of men were now building more. All of this construction was being carried out on a surface scraped clean of vegetation. It looked dusty and dirty. All the tarpaper buildings and even the soil looked black. I gave no thought to who was living in these barracks, for I was only thinking of myself and my complete despondency at being forced from my home in Redondo Beach. I recall there was nothing attractive about this place. I had always looked at Owens Valley as a place lightly populated–very small towns surrounded by huge mountains. Now, here was this massive construction project with scores of people, making it unlike anything I had seen there before.

During my first summer in Independence, the summer of 1942, I felt a deep sense of loss for everything I had grown to love in Redondo Beach: the ocean, my friends, my freedom, my paper route and the earnings that it provided, and more. I count the summer of 1942 as my loneliest ever in over eighty years. Independence was and is a small town where everyone knows everyone. I knew no one. For me, Independence was just a hot, dusty, lonely place.

When school started, I met Bud Abbott, and he and I had something in common— an interest in hunting. That first fall we would go hunting every afternoon after school and all day on the weekends. This would be the first pleasure I found in Owens Valley. It heightened my appreciation for nature and the outdoors—an appreciation I have never lost. Sadly, my first friend in Independence moved away after a few months. His departure was another loss.

Don Nail, Art Williams, and Pat Nail, with Thomas Williams in front

We lived in Independence until early 1943, and then moved into the staff area of the camp. It was shortly thereafter that staff families were moving out of their tarpaper barracks and into the staff area. Manzanar's new staff housing brought in more teenage kids which was very comforting for me. Don and Pat Nail, Don and Bruce Inman, Rick Collins, Fred Causey, David Oille, Bud Gilkey, Dan Cox, Harold Dennis, Bill Hayes, and Bill Boczkiewicz and I became good friends, as our families moved into the camp. I will never forget the hilarity created by the chemistry teacher as he tried repeatedly and finally gave up trying to first spell and pronounce Bill Boczkiewicz's name on Bill's first day of school in Indenpendence. Because we were all new, it was much easier to form friendships. There were no established cliques and nobody there harassing the new kids. We were also each trying to adjust to a completely different life from the one we had known. The shared new experiences accompanying our life in camp gave us something in common. We not only lived in the confined small corner of the camp together, but traveled the same path at the same time every day: walk out to the main gate, catch the bus to school, at night reverse the procedure. Joan DaValle remembers being teased her first semester by the local town kids—a new experience she had to tolerate for the first couple of months. All of us kids from the Manzanar camp were called the "Jap Camp Kids." That label stuck with us as long as we lived in the camp. I will always remember the other staff kids as my life savers, for without them, camp would have been intolerable—the loneliest place on the planet.

CAMP LIFE MEMORIES

I have many memories of my time in Manzanar. Clearly, it was not as pleasant living in Manzanar as it had been in Southern California. Everybody had to adjust and accept where they were and try to make the best of it. I had some good moments and even times I would call great. The longer I lived in Owens Valley, the better it became. The most vivid memories I retain are of the weather, the mountains, and the staff teens. Coming from the ideal climatic conditions in Redondo Beach, Manzanar was anything but. It was freezing cold in the winter and blazing hot in the summer. All of us remember and talk about the wind which seemed to rage every day and would some days get up to 60 miles per hour and more, creating terrible dust storms. Like many things, in time you learn to live with and accept it. I looked at the magnificent Sierra Mountains every day and could not get over their size and beauty. In the fall we would look for the first snow on the mountaintops and watch as the days got shorter and colder, and the snow line crept down the slopes, hoping soon it would reach the valley floor. As a teenager, snow on the valley floor was always exciting, but after a few days of it, the fun was gone, and we grew weary of the wet and cold. I never go back to Manzanar that I don't visit the main gate, and remember the MP's standing there in the cold, and remember walking out to Highway 395, freezing, waiting for the bus. The wind would blow and it would be so bitter cold that I never felt I had enough clothes on. In truth I probably didn't. We had never heard of chill factor, but I have to think it originated in a place like Manzanar with its cold, harsh winters. Coming out of winter, the snow line crept back up the Sierras, exposing green vegetation as the days got warmer. Owens Valley had four distinct seasons that could be seen and felt, giving it a beautiful, natural cycle that never grew old.

In September 1942, the new staff mess hall was opened in the staff housing area. There were a number of families who continued to eat dinner at the new mess hall, even though most now had kitchens in their new apartments. Bachelors had no option but to eat at the staff mess hall, as their apartments had no kitchens. Because my mother's work as chief dietitian in the hospital had her up and gone early every morning, during school I was at the staff mess hall every morning as it opened for breakfast. My parents were concerned that I was too skinny and needed a good breakfast and felt what I would fix myself would not be enough. I remember that first morning in the staff mess hall, for I was the only kid and a bit nervous around all the grown men there. The women never ate breakfast that early. They arrived about the time I was leaving. That first, uninitiated day, I ate nothing more than a bowl of cold cereal. The amused men at the table told me what was available: cereal hot or cold, hot cakes, French toast, ham or bacon, eggs, hash browns, orange juice, and milk. This is where I was introduced to a working man's breakfast and have loved it ever since. Doug Cowart who worked in accounting and I were usually the first two in line waiting for the door to open. I knew Mr. Cowart's son, David Ollie, who was a friend, and over the breakfast table I got to know Mr. Cowart. I found out he was from Scotland, had served two years in the marines, lived in Texas twenty-five years, did some bronco busting in his younger days, and that he had worked at the Fresno Assembly Center before coming to Manzanar. He was interesting, personable, and I liked him. I had just forty-five minutes to eat breakfast and walk out to the highway to catch the bus to school. It was a tight schedule, but it was worth it for those great breakfasts.

During WWII families were encouraged to farm any small area of land they had available to them to help produce food for the war effort. These small family plots were rather grandly called victory gardens. The WRA set aside bare ground within the staff area for several. It was a patriotic thing to have a victory garden, and the Japanese Americans had many of them in camp. My father became very patriotic on my behalf and signed me up for two plots which came with a rake, a shovel, and a hoe. Unfortunately, I had as a youngster on our Manzanar farm, developed a dislike for farming and the tools that came with it. I found it to be punishment, and something at which I wasn't very accomplished. Through all of my sweat and grime, the only things I could manage to grow were radishes and carrots. I'm afraid my contribution to the war effort in this arena was extremely minimal at best.

Over a few summers I worked with other teenagers on nearby farms baling hay and was provided room and board. The farmer would take a group of us into Independence on Fridays after working all week. I made a straight course to the local soda fountain and ordered a milkshake every Friday. After working all week in the heat, that milkshake was without comparison. After our reprieve, it was back to Manzanar camp for weekends with our families, followed by another week of farm work. The farm job did not last all summer, so I worked at various jobs during the summers. My least favorite job was working with a beekeeper named Merle Howard, who later became the Sheriff of Inyo County. I got stung every day without fail. After being stung about thirty times one afternoon I called it quits, never to go back. On the other hand, I really enjoyed my work for Archie Dean who owned a pack train that ran out of Onion Valley. Jack Hunter and I cleared trail over Kearsarge Pass (11,709 feet) in the Sierras for Archie and his horses and mules. This job took place out-of-doors and I loved that. Along with those jobs, I worked in a service station, and at a grocery store. The pay was always fifty cents per hour. At the end of summer I would take the Orange Belt Stage to Southern California, visit my Uncle "Mac" McLeod, Aunt Hazel, and cousin Warren, and spend my hard earned money. My cousin and I were close to the same age and had been friends since birth. This was the time I looked forward to all year. We would spend a week on Balboa Island going to the beach every day. We would then spend a week in Burbank, swimming at Toluca Lake's Lakeside Country Club pool, and hitting all the newly released movies in Hollywood. I remember at the end of my visit one year when I was about 14, my aunt had taken me to San Fernando to catch the Orange Belt Stage back to Manzanar, and I started crying. I wanted to stay and never go back to the camp. I was embarrassed to have her see me cry and tried to hold it in, but it was impossible. Those riding on the bus looked at me like something terrible had happened. To me it had; I was, for another year, leaving the place I loved. When I got back to Manzanar it would always take time to get Southern

California off my mind. It was a place I deeply loved and missed. It never occurred to me that other kids were having a rough time adjusting to camp life as well. It was not until fifty years later that Bud Gilkey shared with me the difficulty he went through. It was so bad in his case that his parents sent him back to Palo Alto to live with his grandparents before he made up his mind it was better to be with his parents in Manzanar than without them in Palo Alto. Richard Collins and his mother, Pauline, both felt they had enough of camp life after one year and returned to Fresno. Richard's dad, Henry, would stay until the camp closed. What I find interesting is that each of us kept hidden our true feelings of unhappiness at leaving a world we preferred for a life in camp. We never shared them with each other until many years later. There is no way of knowing how many others felt like Bud Gilkey, Rick Collins, and me. Conversely, Marjorie DaValle, who taught algebra and geometry to the evacuee students in Manzanar High School, made going to Manzanar sound like a vacation—an exciting adventure. Therefore the DaValle sisters, Joan and Shirley, seemed to enjoy it more than most. Probably growing up with Mrs. DaValle's spirit of adventure and positive attitude made a world of difference for her girls.

FRATERNIZING

Before going to Manzanar I knew very few Japanese Americans. Between first and sixth grade one of my two best friends was a boy named Katsumi. I never thought of him as anything but a friend. Everybody's family came from somewhere and the fact that his was from Japan, or mine was from elsewhere never occurred to us. We were just too busy playing and being kids. I wondered many times if he had also ended up in Manzanar, but the way the camp was organized, with the staff area at the front corner, the sheer number of evacuees in camp, and an unspoken code that kept us staff kids out of the evacuee area and vice versa, quelled any thoughts of finding him. Additionally, I feared he might be embarrassed about being there, and I was concerned about being perceived as part of that group of people keeping him there. In reality, if we had run into each other I would have welcomed finding a friend in camp, but I'm not sure in which side of camp we would have both felt comfortable hanging out—certainly not before the segregation calmed down people's nerves. Many years later, after the camp closed and the Manzanar National Historic Site came out with a list of all those incarcerated there, I found he had indeed been in camp near me.

In Redondo there had been a Japanese-American family who raised flowers at the end of my paper route. In fact, they were my last customers on the route. They noticed I had newspapers left over each night and asked to have them to wrap around their cut flowers. They refused to take them without giving me flowers in exchange. I remember how surprised my mother was the first time I walked into our home with a large bunch of gorgeous flowers. The only member of the family to talk to me was the father. He was always extremely serious. I knew absolutely nothing about them other than they always paid for the paper on time. There were children in the family, but they were younger than me and not at my school. It seemed the complete family was always bent over working in the fields. In my junior high school we had about six other kids of Japanese heritage, but none were in my classes. I remember when they disappeared from school. No one seemed to know or talk about where they went or why. It never occurred to me that they might be in Manzanar. I do not remember exactly when I first discovered the Japanese Americans were being evacuated, but it was probably when the students all disappeared on the same day. I was not emotional about it, for I certainly did not understand their plight. It was not until I found out I was going to a camp that I became emotional—especially when I found out it was at Manzanar, a place I had disliked for years.

Often when I am talking to people about my time in Manzanar, and they discover that I lived inside of the fenced camp with no physical separation between the evacuees' apartments and my family's, they assume I had many Japanese-American friends. They find it difficult to believe that I had none. In reality, we lived in our little corner of camp. I saw Japanese-American adults daily in the staff area and they worked side by side with both of my parents, but at least for the first couple of years, the Japanese-American teenagers, who I might have become friends with, rarely came into the staff area, and I rarely had reason to go into theirs. When we did meet in passing we were always polite to each other, but I never got to know them. For me it equates to the difference between living in a small town—like our tiny staff area—where you know everything about everybody, and living in a big city—like the evacuee area—where you likely don't even know your next door neighbor, and you certainly don't randomly pick a stranger on a busy street to strike up a friendship with. The only time I entered into the area where the evacuees lived, I was either going to an outdoor movie, going out the west gate for a hike up to the Sierras, on a very rare occasion when I went to buy something in the commissary, or when I went to watch one of the evacuee football games. Occasionally, I would walk through camp to the hospital about a mile away to see my mother. I would be walking in an area of the camp where I was the only Caucasian. The Japanese Americans would not wave or say hello. They ignored me as if I did not exist. We staff kids, as a minority, hung out together probably for some of the same reasons the Japanese Americans as a minority on the West Coast stuck together. We were in a comfort zone. We staff high school students arose each morning, took our books and identification passes, walked directly to the main gate and headed to school together each day. We were a small group of teenagers with much in common including considerable travel time back and forth. It was the perfect formula for friendships to develop, and many of those friendships still remain strong today. We just never experienced this type of time together with the evacuee teens. Perhaps if we had gone to Manzanar High School with the Japanese-American teens we would have developed friendships more readily. Although internee and staff teenagers in camp seldom intermingled, working adults were a different matter. Dad's closest Japanese-American friends were those he met working in internal security. He corresponded with some for years after they relocated to the East.

There is another issue regarding the staff kids socializing with the evacuee kids. In the first nearly two years of the camp, the Japanese Americans were having problems within their own section of camp. Due to the internal conflicts between those remaining loyal to the United States and those claiming loyalty to Japan, gangs developed, and there were beatings, violence, and fights amongst themselves. In those early, scarier days, I believe if a Japanese-American teenager had ventured to the staff area to make friends with a staff kid, he might have been met with violence from the anti-American and anti WRA element in camp. As time passed, the angry, anti-American element was removed to Tule Lake, the camp's population dropped in half, and there was definitely a greater calm surrounding the camp. By the spring of 1945, Manzanar had become a much more peaceful, friendly place for all of us and we did have a bit more exposure to the Japanese-American kids in camp.

The closest I came to having a Japanese-American friend in camp was my younger brother's babysitter, Esther Ando. I would like to think of Esther as a friend, but I was just a young teenager and she was an adult. She was a very special person that everyone in our family loved. When she and her husband relocated, it was a very sad parting for us. I can't tell you how much we missed her. Once she left the camp, I never heard from her again, although it is possible my mother did. The closest I came to daily contact with Japanese Americans other than Esther was when I caught the measles and was in the isolation ward at the hospital for ten days. My parents were on vacation in Mexico during this time, so I had no family to keep me company. Many days the young adult, Japanese-American nurses' aides would break up the monotony of my days, asking question after question about life outside of the camp. They wanted to know things like what clothes the high school girls were wearing and how they were wearing their hair. They were cut off from the world they had known and wanted to know what was going on outside of their lives of confinement. The only problem I had was their insistence that they were going to give me a bath every morning. Measles or no measles, at fifteen, I made it each morning to the showers way before they arrived. They were the bright spot in my ten day stay in the isolation ward. Other than when I was brought meals, they were the only ones to enter the isolation ward. No one else wanted to go near the place. Frankly, I enjoyed talking to them, for it was boring and lonely without them. After my release from the hospital, I never saw them again.

The first staff teenage girls to arrive in camp were Lynne Hayes, and Joan and Shirley DaValle. They joined Japanese-American girls' clubs and participated in some of their activities, but they never developed close friendships.

Girls' Club with Lynne Hayes and Joan and Shirley DaValle

Joan stated she thought the evacuee girls were polite but not excessively friendly. After more staff kids arrived and they were all living in the staff area the Caucasian girls dropped out of the Japanese-American girls' groups.

Manzanar was equipped with classes for evacuee children from kindergarten through high school. The staff children that were in elementary school during their Manzanar years attended the same school classes in camp alongside of the Japanese-American children. It wasn't until junior high school and on that the two groups were separated. I had a strong feeling that this system was set up by the WRA to purposely keep us hormonal teens away from each other. I was never told this, but it was something I felt. With interracial marriage expressly forbidden, especially under the circumstances of the war with Japan, it was extremely unpopular for Asians and Caucasians to fraternize romantically. Removing the staff teens to Independence might have been done to prevent potential mixing. Beth Kincade's parents, though, insisted that Beth attend school in camp, which she did. She was the only staff high school student who attended school with the evacuees. She was proof that the WRA didn't strictly prohibit the two student groups from commingling. There is another, very real reason we went to school in Independence. The high school there was so low on students it was threatened with closure. This was the one benefit the camp brought to that small community, and I suspect the Independence School Board made a strong pitch for the Manzanar kids to be sent there. We nearly doubled the Independence enrollment—as pathetically small as our numbers were. As further evidence for this theory, there was a family named

Gates that lived just four miles from Lone Pine, but all the Gates children were bussed to school twelve miles away to Independence. Once the camp kids saved the Independence school with their enrollment, the Gates kids were permitted to go back to their own neighborhood Lone Pine School.

Beautifully maintained staff bachelors' quarters

HOME SWEET HOME—STAFF HOUSING

In the beginning there was a depressing monotony to the camp's appearance. Over time, though, the staff housing area was improved greatly with beautiful lawns maintained by the best gardeners from Southern California—very skilled evacuees. The area was pristine. The biggest problem with keeping lawns, turned out to be gaining access to a lawnmower. There was over 450,000 square feet of lawn scattered throughout camp and only one mower. Besides the striking lawns, the only plantings were a few young, thin trees—no flowers existed except for the few that each family planted themselves. Each spring, my family planted sweet peas on a trellis against our rock walled patio. As for color, all the staff area housing was painted white in contrast to the black tarpaper barracks. It was attractive but a bit stark. The walkways throughout the staff area were lined with precisely arranged, white painted rocks. There was ample room between buildings to give an open, uncrowded feeling to the area.

As for the housing itself, it was comfortable, but very small. I know in our case, the house we had in Redondo Beach was considerably larger and nicer than our Manzanar apartment. To alleviate the icy winters, we had one oil fired heater, but the partitioned rooms away from the heater never felt the meager heat produced. There was no relief from the heat in the blazing summers that got to well over 100°. I remember how difficult it was sleeping during those hot, summer nights. There were many evacuees and MPs who slept outside in the summers, but my parents objected. Authors of books like *Personal Justice Denied* who have made statements about air conditioning in the staff area never lived in the camp I was in. There were no air conditioners or evaporative coolers in the staff apartments except for the project director's unit.

Our kitchen was very small. One person could stand in the kitchen and fill it. We only had one bedroom, so with my parents occupying the bedroom, my brother and I slept on a couch that opened up into a bed. Each evening we had to make the bed, and each morning we turned it back into a couch. There were some two bedroom apartments, but my father chose instead the project director's original residence with the rock wall patio, a relatively large living room, and varnished plywood interior walls. It was different from all the other staff housing.

Family is important to us, but visitors to our Manzanar home were few. Because the apartment was so small, there were no provisions for overnight guests. Those relatives who did come, stayed overnight in either Lone Pine or Independence. For those staff members living in tarpaper barracks, I certainly can't picture inviting grandmother over to share in the communal showers and toilets (and yet, indeed, the Japanese-American grandmothers were forced to endure this very humiliation). Besides the issues of space and convenience, the stark, prison-like appearance of the camp did not encourage visitation. Additionally, visitors were confined to the staff area, and with no staff recreation room, there was essentially nothing to do there. The biggest obstacle to visitation was the written approval required from the project director or his assistant to get a pass. All visitors were logged in and checked out. Consequently, for the Manzanar staff, family reunions were best saved for after the war.

Manzanar in winter

Just as in the rest of the camp, weather and high winds took a toll on our housing. With its dust storms, I'm convinced Manzanar was not far from the dustbowls of the twenties. Every few years in Owens Valley, there is a hard winter in which the snow covers the valley floor.

This very thing happened in February 1944, when the WRA camp was inhabited. The storm came from the South on a driving wind that blew snow into all the north and south facing barracks' attic vents. This included practically all the barracks, since they were all lined up facing the same direction. As the snow melted in the attics, the water trickled down into the living quarters. In short, hundreds of barracks were a mess, including the one my family and I lived in. Along with issues of wind and snow came the aforementioned one of the bitter winter cold. I read a profile on the head nurse at Manzanar, Lillian Josephine Hawes, and the problems she had with trying to sleep at night. By November 1942, the government had not received a heater nor any other furniture for her room. She was using a box as a table and to store personal things in. Her bed was an army cot, and the heavy, army issue blankets were not keeping her warm. She said she learned to put paper under her bottom sheet because it was a better insulator. It was very rough for anyone living in camp during its start up. I can tell you from personal experience that Josephine Hawes was one tough cookie. When I was alone in camp with the measles, I did not want to spend my time in an isolation ward hospital bed eating Japanese food, so I vehemently refused to go there. When she heard this, Ms. Hawes came to our apartment, forcibly put me in a car, and hauled me to the hospital. For the ten days I was in the hospital, she never came to visit me and I was happier for it.

RECREATIONAL OPPORTUNITIES

Except for a single basketball hoop installed two and a half years after the camp was built, recreational opportunities were simply not provided for the staff children at Manzanar. At Tule Lake the staff had a recreation room complete with pool table, but not at Manzanar. I never could figure out how the camp plans called for a recreation room for each block of the evacuee section and a rec room in the MP camp, but none for the staff area. There was virtually nothing arranged for the staff or their children with the exception of a couple of family picnics at Bair's Creek and a swim party someone organized at William "Hopalong Cassidy" Boyd's cabin and swimming pool in the Alabama Hills. It was no wonder we created our own recreation, usually outside of the fenced camp, often foolhardy.

In the era before computers, video games, and television, the radio became an important form of entertainment at home. Unfortunately, radio reception was terrible, so we missed out on all the great radio broadcasts that had kept us on the edge of our seats in Southern California. That was one thing I really missed. We did have a record player and a number of 78's to play. I could restack and shuffle the records, but very soon the same old songs got pretty boring. Besides the repetitiveness, the deterioration of sound quality caused by unavoidable scratches from the dust made listening to records less than an ideal pastime. Some evacuees ran a radio repair shop in camp to which our old radio should have made a visit, but never did.

The one form of entertainment we had in Independence while I lived there, and which was not available in Redondo Beach, was an outdoor skating rink—and it was free! I went every night during the summer of 1942 to the grammar school grounds that housed the rink, and skated to the music from their record player. They too had a limited number of records, one of which was a Glenn Miller recording of *A String of Pearls*. I must have heard that song a hundred times that summer. Today, whenever I hear, *A String of Pearls*, I flash back to the summer of 1942 and the outdoor skating rink in Independence. Because it was so far from Manzanar, and transportation was unpredictable, sadly I never made it back to the skating rink once my family and I moved into the camp.

For the first few years of Manzanar's existence, movies were shown outside on the east fire break near its intersection with the north fire break. Later, an outdoor theater with seating and a stage was built. Evacuees attended showings along with staff and their families, and as long as the movies were held in one of these outdoor venues, they were free of charge. The bad news was I had to stand in the back throughout the movie. In 1944, the movies were moved inside into the newly built auditorium. Once this occurred, seating became limited and a ticket was required to get in.

Manzanar movie ticket

I always assumed that the WRA owned the projector, paid the operator, and rented the movies. In actuality, the camp had a commissary owned and operated by the evacuees, and they—not the WRA—also owned and operated the projector. They also selected and provided the movies. One of the very first movies presented in the auditorium had a newsreel in which Emperor Hirohito was shown on his white horse. The Japanese Americans in the theater went wild at the site of Hirohito whom they considered a spiritual leader. At this, the WRA staff along with their families quickly exited the theater. Where the Japanese Americans saw a leader, we saw a ruthless dictator. Not understanding this vast cultural disparity changed the attitudes of a number of the staff and their family members towards going to the movies in camp. Many simply stopped going altogether, and in the end, elected to pay the price of going to the nearby community movie theater which was located in Lone Pine.

Since there was so little for staff kids to do in camp, the greatest year round recreation for us had to be going to the soda fountain in Independence or attending the movies in Lone Pine. The soda fountain, popular with flight school cadets and school kids, came complete with a white marble top, black covered bar stools, and a jukebox. For a dime we could hear one of our favorite songs. High school girls worked as soda jerks. Betty White, Dorothy Wilson, and Gladys Mitchell were masters at turning out a great soda or milkshake so thick we had to eat it with a spoon. If we did not have money for a soda or shake we might get a cherry phosphate. To get to the movies we would hope our family was going, but if they weren't, we would rush to the main gate and ask each car leaving camp if they were going to Lone Pine and if they had room for one more. It was rare to not get a ride. The next available option was hitching a ride with a car passing by from Independence. Often they too were headed to the movies in Lone Pine. The site of boys hitchhiking was not that uncommon. You do not see it today for it has become dangerous, not to mention that now most kids have a car or access to public transportation. We had neither. There were a number of teachers without a car and on occasions we would see one or two of them hitchhiking as well. They were tough competition and always got the first ride.

During WWII most boys I knew were interested in airplanes, especially fighter planes, so when one set down at the nearby Manzanar airport, which was not that often, it was a big deal. We would all take off running to see the plane and talk to the pilot. I still remember going to see a Grumman F4F Wildcat, nine P39 Bell Aero Cobras, and a P51 Mustang. The pilots would usually put on an air show of sorts by buzzing the field. This was always very exciting. One night, out of the blue, the Manzanar airport operator turned on the landing lights. A lost B-24 bomber pilot and crew saw the lights and approached the runway from the South. On final approach the airport operator, again for reasons unknown, turned off the lights. The plane hit the runway but ran out of paved surface and plowed into a dirt bank. Some of the crew members, as previously mentioned, were hurt and treated at the Manzanar camp hospital. A few days later the plane was repaired and flown out.

Fishing was an activity that kept more than a few people in camp occupied. I was not an enthusiastic fisherman, but some of the staff kids were. Don Nail in particular seemed to always be out fishing. He liked his alone-time and it was amazing how far he would hike in order to fish. We used to call him "GI" for his dad had been the Army Military Police Captain, and somehow Don seemed to be always wearing Army GI issue boots and a pith helmet. He loved his fishing and was very likable.

In the fall once we saw the snow line creep down the slopes of the Sierras to the base, we would hike to it. Just about every staff teenager in camp would go. We would take a lunch for it would be a full day's hike up and back. This became an annual event. Most of the WRA staff and their families had never lived where they had such ready access to fishing, hiking, exploring the country side, camping out in the mountains, and hunting. What made it even better was that gas rationing cut down the influx of tourists so the whole valley and its surrounding mountains felt like our own private sanctuary.

One of our less-well-thought-out activities was catching and riding wild horses and burros. The rides were dangerous, but no more dangerous than a run in with their owner might have been. He was a weaselly looking cowboy who had been married three times and all three wives had died of unnatural causes—or so the story goes. This fellow had a bad attitude that matched his bad reputation, and he carried a revolver. He looked menacing. In spite of the thrill of the adventure, our wild riding days halted abruptly once we found he was the owner of the mounts and that he was looking for the culprits that had been on them.

In the summer, as there was no pool around, a favorite activity was to swim in the aqueduct. Much like riding the horses, we also weren't supposed to be swimming in the aqueduct. There were some close calls avoiding the rider, Frank Lawrence, hired to keep kids out, but we managed. Harold Dennis's mother had told him he could not swim in the aqueduct so we used him as a lookout. One time Lawrence came by and we all dove in and hid under the bridge. I could hear every word exchanged between him and Harold.

"Is anyone swimming in here?" the rider asked.

"I don't know, but I think so," Harold responded.

"Well," Frank Lawrence was yelling, "you boys come out of there right now!" We stayed in the water under the bridge, knowing we were safe.

Finally, Lawrence demanded, "You better be out of there when I come back!" We were, but it never stopped us from going back, although, if we were going swimming with the girls we would go to the sand trap and not the aqueduct. It was a safer place to swim. Lone Pine did get a pool near the end of WWII, and it was opened by none other than Johnny Weissmuller, the Olympic champion who starred as Tarzan in the old movies, but it was too late for us to enjoy.

Duck hunting was my greatest love while living in Owens Valley. I would either hunt with my father or my camp friend Rick Collins. We would always start before daylight and would not come in until dark. Because most men had gone off to war, there were very few hunters and quite a few ducks for those who knew where to look. It was ideal. I loved the sport and my mother loved the free, fresh meat. The trick was in getting our guns in and out of camp. Rick and I would roll our shotguns up in a blanket and hide them in the trunk of the car and have one of our dads take us out through security. Coming back we had to wait for them to get off work to pick us up to smuggle the guns back in. Having guns in camp was not something approved by the WRA, but my father would have given up his kids and wife before he would have given up his guns. There was a notice put out by Capt.

Nail, head of the military police, stating there were to be no guns in the camp. It never got enforced in our apartment. Because our dads worked in internal security it was easy getting our guns in and out through the main gate.

Having my dad in a prominent position with internal security worked in my favor when it came to hunting, but in cases of youthful recklessness, I was at a clear disadvantage to those kids who could remain slightly more anonymous. On one of our adventures, a number of us boys decided to dam up Bair's Creek to make a swimming pool.

Young Japanese-American boys enjoying Bair's Creek

We had never swum in this creek before, preferring the aqueduct. Because we felt it was too shallow for suitable swimming, we decided to deepen it. The stream was dammed up by our handiwork and left to fill. Three days later the water reached to nearly the top of the wall of the canyon (shown above with young Japanese-American boys enjoying the water) and backed up the canyon for several hundred yards. We were going to go swimming but began to feel the dam might wash out. We decided to gently breach the dam, thinking we could release the water slowly, but in minutes it washed out the entire fill material, releasing a wall of water ten to twelve feet high at the dam site and heading rapidly toward camp. It created a flood of notably spectacular proportions. The wall of water passed under Military Police Guard Tower #5 which we were thinking was doomed to go over. Next the water rushed down through the chicken farm pinning hundreds of chickens against the wire fencing at the downstream end of their pens and drowning them.

Future victims of the Bair's Creek flood

One cannot imagine our sense of fear and our desire to go anywhere but back to camp. When we arrived at the south gate to enter the camp, we were met by internal security. My father felt—and shared—the pain of being in something of a prominent, law enforcement position and having had his own son cause so much damage to the camp—predominantly to the poultry supply. You might have believed that the WRA would have thought at this point they should organize some sort of recreation for the staff kids to keep them out of trouble, but it did not happen. Maybe that would have been a bit too much like rewarding our devastatingly poor choice.

Approximately two years after moving into the camp, recreation hall opportunities opened up for us. Even though we had no recreation hall of our own, after a couple years of passing the main gate sentry post twice each day, to and from school, we had gotten to know a few of the sentries there quite well. By this time the number of MPs had been reduced from a maximum of about 135 to about sixty. On bitterly cold mornings, while waiting for the school bus, the girls got to share the heater inside the MP's sentry post with the Military Police. We boys never seemed to get the same privileges and had to stand out in the cold waiting for the school bus, but it still provided the opportunity to visit with those MPs at the main gate. Eventually they felt comfortable enough with us to invite us to enjoy their rec hall. Some of the single female teachers would also go with us to the MP's recreation room. Since the room had been designed for 135 men, it was not crowded and the MP's seemed to enjoy us being around. Well, honestly, probably not us teenage boys as much as the single school teachers. For those of us staff kids living in the camp, this was our first opportunity to enjoy a recreation room even if it was not ours. As the number of MPs dropped even further to fifty and then to forty, we went to the MP rec hall even more frequently. I do not ever recall the girls going with us. I can only imagine their parents felt it inappropriate and unsafe for their young girls to be hanging out with the older MPs. The rec hall was equipped with nothing more than a radio, a pool table, and a soda machine, but it also provided a space for us to just visit without standing in the burning sun or cramming into a tiny apartment.

On a few instances, the MP's arranged for an army truck to take some of the school teachers to dances in Independence. There were a few adventurous, young school teachers who dated Military Police. On a few occasions, the Military Police jeep patrol would take the staff's teenage girls for a ride around the perimeter of the camp. One time they let them climb one of the unmanned guard towers.

For the first two and a half years of camp there was no recreation provided by the WRA for the staff and their families until the staff organized a club called "MAP" which stood for "Manzanar Appointed Personnel." MAP provided the opportunity to play badminton, shuffleboard, and cards, and organized parties and dances. The first chairman was Aksel Nielsen and his committee consisted of all adults—Dr. Little, Mrs. Virgil Morgan, David Bromley, and Douglas Cowart. They prepared by-laws and immediately denied membership to anybody under the age of fourteen, and established a monthly fee of $1.00 per member. I do not know if the purpose of the monthly dues was to keep kids out, but that's certainly what it did as a dollar was considerable money back then. The first MAP function was a dance held at the staff mess hall and included soft drinks and snacks. Hard liquor was not permitted in camp, although several evacuees had been arrested for imbibing. Later, a tarpaper barrack was assigned as the MAP clubhouse. Once, the staff teenagers were permitted to hold a dance to which I took LaPriel Strong. I did not know my right foot from my left, but she was kind enough to teach me the Balboa Hop. The thing I remember most about that dance is that no two bodies were ever allowed to touch. In other words, for a hot blooded teenager accompanied by a pretty girl like LaPriel, this dance was a letdown. Before school was out in 1945, the club's location was moved to D-4 in the staff area. The club, for the first time, had a bathroom and a kitchen.

Even sports were not as readily available then as they are for the average high school student today. After MAP was formed, members did participate in softball. There was a staff men's team that played a Japanese-American women's team and there was a coed team of young staff women and teenagers who would play each other.

Joan DaValle and Lynne Hayes, both teenagers, each pitched for one of the two teams. Again, these games were primarily for the MAP members. All the games were played on the evacuees' baseball fields for there was no field in the staff area. The significance of this was, for the first time, the WRA families were now going out into the Japanese-Americans' part of the camp to join in athletic activities with them. Prior to this there had been adult square dances with the evacuees in camp, but not sports activities.

For the teenage boys in camp, athletic activities mostly took place at Independence High School, however, not until the fall of 1944 were there team activities with other schools. The government stopped interscholastic sports in our area for two years to save rubber and gasoline for the war effort. After the restriction was lifted, the only full schedule was basketball, although we did have one football game with Big Pine and one tennis match with Burroughs High School from Inyokern. In camp we would play touch football on the lawn in the staff area. One day, after those stating loyalty to Japan had been moved to Tule Lake, some evacuee boys came over and joined in our game. This had never happened before, but after the segregation the entire atmosphere of the camp became vastly less tense and more relaxed. A few days later the boys asked us to play over on the fire break. When we got there, we found ourselves facing several thousand Japanese-American spectators lined up along the sidelines. This was taking on the look of a big game. Interestingly, the young Japanese-American boys our age who had played earlier in the staff area disappeared when we got to the fire break. Four of us, Bill Boczkiewicz, Rick "Bird legs" Collins, Fred Causey, and myself, all under sixteen years of age, were facing older, bigger boys and an organized team with substantial depth. We felt we had been set up. We quickly got support from Lee Poole who worked for the WRA and had played college football, and Bill Adams, a visiting college student. It was a rough, bloody game of six man tackle on dirt without uniforms which we lost 42 to 6. Big Pine's high school football team, at one point, played the evacuees also. Manzanar High School, with an enrollment of over a thousand students to draw from, tromped little Big Pine with fewer than a hundred students. Bishop High School was invited to play basketball against Manzanar, but the administration declined on behalf of the students. The student body president followed with a letter of apology to the Japanese-American youths, stating that the athletes had not been allowed the choice to play.

Boredom combined with hormones can lead to dangerous exploits in some teens. One evening a group of us high school boys from the WRA camp were walking back from a game of pool in the MPs' recreation room when Rick Collins, the same staff teen responsible for destroying the Mastipave in the staff dormitory, decided to take a short cut rather than walk to the main gate. Rick was a talented high jumper and high hurdler, coming in third in the California State Finals behind Hugh McElhenney and Bob Mathias. Rick took off running along Highway 395 just north of guard tower #7, darted toward the camp, and jumped over the five-foot barbed wire fence and was off into the darkness while the guard in the tower scrambled to get his gun. It was a spontaneous yet dangerous move, but Rick was always wild and very sure of himself. It has always remained a question in my mind if the guard in the tower would really have shot Rick, had he been quick enough. I'm sure it all depends on which MP was on duty at that time. Luckily, we will never know. Rick's bravado came in handy as he later ran track in college, graduated, and spent most of his life flying for the air force. He retired a Lt. Colonel.

None of the evacuees or staff teenagers had cars and there was no public transportation in the area, so we had to be creative in getting to our destinations. In camp, everywhere you looked people were walking—staff and internees, young and old. For the staff kids it was the same outside of camp. We walked to fishing, walked to hunting, and walked to the mountains. There were only a couple a teachers and some staff kids who had bicycles. The teachers, particularly Lois Ferguson and Martha Shoaf, used theirs, but we seldom did. What few bike rides we did have were out of the camp on Highway 395. In those days it was lightly traveled. One night, Bud Gilkey, another staff teen, and I rode home tandem on a bike six miles from Independence to Manzanar in the dark with no lights. Not one car passed us. Today the traffic is so heavy it would be suicide to duplicate that bike ride. That was not the case during WWII with gasoline rationing. Fred Causey's dad bought a model T Ford and a couple of times he let Fred drive it in camp. After a few years living in camp, Bud Gilkey, who was older than the rest of us, got a car. He was the only one of us who had one, and he was very good about giving us a ride. He shared it so willingly it felt like we all had gotten a car.

Coming and going from the various activities outside of camp required us to have a gate entry pass. According to General DeWitt, no WRA camp was allowed to issue a pass for longer than one month, and each pass had to be approved by the project director. Soon after, the approval level was reduced to the assistant project director, but monthly passes were still required right until the camps' closures.

Gate entry pass

All WRA employees and each of their family members were issued a new pass each month which we picked up at the Internal Security Police Station. Initially, every time we entered or left the camp we had to show our pass. After a while, if the MP knew us, he might not ask to see our passes. Those of us who went to school in Independence and passed through the gate twice each day were seldom asked to show our passes, but we carried them with us always because we were never sure when we might be asked.

IN SUMMARY

As one might expect, for the staff and family members, living in Manzanar was viewed differently by each person there. From the ever positive DaValle sisters who saw everything in the brightest possible light, to the ones who just couldn't make it work and moved away, everybody's previous experiences brought a unique perspective to the table. Those who had it rough during the depression—and most people did—might have viewed Manzanar as a promising end to their unemployment. Those who had recently divorced or been widowed might also have been thankful for the job opportunities afforded them by the WRA. There were many reasons for taking a job in Manzanar. For the WRA employees, working and living in Manzanar was a choice—one which they could rethink if they chose to do so. My father loved Owens Valley hunting and fishing so much that working in Manzanar was a blessing. He could not have been happier anywhere else; after all, he was back in the place he had loved as a kid. Fred Causey, Jr., a staff teenager from the East Coast said, "Living in Manzanar was one of the happiest times of my life." Joan (DaValle) Beyer a staff teenager from Southern California said about moving there, "I hated to lose my friends and home, and I hated the tarpaper barrack and latrines, but once in new housing and more Caucasian kids moved into camp I liked it. The mountains and the camp turned into an enjoyable experience. Coming from a large school where I was a nobody to a very small school, I became, in time, a somebody. There were six of us Caucasian girls in camp and we became very close. We corresponded for many years after leaving camp. As to the Japanese-American girls in camp, they treated my sister and me with respect. They were nice. I look back on all of it as an adventure, a wonderful experience." The son of a very successful Japanese American told me his father said, "Manzanar was the only time in my life I had a paid vacation." In truth, he and his family were only in the camp a little over a year before relocating. Had he stayed longer he might not have looked at it as a vacation, but it exemplifies a positive attitude. Martha Shoaf, a fourth grade teacher, said, "I hated to leave Manzanar for I loved working and living in the camp." In the interviews I have read, by far most WRA employees enjoyed the experience. This is particularly true of the teachers. Let's face it, it was different, challenging, and exciting. Although many of us gave up something we loved when we moved to Manzanar, and it was certainly a challenging environment to learn to enjoy, time has transformed our frustrations and discomforts into positive feelings and fond memories. Some bad memories we can't seem to forget, but at least we can now laugh about them. For fifty years most of us rarely if ever thought of Manzanar. Now that it has become historically recognized, we have been reminded of the good times and good friends we had there. Never while living in camp would I have fathomed that this place we lived would become a historic site. For me it was just the place I lived out the war.

CHAPTER XI
VIOLENCE IN CAMP

DIVERSITY CREATES TENSION

As discussed in Chapter VII on the diverse makeup of the evacuees, the different groups of Japanese Americans did not always agree on social or political issues. To give you some idea of the clash of cultures represented in Manzanar, keep in mind that some evacuees spoke only Japanese and some only English, while others spoke both; some were raised on a Japanese diet, while others preferred American food; some enjoyed American music, yet others preferred Japanese music. I was introduced to Japanese music in the camp; it was played over loud speakers—VERY loud speakers—at night. We could not get away from it. I can confidently say, our family never developed an appreciation for Japanese music and we had considerable exposure. It sounds nothing at all like Bing Crosby, Glenn Miller, or the Andrew sisters whom we enjoyed. Furthermore, some evacuees had US citizenship, some had Japanese citizenship, and some had both. There were Christians, Buddhists, and atheists represented. The camp had a few Communists, some pro-American, anti-American, anti-WRA, pro-Japanese supporters and many who, due to their current treatment by the American government, understandably were not sure where they stood. Some evacuees were college educated and professionals while most were farmers, gardeners, and fishermen. The fishermen and their families from Terminal Island took up several blocks in the camp, and they truly stuck together. Being the group considered most likely to assist the Japanese fleet if they were to attack the West Coast, they became one of the first groups evacuated from their homes and received probably the worst treatment before reaching Manzanar. The FBI rounded up many men identified as having the opportunity to spy, and shipped them off to prisons for interrogation. The wives were left with little time to liquidate their families' holdings before vultures swarmed in to take advantage of the families' inexperience and insufficient time to recover a decent price. Most buyers showed no mercy and took every advantage of the opportunity to score a profitable deal at the expense of their Japanese neighbors. It is questionable whether any group of Japanese Americans lost more in proportion to their financial holdings than those from Terminal Island. They were bonded together before the evacuation, but afterward, they became an extremely tight community within a community. Initially, the fishermen were considered at the lower end of the social ladder within the Japanese-American community. At first, the Terminal Island boys had difficulty dating Japanese-American girls in camp. They held a general defensive feeling towards others, and they were determined to take care of their own, physically or otherwise.

Some evacuees were strong union members while others were not. There were social-political groups like the pro-American, Japanese American Citizens League (JACL) formed by college educated Nisei in 1930. Pre WWII, the JACL was the largest Japanese-American political group in the country. Their motto was "loyalty, patriotism, citizenship for all Japanese Americans." They turned their backs on the very things most admired by the Issei: Japan and its culture. They initially thought because of their citizenship and love of the USA they would not be evacuated. They were mistaken, but once they knew they were to evacuate, most supported it as another way to prove their loyalty and love for this country. Some quickly joined the army to further show their loyalty to the USA. They tried to play the role of spokesmen for all Japanese Americans in the camp and the government supported this while the Issei and Kibei resisted it.

With their Japanese education, some Kibei who had attained a high rank in the in-camp judo club would recount to young Nisei who had never been to Japan, the power and superiority of Japan in an attempt to persuade Nisei to switch loyalties. As a result, these Kibei were disliked and mistrusted by the WRA authority. Sometimes, however unfairly, this distrust spilled over to the Kibei group in general. As happens in the application of a label to any considerable group of people, a part is often mistaken for the whole. Some Kibei clung together and tried to form a Kibei-only organization within the Manzanar camp. There was no lost love between the Kibei and the Nisei members of the JACL, or its offshoot, the Manzanar Citizens Federation. There were persistent power plays by both to take over and organize Japanese-American workers in various operations within the camp, such as the kitchen workers group composed primarily of Kibei. A kitchen workers union was formed, but the administration never recognized or accepted it.

The countless social separations between the Japanese-American factions within camp, combined with the stress of the entire situation led to consequences that had not been predicted—gangs. Gangs were a prominent feature within Manzanar which unwittingly hosted such ones as the Blood Brothers, the Terminal Island Gang, the Black Dragons, and the Dunbar Boys—a gang that had operated in West Los Angeles and continued their criminal ways in Manzanar. Many Dunbar Boys had police records before they reached the camp. There were even gang members wandering about camp with their pachuco haircuts—typical of juvenile, Mexican-American gang members—and the 1940s zoot suits. Some of the camp gangs were on a mission to stir up trouble, start rumors, and arouse hatred and they were good at it. They had an underground in which messages attacking self-government, cooperative stores, an American education, Caucasians, and the WRA administration were posted in latrines and signed by the Blood Brothers and Black Dragons. Other gang members were involved in more serious criminal activities. A letter dated December 30, 1942, from internal security to Project Director Ralph Merritt, said this about gangs in Manzanar, "Like hyenas these gangs travel in packs, and when a member of a rival gang falls behind, they fall upon him in force. Odds of twenty-five to one is the rule rather than the exception." The letter went on to say, if not stopped, someone was going to be killed, and if that were to happen, the army would have the excuse they needed to take over internal policing.

The diversity expressed throughout camp sometimes led to a wholesome exchange of ideas, but at other times led to extreme tension and violence as predicted in the letter from internal security. In addition, the incompatibilities of many of the evacuees created special challenges to the WRA staff in regard to housing, supervision, and training of the evacuee workforce. To give some idea of the extremes that existed within this confining, one square mile fenced camp, let's take a look at two Japanese-American Issei with remarkably similar upbringings who ultimately came to hate each other: Tokie Slocum and Joseph Kurihara. Both men were born, raised, and educated in Japan and arrived in the USA about the same time. They were Issei, both without U.S. citizenship, so both joined the US Army during WWI. They both saw combat and were decorated. Tokie Slocum served in the same outfit as Sergeant York. As a result of serving in the Army, they were given US citizenship. After the bombing of Pearl Harbor, Joseph Kurihara volunteered to serve again but was rejected and sent to Manzanar, where Slocum was also sent. Kurihara would later come to say, "The blood that flows through my veins is Japanese," and from that day on he rejected the USA. Tokie Slocum, on the other hand, became an outspoken patriot, and an informer for the FBI. Thrown together in camp and with such disparate feelings towards their country of residence, they would become mortal enemies. Since the removal of Japanese Americans from the Pacific Coast there has remained an important, unanswered question; how many loyalties did this country lose as a direct result of the evacuation? No one has the answer, but we do know of one, Joseph Kurihara, and we know there were many more.

In the midst of the Nisei was a new group called the "Citizens Federation" which was vigorously pro-American and led by the strongest of the Nisei. The FBI recognized the love that the Nisei held for this country and depended upon those still in Manzanar for information in uncovering fascists among the Issei and Kibei. Once this spying by Nisei on others in camp was uncovered, the very type of violence most feared by internal security erupted into a riot of greater proportions than any had anticipated. Many loyal Nisei left the camp in November 1942, and volunteered as intelligence officers in the army. Some served in the US military in the Pacific interrogating captured Imperial Japanese prisoners. Incidentally, Kibei were also valued as superior interpreters as their accents were nearly flawless due to their time growing up in Japan.

Controversy in camp surrounded another internee, Harry Ueno, who remains something of a hero to many Japanese-Americans. Ueno, a Kibei born in Hawaii and educated in Japan from the age of eight was unpopular with the WRA staff. He organized the previously mentioned kitchen workers union that the administration refused to acknowledge, in an effort to lead the workers in a strike. He was especially troublesome for Assistant Project Director Ned Campbell and for Joseph Winchester who was the head of all thirty-six camp kitchens and warehouses. Harry had been disruptive during staff and kitchen workers meetings on numerous occasions, and he and Ned had nearly come to physical blows. The final insult came when Ueno reported to the FBI that both Campbell and Winchester were stealing sugar, meat, and milk slated for the evacuees' kitchen and selling it on the local black market. I question whether any such thefts truly took place. It's fairly common knowledge that there was quite an illegal saki production going on behind closed barrack doors. Saki is a Japanese alcohol made from rice and sugar. Certainly the sugar used in making this saki could only have been acquired through the kitchens' stores. Don Inman, whose family was the last to leave camp, and whose father turned the power off there for the last time, related to me that he and his brother had gone exploring through the camp after it was vacated. What they found were a number of hidden cellars built underneath the evacuees' barracks, and in these cellars were numerous bottles of homemade saki. It's highly probable that sugar shortages in camp could be traced directly to the saki operations. As for the milk shortage, according to Jack Hunter who worked for the local dairy in Independence, there was no rationing of milk in the area like there was in other areas during WWII. In fact, there was a milk surplus which was sold to the WRA at Manzanar. It seems highly unlikely that one could sell a product on the black market in an area in which the product was abundantly available legally. Finally we arrive at the accusation of stolen meat. Meat shortages were strongly felt in the large cities during the war, and this is exactly where the black market on meat thrived, not in cattle country. Ranchers in Owens Valley raised great herds of cattle. As was the case with the milk, it is doubtful that anyone could find buyers willing to risk buying meat illegally when there was so much of it around. Additional support for the innocence of Campbell and Winchester lies in the two separate investigations held in 1942, both finding the men innocent of any stealing. It's too bad the barracks' saki cellars had not yet been discovered. It appears that Harry Ueno recognized the shortages and used the partial information at his disposal to fit his purpose of accusing Campbell and Winchester, and then spread rumors throughout camp to incite anger amongst the internees. In short, Harry Ueno was disruptive to camp life and antagonistic. Riling up several thousand people on rumors also made him unpopular with the project director. Despite his unpopularity with staff management he was very popular with and had a large following amongst the Japanese Americans who were happy to see him take on the establishment.

SUMMARY OF CONDITIONS

Contented citizens who feel they have been treated fairly rarely riot as a means of expressing themselves. In Manzanar, the perfect set of factors came into play to cause a riot. Within camp and in crushing proximity to each other were housed extremely diverse groups of people including loyal citizens, political extremists, and gang members. To these groups of people were done countless demoralizing things. The government had misled Japanese Americans about the ramifications of evacuation, telling them one thing and then doing another. Those affected were given such short notice about the evacuation that they had no time to liquidate their assets and many lost most if not all of what they had worked their lives to build. They were herded like cattle to an unfinished camp in one of the hottest and coldest places in America which was lacking in medical facilities, proper food, nutrition, and sanitation and were crowded into tarpaper buildings which allowed free access to blowing dust and temperature extremes. Forcing them to stand in line for hours to receive food they were unfamiliar and certainly unhappy with, and worst of all, to perform the most private of necessities—going to the bathroom—in full view of their friends, relatives, and perfect strangers dealt a crushing blow to their self-worth and to their tolerance for the government that forced all of this upon them. Another blow came as the government expected internees to maintain jobs that were often hard work and paid next to nothing, after months of no pay. The final straw came with the FBI choosing to use Nisei informants to spy on their neighbors in camp making it obvious why a riot erupted in fewer than nine months of the camp's opening. Many people, including Project Director Ralph Merritt, felt this in-house spying was the single biggest reason for the Manzanar riot. So many poorly thought out policies were enacted, and with such little knowledge and concern for those people affected by them, it is surprising that it took nine months for a riot to occur and surprising that more people did not participate. Rioters were estimated to total two to four thousand people, many of whom were thought to be more spectator than actual rioter, out of a camp total of ten thousand.

INTERNAL STRIFE LEADS TO VIOLENCE

The first recorded violence against authority within Manzanar's fenced-in area was the beating of a Japanese-American member of Manzanar's internal security force. This beating was carried out by a gang of Japanese Americans after the security member assisted security officers and the Military Police in taking away liquor from a returning evacuee furlough worker. This was followed by the beating of two evacuee staff members of the camp newspaper, the Manzanar Free Press, after the newspaper wrote pro-administration and pro-American articles. Joe Blamey was beaten by a group of pro-axis youths and John Sonoda, a pro-American Kibei was severely beaten by a gang with clubs. Japanese posters were appearing in public places against the administration. The anti-American and anti-administration feelings within the evacuee community progressively got stronger during 1942. Things were heating up as it became easier to find fault with the government.

Joseph Kurihara, the Japanese-American referred to earlier that had fought for the USA in WWI and then been sent to Manzanar where he denounced all loyalties to the United States, was fed up. He hated the treatment he had received at the hands of the Americans and he wanted out of the camp. He was a natural leader with a special talent for rousing anger and building a mob. In a later interview with Ralph Merritt at Tule Lake after the war, Kurihara stated that in late 1942, he came across correspondences revealing that Fred Tayama, a JACL member, was transmitting information to the FBI on Japanese-American meetings in the camp. Specifically, Tayama was reporting to the FBI on certain individual Issei and Kibei attitudes and plans. At that time before the riot, FBI employees were making frequent visits to the camp to keep a close watch on the internees. When Kurihara found out about Tayama's spying, he stated he wanted Tayama killed and organized a group of men to carry out the job. Several people gathered, entered Fred Tayama's barrack wearing hoods, and beat him with clubs. Tayama was not killed, but he was badly beaten and taken to the hospital. He and his wife both reported to the Internal Security Police they recognized the voice of one of those doing the beating as Harry Ueno, a Kibei. Following the incident, the Internal Security Police interrogated a suspect in the Tayama beating who stated he thought Harry Ueno was involved. Based on these two separate reports of Ueno's participation, the Internal Security Police arrested him. Assistant Project Director Ned Campbell escorted Ueno to the Inyo County Jail in Independence six miles away. Interestingly, to this day, it has never been proven whether Harry Ueno took part in the beating of Fred Tayama. If Kurihara knew the names of those that participated, he never revealed them to Ralph Merritt during the interview. However, Harry Ueno was a prime suspect and there was suf-ficient evidence to suggest he was involved. As for Joseph Kurihara, who admitted instigating the beating, it appears he very well could have led the group and Harry Ueno was one of the members he wanted to protect. Kurihara was a natural born leader and not one to send someone else to carry out his plan. Additionally, both he and Harry Ueno had the motive, desire, and deep hatred for Fred Tayama to want to personally carry out such retaliation.

Before the ensuing riot, two more Japanese Americans who were loyal to America suffered beatings at the hands of their club-wielding neighbors. The internal social/political tensions were coming to a boil.

RIOT

*A complete, original, word for word internal police report of the riot at Manzanar can be found in Appendix #5

On December 6, 1942, Harry Ueno's followers quickly organized a meeting in Block 22 where he had lived. This meeting had a small attendance, but the one to follow a few hours later drew several thousand people. A "Committee of Five," as it came to be called, was established with Joseph Kurihara as the spokesman. The meeting resulted in two objectives. The first goal was to get Harry Ueno returned to the camp with an unconditional release from jail, and the second to prepare a blacklist of those to be beaten. Along with the Japanese Americans serving as security police, members of the Manzanar Free Press, and a half dozen JACL leaders, Campbell and Winchester were on the blacklist. About 1:30 p.m. the Committee of Five along with several thousand supporters marched to the administration building to meet with Project Director Ralph Merritt. About thirty armed MPs had previously set up a line between the police station and the administration building. The only physical violence that ensued was that Ned Campbell got punched by one of the evacuees. Ralph Merritt asked Campbell to leave, which he did, to avoid further physical conflicts. The Committee was allowed to meet with Merritt and together they agreed on the following:

- The crowd was to disperse immediately.
- Harry Ueno would be returned to the Manzanar camp jail within one hour of the crowd dispersing.
- There would be no mass meetings without Ralph Merritt's consent until after the Ueno case was settled.
- There would be no attempt to free Ueno from the Manzanar camp jail.
- All future grievances would be discussed and negotiated through Merritt.
- The Committee of Five would aid in finding the assailants of Fred Tayama and aid inkeeping law and order within the camp.

Ueno was returned to the camp jail by the WRA staff as promised at 3:30 pm, but the part of the agreement the Committee of Five was responsible for committing to was very short lived, for at 6:00 p.m. the Committee confirmed to a crowd of two to four thousand people that Harry Ueno was back in the camp jail. At that point in time a violent mob attitude surfaced. They organized half of the mob to go to the hospital and kill Fred Tayama while the other half were directed towards storming the jail and releasing Harry Ueno. One report stated the mob members armed themselves with hatchets, knives, hammers, and whatever else they could find as weapons, yet I found no written evidence that weapons were present. In fact, I never heard my father, who was at the riot scene, ever say the evacuees were armed with anything other than a few rocks which were thrown at the Military Police. Word preceded the mob to the hospital and Internal Security Police Station. The hospital was able to hide Fred Tayama from a small portion of the mob doing a search of the premises. An ambulance safely spirited Tayama from the hospital out to the Military Police camp just as things started to happen at the police station. When my father, Arthur Loren Williams Sr., came to work that afternoon he found Harry Ueno out of his jail cell. The Japanese-American Internal Security Police officers were afraid of Ueno's mob and had released him. A scuffle between Harry and my father followed when Harry refused to voluntarily go back to his cell. My father had to physically put him in his cell but in the process received fingernail scratches to his face and a cracked rib. With Harry Ueno back in his cell and word there was a mob on its way, my father told the Japanese-American officers on duty to go home to their families, for word had reached the police station that the mob was going to kill all the Japanese-American police for participating in the arrest of Ueno.

Williams, unarmed as were the five Japanese-American internal security policemen—three of whom were there seeking protection from the mob—was the only Caucasian that night to face the mob. The Internal Security Police sentry post was unstaffed and the police station was swarming with rioters who had opened Harry Ueno's jail cell, but Ueno refused to leave it until Ralph Merritt arrived. At that point, Merritt and Ned Campbell were safely in staff quarters "A" or "E" watching the mob through the window and communicating by telephone with Williams who was in the police station. Williams first talked to the Committee of Five, reminding them they have broken the agreement reached with Merritt earlier the same day. He next called Ralph Merritt, advising him not to come to the police station as the situation was dangerously out of hand. Merritt advised Williams to call out the Military Police, and if he deemed it necessary, have marshal law declared. Seeing the arrival of several thousand rioters caused the MP in the main gate sentry post to fire three shots into the air as a signal for help. The MP sentry post was about seventy-five yards east of the police station. Armed MPs numbering 135 arrived and removed the rioters from the police station without violence. The MPs were instructed not to fire unless ordered by an officer or rushed by the mob.

The Committee of Five was permitted to remain in the front portion of the police station where Capt. Martyn Hall, commanding officer of the MPs at the time, talked to them for thirty minutes, rejecting all of their demands. He reminded them, as Williams had, that they had not lived up to the agreement reached earlier with the project director. He walked out of the police station at which point he and Lt. Stanley Zwaik tried to persuade the mob outside to return to their quarters. The mob responded with threats, insults, and rock throwing, all the while singing patriotic Japanese songs. Someone threw a rock that barely missed Capt. Hall, causing him to order tear gas, but the north wind blew it harmlessly away. As a result of the tear gas, the crowd dispersed to the North, regrouped, and advanced toward the MPs. Fire Chief Frank Hon's car, parked on the northeast side of the police station, was started by the mob and aimed at the north end of the building where MPs were lined up like dominoes, and where Harry Ueno was in his cell. The intended target is not known for certain, but it is possible those involved were thinking the car would knock a hole in the jail cell and assist Harry Ueno in an escape. Capt. Hall ordered Lt. Zwaik to fire at the approaching car. The car hit and then careened off of the northeast corner of the police station and hit an army truck where it came to rest.

RIOT SCENE

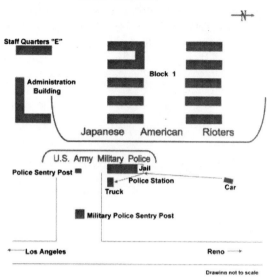

Diagram of the riot scene

Although struck, the jail cell was not penetrated, but at that time, two panicked soldiers fired into the crowd—Pvt. Tobe Moore with three shots from a 12 gauge shotgun and Pvt. Ramon Cherubini with three bursts from a 45 caliber Thompson submachine gun. The cause of the gunfire still remains a mystery. Did the two soldiers think the order to fire had been given because they heard Lt. Zwaik fire at the car, or did they fire because the mob advanced after the tear gas had been deployed? The soldiers claimed they felt threatened when the crowd advanced. What makes their story hard to believe, is that, according to reports, all the wounds were inflicted in the back extremities or side, indicating the crowd was moving away, not advancing.

After the dust had settled it was discovered that one Japanese-American youth, a seventeen year old named James Ito from Los Angeles, had tragically been shot and killed instantly. Ten others, one of whom later died, were wounded by gunfire, and one had to be treated for overexposure to the tear gas, bringing the total number of riot casualties to twelve. All the victims of gunfire had been shot by the same two MPs, and all at close range. When Ito's older brother came to Manzanar for the funeral, he was allowed to walk right through the main gate, past the MPs there without having to show any identification or permission for entry. Why? Because he was serving in the US Army.

As with many tragedies, out of the ashes often emerge the most heartwarming stories of heroism and patriotism and the Manzanar riot is no different. Although the validity of this story remains unsubstantiated, I love the idea of it and hope it is true. On the night of the riot, it is said that a Boy Scout troop made up of evacuee boys caught wind that the rioting mob was headed to the internal security jail and to tear down the American flag in front of the administration building. These young Japanese-American boys put their very lives on the line to run to the flag pole and surround it, arming themselves with rocks to protect themselves and their flag against an angry mob of thousands. The flag did not come down that night, and the question of the loyalty to country that at least some Japanese Americans felt should have been no longer in question. In my view, if this story is true, these young Nisei Boy Scouts were an honorable representation of their generation.

IMMEDIATELY FOLLOWING THE RIOT

Before going further, I'd like to point out one important fact. It has been estimated that 2,000 to 4,000 people were down at the police station, leaving 6,000 to 8,000 others who did not take part in the riot. It is also clear that not all those down at the police station were there supporting the release of Harry Ueno. Many were curious onlookers, some of whom were WRA staff members. The vast majority of internees at the time, despite their harsh, unfair treatment were simply going to work or school every day, peacefully determined to make camp a better place to live.

Those treated at the hospital consisted of two Issei, seven Nisei, and three Kibei. The responsibility for dead and wounded lies firmly with the FBI that encouraged in-house spying, and the men who participated in the brutal beating of Fred Tayama, which led to the arrest of Harry Ueno and the subsequent riot. It is not surprising that those who took part in the various beatings never came forward. There was a funeral held in a grove of trees outside of the camp. Those attending prayed the lives of the two boys might be a sacrifice for the sins of the whole community. The riot was a product of anger, fear, and poor judgment by many, and a tremendous tragedy.

Frank F. Chuman was the hospital administrator at the time of the riot, and in an interview dated January 27, 1987, outlined his recollections of the night of the riot. I found a few inaccuracies, but otherwise his memory was very good.

"I was at the hospital and received a telephone call that the Military Police had shot into a crowd of evacuees. I sent all available ambulances to the scene and within minutes there were eleven persons admitted into the hospital. The most seriously shot were immediately placed upon the operating table for surgery and others were placed on army canvas and lined up outside the operating room. All doctors and nurses and hospital personnel off duty were recalled to duty. A large crowd had quickly gathered outside the entrance of the hospital. None in the crowd were belligerent or hostile but were concerned for the ones shot. They were quiet. The chief of medical staff, Dr. James Goto, who performed the surgery on the wounded, stated to me that all the wounded had been shot either in the back or the side, but definitely not from the front. Dr. Goto was asked at a military board of inquiry on the shooting to change his testimony that the shooting was from the front to justify the shooting. He refused as did others on the medical staff. He was dismissed as Chief of the Medical Staff and exiled to go out of the camp within one week."

Dr. Goto transferred to the camp at Topaz although there could have been other issues influencing this move, such as his known rough behavior with the medical staff, although doctors being rough on nurses is nothing new. His skill as a doctor was not the issue.

TIMES OF TURMOIL FOR STAFF AND FAMILIES

While several thousand evacuees gathered in the afternoon of December 6, 1942, hours before the rioting began near the main gate, some WRA employees and their families saw this as a sign to temporarily evacuate themselves and their families from the camp. Most fled into the two small towns of Lone Pine and Independence. There were some staff members and their families who stayed in their quarters during the riot. Many either did not have transportation or failed to recognize the severity of the rioters impending actions. None were threatened. The majority of remaining staff were in blocks 1 and 7, which the rioters passed through on their way to the jail. The next morning they were evacuated and remained out of the camp for a few days. School was closed from December 6 to January 10, 1943. After classes resumed at the Manzanar school, some WRA teachers were victims of harassment and threats and were locked in their classrooms by Japanese-American students. Although this was undoubtably intimidating, nobody was physically attacked. A number of public services came to a screeching halt following the riot, as evacuees stayed indoors. There were a significant number of staff members who volunteered to take on second jobs just to make sure the basic services such as food, water, and heating oil deliveries to the evacuees were not interrupted.

When Marjorie DaValle, an adventurous, single parent, accepted a high school math teaching position at Manzanar, little did she know what was ahead. She arrived in 1942 with her two daughters, Joan and Shirley, and was assigned to the tarpaper barrack shown here.

The night of the riot, the evacuee mob of several thousand passed in front of their doorstep carrying torches and shouting in Japanese. It was a frightening night for a single mother with two young daughters. The next morning, when the remaining staff members and their families were escorted out of the camp by Military Police, Marjorie DaValle took her daughters and went to Independence looking for a place to stay, but every lodging had been filled. The local sheriff came to her rescue, allowing Marjorie and her daughters to stay in the Inyo County Sheriff's women's jail until they could return to Manzanar. If in moving to Manzanar, Mrs. DaValle was looking for adventure, she had gone to the right place.

Shirley and Joan DaValle in front of their barrack

RELOCATION AND SEGREGATION

After the riot, the MPs were reinforced with troops from Bishop and immediately took over peacekeeping inside the camp in coordination with the Internal Security Police. Arrests and the permanent removal of suspected troublemakers by internal security were backed by MPs. This joint action by both the WRA Internal Police and the MPs avoided marshal law. JACL leaders and their families were moved to a Civilian Conservation Corp (CCC) camp in Death Valley until they could be relocated to the relative safety of the East. Having the riot leadership and JACL leaders removed from the camp, the atmosphere calmed down and peace was restored. This was, however, not the end to problems caused by the internal strife, for total segregation was to follow. The riot played right into the hands of those in Congress who felt the WRA was too soft on the evacuees, running the camps like social clubs. They felt the camps should be run more like prison camps. They had been waiting for the first sign of discord to pounce, to turn the camp over to the War Department. In the January following the riot, a congressional investigation was put in motion in response to a bill to place the War Relocation Authority under the War Department. Senator AB Chandler from Kentucky was appointed chairman of the Military Affairs Committee to investigate. After several months of investigations, the full committee rejected moving the WRA to under the War Department. They did, however, come up with several recommendations:

- Develop a "loyalty questionnaire" for internees to take.
- Place into a segregated internment camp at the earliest possible date those determined to be disloyal to the USA.
- Send away at the earliest opportunity those asking for repatriation to Japan.
- Move out of camps to a safer area, Japanese Americans loyal to the US.

These decisions by the Senate committee closely paralleled that which the WRA had previously requested and been denied. The Senate committee's decision was a benefit to the WRA and would eventually prove to be so for many of the evacuees. This was not the end to the investigations from Washington D.C., for true to the nature of politics and politicians, the House put a committee together to make further investigations. This committee was more critical of the WRA than the Senate committee had been, but also came around to supporting segregation. These two committees would expose strong anti-Japanese-American feelings by some members of Congress.

Through the process of relocation, many internees deemed loyal to the US were able to relocate from the camps to east of the Mississippi River. The WRA established a screening process in the ten camps and a college and job placement system in the East. For example, college students evacuated from west coast universities were screened and their transcripts were reviewed. They could then be vouched for by the WRA for acceptance to east coast universities. Job placements were handled in a similar fashion. A person's loyalty, job skills, and other factors were examined at their camp before the person was released for relocation to the East. Once in the East, they could be assisted by those working there to find jobs for the evacuees.

Segregation was a much more insidious and disruptive process than relocation. In February 1943, the War Department and the WRA required all internees seventeen years old and over to complete two questionnaires which were meant to establish which Japanese Americans were loyal to the USA and which were loyal to Japan. Through a questionnaire and personal interview, each eligible draft age Japanese-American male was evaluated by the army to determine those loyal to the United States and willing to serve in the US Army. At the same time, due to the riot, the WRA prepared its own questionnaire for all evacuees of age to determine loyalty, only this set of questions would determine whether evacuees would stay in their own camps, or if deemed loyal to Japan, be segregated to Tule Lake. Two questions in particular, each requiring a simple yes or no answer, were the most confounding and difficult to answer. Question #27 asked, "Are you willing to serve in the armed services of the United States on combat duty, wherever ordered?" Question #28 asked, "Will you swear unqualified allegiance to the United States of America and faithfully defend the United States from any and all attack by foreign or domestic forces, and forswear any form of allegiance to the Japanese Emperor or any other foreign government, power, or organization?" For many young men this question yielded an enthusiastic "Yes-Yes" answer, indicating to the War Department that these individuals were loyal and faithful to the United States. For others, the questions were perplexing, often misguidedly leading to a "No-No" answer, indicating, in the eyes of the American government, loyalty to enemy Japan. There were many more reasons for answering "No-No" than disloyalty to the US. Many were simply confused about the phrasing of the questions and misguided about the consequences of their answers. Should the elderly answer "Yes-Yes" thinking they were potentially volunteering for active duty? What if they were to forswear allegiance to Japan only to find that, after the war, they were to be deported back to that very country. Forswearing allegiance to Japan would leave them homeless and with citizenship nowhere, since United States law denied them citizenship in the US. Some marked "No-No" in refusal to volunteer for active duty until their legal rights as American citizens were honored. For some American citizens of Japanese descent, answering "No-No" seemed a simple, nonviolent way to protest the treatment they were receiving at the hands of their own country. Maybe they weren't swearing allegiance to Japan as much as rejecting an America that had treated them so badly. Another issue was the question of forswearing allegiance to the Emperor of Japan. As emperor, he was the great spiritual leader of the Japanese. Should they be asked to abandon their religion to prove their loyalty to America? Others answered "No-No" to not be separated from their Issei parents who, at the end of their productive lives, had planned to return to their own families in Japan. Many young Nisei begged their parents to answer "Yes-Yes" to no avail. Their parents were just too confused over the questions and the consequences of their answers, feeling "No-No" was the only way to maintain a connection to one country or another. In spite of their individual reasons for giving a "No-No" answer, those that did were either sent to the segregated camp at Tule Lake for the disloyal, or sent to prison as "resisters." While the "disloyal" were en route to Tule Lake, those already there expressing loyalty to the USA were given the opportunity to move to one of the other nine camps to avoid being housed with potentially dangerous factions. Many chose to stay, although whether due to confusion over the move, or simply to avoid one more uprooting, or due to some other motivation, is varied and unknown. Regardless, many loyal, peaceful, unsuspecting people found themselves jammed into a small confined Tule Lake camp with some angry, disloyal agitators. Tule Lake became filled with hatred and tension, while the other nine camps became calm places to sit out the war. In summary, both the army and the WRA did poor jobs in developing their questionnaires and conducting interviews, resulting in confusion and the implication of loyalty to Japan by many more people than actually felt such loyalty.

The physical segregation took place in Manzanar between February 19 and 25, 1944. Evacuees were moved in trucks from Manzanar to the train station in Lone Pine eleven miles away. A blizzard raged over the Manzanar camp, yet the Army Ninth Service Command (escorts) demanded the evacuation take place as scheduled. Ralph Merritt resisted their demands and did not comply, but was able to meet the time schedule and avoid undue hardship on the more than 2,000 evacuees which included elderly people and little children. It is important to recognize that, by this time, Tule Lake had received from the other eight camps most of those indicating a desire to leave this country for return to Japan. Once the move was over, one camp instead of all ten contained all the gang members, troublemakers, and sympathizers of Japan. Along with them now lived over 4,000 Japanese-American men, women, and children who had declared their loyalty to the United States but didn't think it necessary to move to a safer camp.

Through the questionnaire and personal interviews of each eligible draft age male evacuee, the men of the JACL were again able to prove their loyalty to the US, as they became qualified to serve in special all Japanese-American US Army units.

There were no winners as a result of the riot. The Japanese-American families who lost loved ones in the riot were the hardest hit. The WRA lost respect and trust by not controlling the escalating tensions between the extremists before violence erupted. The young, scared MPs who were responsible for killing people that night had to live with the consequences of their actions. Due to an erroneous statement released by Assist. Project Director Robert Brown, the press reported that the violence was a demonstration in support of Pearl Harbor, as the riot occurred on December 6—almost a year to the day from the attack on Pearl Harbor. Although the riot had nothing to do with Pearl Harbor, public belief in this fallacy certainly presented the interned Japanese Americans in a worse light and created even more public support for the ill-conceived evacuation.

Due to the fallout from the riot, there was a noticeable calm over the camp for the first time. The WRA staff along with those Manzanar internees who had declared their loyalty to the US experienced a new level of comfort in camp. As for me and my life, whether before or after the segregation, there was very little difference. I continued to get up in the morning, go to the mess hall for breakfast, show my pass to walk out past the two sentry posts, and wait beside Highway 395 with the other staff high school kids for the bus to take us to school in Independence. In the afternoon the process was reversed with the addition of my usual dinner in our apartment and listening to my parents discuss the day's events. If they discussed the segregation, I do not remember it. My father, who had gone through the riot, wrote in a letter how he looked with anticipation to the completion of segregation. His wish for an end to all the tension and crime caused by the gangs in camp was finally fulfilled.

Following the riot, many of the Japanese Americans working in internal security resigned. Ralph Merritt recruited replacements from the martial arts classes. It was a good idea, but mostly unnecessary for the troublemakers were then in the Tule Lake camp under tight security, and Manzanar had settled into a very peaceful atmosphere.

The riot at Manzanar was not the first nor the last to occur within the camps. Those distinctions go to Poston, Arizona and Tule Lake in Northern California, respectively. The Manzanar riot, however, proved to be the bloodiest.

HEALING

The following is taken from the biography of Margaret d'Ille, Director of Community Welfare for the WRA at Manzanar. These words were spoken by Ralph Merritt at Margaret d' Ille's memorial service in Los Angeles, in May, 1954.

In the days and nights after the riot, the internees at Manzanar refused to come out of their barracks to do any of the necessary work for a city of 10,000 people. It was a dead city. No children came out to play. No lights burned at night. Days went by and Ralph could find no way to bring about the normal way of living, where children played and went to school, and people went about their daily routines. Two weeks following the riot, Ralph was sitting in his office listening to telephoned instructions to get tough. I stood next to his desk and heard the conversation. Ralph said he had no answer to restoring peace and harmony to the 10,000 people under his charge.

Kindly, I asked him what he planned to do. He said he didn't know, but would only admit it to me. I was startled. "Ralph, have you forgotten your Christian upbringing?" I asked. "Have you forgotten that this is Christmas and what Christmas means?"

I said there was a warehouse full of presents that had been shipped to Manzanar by churches and friends who wanted to give Christmas happiness to the more than 1,000 children living behind our barbed wire fence.

I suggested Ralph send trucks and men to the mountains to cut trees and bring them back to the camp; that they should be set up in front of each barrack, decorated with lights; and that presents should be distributed the day before Christmas so people could prepare Christmas trees for Christmas morning and each child receive a gift.

I reminded him there was a Children's Village at Manzanar which was under my department. Here were more than 90 orphans from babies to boys and girls up to 14 years old.

On Christmas Eve, Ralph, his wife Varina, and I walked through the dark, dead camp to the opposite corner of our mile square, barbed wire enclosure. There alone, our Children's Village was lighted and happy voices welcomed us.

We sat Japanese fashion on the floor in the big hall, surrounded by excited, happy children, while the Christmas scene of shepherds and wise men was enacted upon a little stage. Then there was Santa Claus and presents and we began to sing Christmas carols. As we sang, we suddenly realized that there was more singing than the voices of the little children gathered in that room. Ralph got up and quietly walked out into the night. The clear moon and stars were shining over the Sierras. From out in the darkness, a great volume of Christmas carols was also being sung by children outside the village.

The children suddenly became quiet, wondering what this new government representative would say and do. Ralph called out to them that we should sing for the children inside. He led them in "Oh, Come All Ye Faithful."

Varina and I joined him and, followed by hundreds and hundreds of boys and girls and young people, we marched down through the camp, singing as we went. As they began the words of "We Three Kings of Orient Are," we looked at the faces inherited from the Orient, and knew that we were living again in the spirit of *peace on earth and good will among men*, when kings of the Orient worshipped the Christ Child.

Lights came on throughout the camp, voices in Christmas greetings called out to us, and Manzanar came alive. As we came to the spot where the riot had occurred, where men had been wounded and killed, we stood together, not in the spirit of anger, but in the Christmas spirit that had recreated a new peace and good will for Manzanar.

We called out to wish everyone a Merry Christmas and they wished all of us a Merry Christmas. Christmas carols were still being sung as their voices faded in the distance. Then Ralph, Varina, and I stood alone watching the star that was above us. Ralph turned to me. He said, *"Peace has come again to Manzanar."*

VIOLENCE FOLLOWS THE VIOLENT—TULE LAKE

As the dissidents were moved to Tule Lake Camp, so too was the violence. Where Manzanar became a mostly peaceful place to live, Tule Lake became a powder keg, with many peaceful people caught in this war zone.

The following information was extracted from a government report written by National WRA Director Dillon Myer and presented to a congressional subcommittee investigating what they perceived as total chaos at Tule Lake

During the segregation process some of the arrivals from the other camps began to create difficulties. A small, well organized group of new arrivals had the objective to gain control of the Tule Lake, Japanese-American evacuee community and then disrupt the WRA administration authority. On October 15, 1943, a truck driven by an evacuee and carrying twenty-nine farm workers turned over, injuring most of the workers, one fatally. Following the accident, which occurred during harvest, no farm workers reported to work. For ten days, harvesting stopped. On October 25, a group claiming to represent the Japanese-American community asked to meet with Project Director Clayton Best and submitted to him a number of questions and demands. They wanted to know if the US government regarded the Japanese Americans at Tule Lake as "prisoners of war" and then stated they would not work on the farm for the benefit of the other nine camps—those camps housing the evacuees that were in support of the USA. Clayton answered their questions as follows:

No, they were not considered "prisoners of war," they were considered "segregates."

The WRA does not answer to demands.

The WRA will find another source to harvest the crops.

The WRA brought in Japanese Americans from the other camps to harvest the crops. For their protection, they were housed outside the Tule Lake perimeter, separated from those inside.

On the morning of November 1, 1943, National Director Dillon Myer and Assistant National Director Robert Cozzens arrived at Tule Lake Camp to consult with the staff. Myer was also scheduled to meet with representatives of the Japanese-American camp community in Tule Lake the next day. At 1:30 p.m. on the same day as his arrival, a crowd of 3,500 to 4,000 evacuees congregated outside of the administration building. One Japanese American asked if seventeen representatives could meet with the WRA staff. In that meeting they demanded that Clayton Best and some other WRA employees be terminated. While the discussions were in progress, word was received that a dozen evacuees had entered the hospital and beaten the chief medical officer, Dr. Reece Pedicord; it was later determined, he had been beaten badly. Dillon Myer addressed the crowd and here is what he said:

- The WRA would consider requests by the camp population provided they were within the framework of national policy.
- The WRA would not accede to demands.
- The WRA was of the opinion the majority of the Tule Lake evacuees wanted to live in a peaceful atmosphere.
- If the evacuees could not deal with the WRA peacefully, they would have to deal with someone else.
- Once the segregation was completed with the arrival of those from Manzanar, the community of Tule Lake should select a committee representative of the masses to deal with the WRA.

The crowd dispersed peacefully, and on the next day, November 2, 1943, Dillon Myer left the camp. He would later be criticized for running away from the scene as had the Project Director at Poston when, earlier, that camp had experienced its own internal camp conflict.

On November 4, tempers escalated to violence once again. The WRA started the construction of a tall, solid fence to separate the section of the Tule Lake camp inhabited by the evacuees from the administration building and the WRA staff housing. That evening a crowd of 400 evacuees entered the staff housing area and were met by a lone Caucasian internal security officer who, in attempting to halt their advance, was beaten with clubs. The crowd closed in around the project director's house, leading him to call for the army, who arrived promptly, moving the crowd back out of the staff housing area and taking control of internal security.

In the midst of all of this violence and disruption, Japan did something surprising. The day following the clubbing of the security officer, the Imperial Japanese government asked the Spanish consul to investigate the situation at Tule Lake. What I find interesting is that the Japanese enlisted the aid of the Spanish consul to protect Japanese nationals in the USA. Although the Japanese government seemed concerned for the Japanese nationals in the camp, they proceeded to categorize all Nisei as US citizens, professing no jurisdiction over them, despite those who held dual citizenship and professed their loyalty to Japan.

Over a year later, conflicts within the confines of Tule Lake had yet to be resolved, so in June of 1945, my father was asked to report to internal security in Tule Lake to share details about what Manzanar had experienced both before and during the riot. These discussions were to be held with the Tule Lake Internal Security Police which, by the way, numbered about sixty-five Caucasians. I accompanied my father and ended up spending two weeks with him at Tule Lake. I was totally unprepared for how dissimilar it was to Manzanar. By now, Manzanar camp was down to one twenty-four hour guard at the main gate and an additional jeep patrol every eight hours. No other gates were guarded and all the guard towers had remained unmanned for some time. In contrast, Tule Lake housed tanks, 1,200 MPs, an impenetrable, tall security fence between the internees and the staff, twenty-eight staffed guard towers, and a stockade for prisoners. Tule Lake was what those in Congress had been yelling for all along—an internment camp complete with prison and tight security. Each morning, out of their barracks appeared thousands of Japanese supporters wearing white strips of cloth around their foreheads, preparing to engage in emperor worship and pray to the rising sun. The camp's overall atmosphere was one of hostility. Tule Lake experienced anti-American demonstrations, sit-down strikes, hunger strikes, beatings, and murder.

In Manzanar the pass we were required to display to enter and exit the camp was a printed card with the bearer's name only—not even an identifying photo was on it. To move about at Tule Lake one had to have a badge also, but the badge there was like the camp itself—much more serious and much more restrictive. Badges at Tule Lake were a true photo ID with the bearer's picture on the front as well as their fingerprint on the back. It was to be worn in full view at all times while in the camp.

I was required to wear my badge the entire time I was in Tule Lake, including the time I spent in the staff area, which somehow didn't make sense to me. It made me look and feel like a criminal and I despised wearing it. In fact, I still hate this picture and only included it in this book because it is possibly the only Tule Lake badge still in existence.

My Tule Lake ID badge

Because of the Tule Lake problem, Tokyo became very indifferent about an exchange of American nationals in Japan for the Japanese supporters in Tule Lake. Eventually hundreds of people were shipped out of camp and placed in even tighter security under the Department of Immigration. I witnessed the evacuation by the border patrol of about fifty Japanese Americans from a stockade to a train sitting alongside the camp. I stood on the edge of the road as a border patrolmen marched out in front leading the way to the train. He was just about the biggest man I had ever seen. Behind him came the Japanese Americans who had definitely been roughed up and many of whom were still wearing just their long underwear. Some were bloody, some being helped along by their fellow evacuees. It was obvious the move had been accompanied by physical violence. I asked my father that night what had happened. He told me when it was time for the Japanese Americans to leave the stockade for the train they had refused. Dad said the big guy I saw out in front with the border patrol went into the stockade and grabbed the Japanese Americans in their bunks and threw them at the front door. Some hung onto their bunk beds, but he was so big and strong that he yanked them loose and tossed them at the open door. Clearly, some did not hit the opening. It was a shock I will never forget, and the only time I ever personally witnessed violence in either camp.

After the war, 5,000 Japanese Americans, including 4,406 from Tule Lake, were returned to Japan. Of those from Tule Lake, 1,767 were children. With a camp population that reached 18,000, that leaves a large number of evacuees that never left the USA. Joseph Kurihara, the spokesman for the Committee of Five and man directly responsible for the beating of Fred Tayama and possibly the riot in Manzanar, was one of those who returned to Japan. Before leaving, he denounced his American citizenship, and later still expressed sorrow for his contribution towards the violence which had ultimately taken the lives of two people. He lived out his life in Japan, dying at the age of eighty. Harry Ueno paid a heavy price for his disruptive actions. He was removed from Manzanar and separated from his family the night of the riot, but his inciting behavior did not stop there. He went on to be incarcerated in several different jails and prison-like facilities where he denounced his American citizenship, and was ultimately placed in Tule Lake until December 1945. He was one of the last to leave camp. After the war, but while still in Tule Lake, he changed his mind about moving back to Japan and decided to stay in the United States. He later regained his US citizenship and went on to write a book about his life entitled *Manzanar Martyr*. He lived a peaceful life in post-WWII California until the age of ninety-seven. He was later featured in an article in the Los Angeles Times in which he was described as a peaceful person and has since been memorialized as a selfless whistleblower. Having read and heard the fallout from his tactics as well as the lack of evidence for the crimes he was purportedly exposing, I can wholeheartedly say that Ueno was anything but a gentle, nonviolent activist while in Manzanar. The war between the United States and Japan, along with Ueno's forced incarceration, brought out in him an aggressive, agitated character which history has denied.

CHAPTER XII
MILITARY POLICE IN MANZANAR

Just as the WRA staff have been largely left out of the books on Manzanar's history, so have the hundreds of Military Police who served at Manzanar, yet they too are a part of the WWII Manzanar story. It can be said that the MPs were not appreciated—that they had less than a stellar reputation. Perhaps this accounts for the lack of interest in preserving their story. Sadly, though, as time moves on, increasingly more of the story is to be forever lost as that generation of men succumbs to old age. As we all know, history is not just about heroes. It is about humans with all of our faults, lapses in good judgment, and inconsistencies. As humans we tend to remember that which stands out—the great or horrible—but mostly the shocking, and therefore we remember the MPs for the few who killed or injured other people, the ones who partied hard, caroused, and sullied the honor of the young, small town, local girls. There were, nonetheless, countless, good men serving in the MP companies—good, honest men who were working day to day in less than ideal conditions to do their part for their country.

SELECTED FOR DUTY

*A list of known MPs serving at Manzanar can be found in Appendix #6

The men who served in the Military Police fell into one of two categories—general service or limited service. Men labeled limited service were those considered unfit for overseas assignment for various reasons: age, poor eyesight, etc. Initially, most of the MPs at Manzanar were considered limited service personnel, with a few coming from the general service group. It can be said the MPs at Manzanar were not an elite, combat ready unit. Following the Manzanar riot on December 6, 1942, the balance changed with an increase coming from the general service category. As the war progressed, the standards were loosened and some previously labeled limited service were later considered combat ready. Some from Manzanar, such as men who wore glasses, were reclassified as combat ready and sent overseas. Fortunately, no veterans returning from combat in the Pacific were ever assigned to guard duty at Manzanar, as these men were thought to have had a potentially difficult time separating their feelings for the Japanese they had been fighting against, from the Japanese-American evacuees they would have been entrusted with guarding. Many of the MPs on duty at Manzanar came from east of the Mississippi River, mainly from the East Coast and southern states. There were some from the Midwest and fewer still from the West Coast. One feeling I have always had is that the MPs from the East Coast grew up with no prior relationships between themselves and Japanese Americans, as the Japanese Americans settled largely on the West Coast. They had only really thought of Japan and the Japanese once WWII broke out, and they had no personal knowledge of what Japanese Americans were going through. They had a more difficult time in separating Japanese nationals from Japanese Americans. I have often wondered if the MPs ever reconsidered their views of the dangers posed by the Japanese Americans behind the fence once they realized the over two hundred WRA employees and their family members were living safely within the confines of that same fence.

Manzanar MPs

THE FIRST MPS ARRIVE

The first Military Police unit to arrive in Manzanar, the 747th Battalion of Military Police, Escort Guard Company, arrived from Fort Ord, Monterey, California on March 19, 1942, just two days before the first evacuees arrived. The MP camp was situated outside of the fenced evacuee camp, about 100 yards south of camp along Highway 395. The picture above reveals a couple of things that made Manzanar a less than ideal assignment during its early stages. The first thing is that the troops were issued old, WWI helmets—helmets not popular with the WWII troops. As one might expect, the newly designed WWII helmets were issued to combat ready units first. The picture also shows the tents the MPs lived in for several months until barracks could be constructed. Living in a tent in the Owens Valley in March and April is not pleasant. Imagine trying to eat outside in a wind storm that might reach 70 miles per hour, and trying to sleep in a WWII era, heavy canvas tent in 100° heat. Those that stood watch at night, had to attempt sleep in a tent during the heat of the day, drenched in sweat. To avoid the oven-like temperatures inside, some of the men would move their cots outside, hoping for a cool breeze. The sloppy appearance of the MP camp with cots strewn around, coupled with the slovenly look of some of the off-duty MPs didn't help the ragtag reputation that this group of men operated under.

Sloppy, off-duty look of many MPs

This presented quite a contrast to the look of the men once in uniform and ready for duty as evidenced by the two disparate photos of Pvt. Russell Demo.

Same MP, different countenance

Upon their arrival, General DeWitt gave very specific directions to the army regarding their treatment of the Japanese-American evacuees. Those rules were as follows:

- A firm but courteous attitude to be maintained toward evacuees.
- No fraternizing with evacuees.
- No Military Police permitted within the fenced camp occupied by evacuees, unless in the performance of prescribed duties.
- If an evacuee leaves the camp without approval, the Military Police will make the arrest and turn that individual over to the Internal Security Police in the camp.
- In the event of a fire, disorder, or riot in the camp, director of internal security may call upon the Military Police. If called upon, the Military Police camp commander to take full charge until the emergency ends.
- Military Police to patrol camp fenced periphery for the purpose of preventing ingress or egress of unauthorized persons.
- No one to leave or enter the camp fenced area without written approval. This includes evacuees, staff and their families, and others. Approvals to

come from the camp project director and the information transmitted to the Military Police commander.
- No permit to be issued for more than 30 days.
- The disposition of unmanageable evacuees is not a Military Police responsibility.
- The provost marshal is responsible for actual supervision of Military Police at the center. Military Police to recognize the importance of the assignment and conduct themselves to a high standard.
- There is to be close cooperation between the commanding officer of the Military Police and the camp project director and his assistants to ensure an efficient and orderly operation.

The MPs not only had their camp outside of the fenced area, but they were prohibited from entering it. The only exception to the third rule was the one MP that was assigned to inspect all packages at the post office for contraband. This was the sole army representative allowed inside the fenced camp on a regular basis, although this position became obsolete when, in November 1944, inspections at the post office by the Army stopped. We all know that groups of people kept apart remain unfamiliar with each other, creating an atmosphere of fear, distrust, and contempt. Only when people "fraternize" can they discover their similarities and develop respect for their differences. By design, this did not happen between the MPs and evacuees. In his handwritten recollections of life as an MP at Manzanar, Pat Tortorello, made some very revealing comments. He stated that he and his fellow MPs referred to the people in the compound by the slang "Jap." He went on to state, "We never considered them Americans or Japanese Americans." The MPs were groomed to distance themselves from the evacuees.

SECURITY ASSIGNMENTS

*A list of dates and events pertinent to the MPs can be found in Appendix #7

By March 28, 1944, security around Manzanar was virtually nonexistent. These are the security assignments officially followed in camp:

MARCH 19, 1942 TO JUNE 1, 1942

There were a total of eleven sentry posts which included three gates; the west gate leading to the cemetery, the south gate leading to the farming operations, and the main gate next to Highway 395. All eleven posts were manned twenty-four hours per day, seven days per week. There were eight sentries stationed around the perimeter of the camp outside the five-foot, five-strand barbed wire fence. Each MP would be on watch four hours. Along with the sentries, there was a jeep patrol of the perimeter.

JUNE 1, 1942 TO DECEMBER 24, 1943

Between June 1 and November 1942, the Army contracted for the construction of the eight, forty-foot-high guard towers. The camp built a tower at each corner, and another positioned midway between each two corners. The eight sentries on ground patrol were repositioned to the towers. All eight towers and the three gates were manned twenty-four hours per day, seven days per week. There was also a jeep patrol of the perimeter.

DECEMBER 25, 1943 TO MARCH 27, 1944

On Christmas Day, 1943, Capt. Nail informed Project Director Ralph Merritt that the Military Police were reducing security. There would be no guards in the towers during the day. The towers would be manned from 6 p.m. to 8 a.m., seven days per week. The west gate to the cemetery would not be manned at any time. It would be open during the day and locked at night. The south and main gates would continue to be manned around the clock. There would continue to be a twenty-four hour jeep patrol of the perimeter.

MARCH 28, 1944 TO APRIL 20, 1944

The War Department, with the concurrence of the WRA, agreed on a further reduction of MPs. Staffing was reduced to one half of an escort guard company (approximately sixty men) and two officers. The main gate would be manned continuously. All other gates and towers would no longer be manned. Once every eight hours there would be a jeep patrol of the camp perimeter. At the request of the WRA, the army agreed to leave the lights on at night at each guard tower to give to the local communities the appearance that the towers were manned.

APRIL 20, 1944 TO CAMP CLOSURE

There was a further reduction of Military Police to two officers and forty enlisted men. Security consisted of a sentry at the main gate twenty-four hours per day and a jeep patrol of the perimeter once every eight hours. This schedule continued until the camp closed.

GUARD DUTIES

There were various duties performed by the MPs at Manzanar: guarding the entry gates, staffing the guard towers, driving the perimeter jeep patrols, and escorting evacuees to destinations outside of the camp. The MPs we kids became most familiar with were those stationed at the main gate sentry post. Every person entering or exiting Manzanar camp passed two stone check points. The outermost and largest sentry post shown here was staffed by the US Army MPs. The MP's were instructed to check everyone who passed that point. It was equally important to ensure no unauthorized persons entered the camp and no evacuees left without authorization. This stone sentry post was the only MP post to be manned continuously throughout the life of the camp. The guards at this post were normally noncommissioned officers, giving them more authority than the regular soldiers who were in the watch towers. Initially there were two MPs on duty during the daylight hours. Later, it was reduced to one. It was from this stone sentry post on the night of December 6, 1942, Pvt. Ruggiero fired two volleys of three shots each to alert the MPs in their camp of the massive gathering of evacuees at the police station some seventy-five yards away near the second stone sentry post.

Inner and Outer Sentry Posts

The inner, smaller checkpoint was staffed by Japanese-American Internal Security Police. They may have been serious about checking Japanese Americans leaving the camp, but only occasionally did they check the school kids who passed each day.

The Military Police were involved with escort duties during most of Manzanar's operation. When a group of evacuees needed to transfer from one camp to another, they were escorted by MPs who were accompanied by a Caucasian, WRA Internal Security officer. Buses were chartered and the MPs and WRA officer would escort the evacuees to see they did not escape, but also that they were not harassed or denied public services while en route. The WRA officer's additional duty was to ensure the Japanese Americans were safe from any wild MP behavior.

MP Escort in Winnemucca, Nevada

In the photo above, Manzanar MPs in Winnemucca, Nevada are returning from escorting evacuees from Manzanar to the camp at Topaz, Utah. On this occasion there were two busloads of evacuees. A WRA officer from Manzanar was also present, but not shown in the photograph. After the Japanese Americans arrived at their destination, the MPs were reputed to party at any and all bus stops on their way back to Manzanar.

CONDUCT UNBECOMING

The Military Police stationed at Manzanar were the only military units within sixty miles. When one of the MPs got out of line, everyone within the two small, local towns knew his post was at Manzanar. Problems of overindulgence and disorderly conduct were impossible to conceal from the townspeople. The fact is that Independence and Lone Pine had a number of bars and few positive activities with which servicemen could entertain themselves. Within a very short time, a few wild MPs at Manzanar had given the entire group a bad reputation.

The first company to arrive in Manzanar, the 747th, established a reputation from under which no other MP units could crawl. An inspection of the 747th deemed some of the soldiers unfit to stand sentry duty. Their morale and discipline were low, their outfit was described as being sloppy, and locals considered them misfits. Besides the drinking and general rowdiness, the MPs lost favor with their neighbors when they started dating local girls—some still in high school. With pregnancies added to the list of damages, the locals began to hate the sight of the MPs coming to town. It is believed the locals went so far as to turn their backs on a house of prostitution located just outside of one of the towns hoping this would put an end to the military men's desire to date local girls. The greatest incidents of drinking and disorderly conduct seem to have been caused by the older men—those who had been in the army before the war. Within the camp, a few MPs delighted in tormenting the already exploited evacuees by shining the guard tower search lights into the barrack windows at all hours of the night. Once this practice was discovered, the MPs involved were told to stop, but it proved that at least a few of them showed nothing but contempt for the Japanese Americans in the camp.

Besides the shootings that killed two retreating evacuees during the riot, violence tainted the reputation of the MPs on additional occasions. On March 30, 1942, one MP shot and killed another. It happened that the young man killed was the only African-American man serving in an otherwise all-white, recently desegregated unit. It was reported as an accident, but doubts remain. In another incident, two MPs faced off in a deadly game of quick draw and one shot and killed the other. Another MP shot and injured a Japanese-American evacuee and was later heard bragging about it. In one poorly thought out practical joke, a group of MPs in the back of a 2 1/2 ton army truck tossed out a bowling ball sized rock on the highway, striking the radiator of a following vehicle. Had it hit the windshield it would most likely have killed the driver. In short, these stories of wild and sometimes dangerous behavior made the MPs unwelcome at the camp and in the surrounding towns.

THE SILENT MAJORITY

For every MP that caused a problem and tarnished the name of their unit, there were many more who caused no trouble at all. Some of these were bachelors, some family men who brought their wives along on their assignment. Many MPs attended church regularly, while others were noted locally as being decent, respectful men. Some who had come from the West Coast had grown up with Japanese-Americans—had played football with them as children or purchased produce from then as adults. Although they too had seen the government's anti-Japanese propaganda, some were able to separate Japanese enemies from Japanese Americans. Many MPs performed their duties while treating the internees with dignity and respect. For every tale of misconduct, there is another of honor. I heard the following two stories several years ago at the NPS Historic Society at Manzanar. I believe them to be true.

An internee who was a young boy while in camp was stopped while trying to reenter camp after sneaking out to fish. According to camp policy, the MP reprimanded the youngster for leaving camp. He then asked if the stick the boy was carrying was his fishing pole, to which the boy replied that it was. A couple of days later the boy again snuck out of camp to go fishing. Upon his return, leaning up against a rock at the exact spot where he had been previously stopped was a new rod and reel. This probably occurred after the segregation and lessening of camp security. It was most likely an MP on jeep patrol that caught him and found joy in sharing with a young boy his own love for fishing.

The second story involves Lillian Masumoto and her husband Harry, along with an unidentified MP who were bringing Japanese-American children up on a bus from a Los Angeles orphanage to Manzanar. Lillian was trying to keep the kids occupied by having them sing. They were singing "Row, Row, Row Your Boat" and other children's songs when one of the young, orphan girls walked up to the front of the bus where the MP was seated. No one had a clue what she was about to do, standing at the head of the bus. Suddenly she started singing "God Bless America." Lillian reported that the MP choked up and tears actually showed on his face. He clearly grasped the lunacy of delivering innocent children to an internment camp.

MP helping a child off the train

MP helping a blind man

With the simplest, forgettable act of kindness, such as the one performed by the men above abandoning their roles as guards to assist young and old evacuees off of a train, many MPs showed that human kindness was certainly not foreign to the Military Police. Initially there was an unspoken distance separating the MPs from not only the evacuees, but also the WRA staff and their families. Over time and with increased familiarity, this distance virtually disappeared. The Military Police camp eventually became a place of comfort and recreation for a number of the WRA single female teachers as well staff teenager boys. As time passed and the number of MPs dropped from 135 to sixty and then to forty men, it became easier for MPs and staff to get to know each other. On occasions when the United Service Organizations (USO) came to the MP camp we sometimes were allowed to watch them perform. The MPs recreation room became a major unifying force as the staff and their teenage children were welcomed to use it. On many a summer evening we would walk over to the MP camp for a soda, a game of pool, and a sense of community.

ARMY UNITS THAT SERVED THE MANZANAR CAMP

March 19, 1942 to June 30, 1942	747th Battalion of Military Police, Escort Guard Company
June 30, 1942 to June 1, 1943	322nd Escort Guard Company
December 7 to 31, 1942	753rd Military Police Battalion. Reinforcements for 322nd.
June 1, 1943 to April 20, 1944	319th Escort Guard Company
April 20, 1944 to camp closure	Service Command Unit 1999. Renamed from 319th.

The 319th Escort Guard Company

CHAPTER XIII
DEATH OF A CAMP

A RETURN TO THE WEST

The Japanese Americans who declared loyalty to the USA were understandably eager to return to their homes on the West Coast, and made several requests to be released from the camps for that purpose. Their earliest support came from the California Board of Agriculture who, in January 1944, expressed the importance of their return to farming in California. They qualified their support by stating they felt the Japanese Americans should be able to return to the West Coast "after the war." On January 3, 1945, one year later and with the war still in progress, but the imminent threat of invasion over, the US government granted the Japanese Americans their wish. It is believed the basis for the government's decision was partially financial—to reduce operating costs at the camps. In a time when a person could buy a hamburger and milkshake and take in a movie, all for thirty cents, an annual operating budget of $40,000,000 to run the ten relocation facilities was astronomical. After a dramatic reduction in evacuees through relocations, the fiscal year 1945 budget was still $37,500,000. It is doubtful that the government gave much thought to the safety of Japanese Americans returning to what might be a hostile West Coast environment. California Governor Earl Warren did make an appeal to public officials to cooperate in the rehabilitation of Japanese Americans returning after the army's revocation of their mass evacuation order. This was a start, but it lacked the necessary support and muscle to avoid conflicts. The press certainly could have given support to the returning Japanese Americans by reporting on their ordeal and their loyalty despite the treatment they received, but that failed to happen. The newspapers were all about readership, and support of anyone with any ties to Japan, even ancestral ones, was unpopular.

In deciding to end the incarceration of loyal Japanese Americans, both the government and many Japanese Americans themselves overlooked one important fact; the war was still on in the Pacific and there had been nothing to change opinions about Japan or Japanese. It had been easy for the press to sustain hatred for Japan, for the Japanese Imperial Army had committed heinous acts to civilians and military prisoners. Through ongoing press reports, hatred for Japan was still at a fever pitch. During the very time the Japanese Americans were returning to the West Coast, the battles for Iwo Jima and Okinawa were taking place. In February and March of 1945, the battle for Iwo Jima experienced extremely heavy casualties. There were 6,821 military personnel killed and 19,217 wounded. The battle for Okinawa followed in June 1945, with an additional high casualty count and ferocious fighting. For the first time, in desperation, Japan was using Kamikaze (suicide) attacks on naval vessels resulting in the deaths at sea of over 3,000 US naval personnel. In this climate, it should not be a surprise that Japanese Americans leaving the safety of the camps could face serious problems. In some cases, returning Japanese Americans were welcomed back home by neighbors. Unfortunately, there were too many others who experienced verbal and physical abuse. There are numerous stories about the abuse some Japanese Americans received upon returning to the West Coast. There were twenty-four cases of abuse or violence brought before the courts before a judge ever sentenced a Caucasian perpetrator to actually serve time in jail. That sentence resulted in a mere thirty days in jail. The Caucasian had threatened to burn the home of Pvt.Yoshio Matsuoka who had just been released from a Nazi prison camp. This returning soldier, threatened for being a Japanese traitor had, in fact, been fighting for his country—the United States—in Europe. It is not surprising that in the first six months of 1945, out of 10,000 Japanese Americans leaving camps, 7,000 elected to relocate east and not back to the West Coast. It is also not surprising that there were thousands who did not want to leave the camps. There is clear evidence to support the assumption that the total evacuation of Japanese Americans from the West Coast gave the evacuees greater safety and saved lives. The question remains, even with the wisdom of hindsight, what would the optimum choice have been—to incarcerate people against their will knowing that this would have saved more of their lives, or allow them their freedom knowing many would be endangered by an angry public. I'm convinced there was a better, alternate course that was never explored due to the hysteria of the public and the prejudices and haste of those in power.

The State of California was very slow in coming to the aid of those returning Japanese Americans. It was six months after the Western Defense Command's approval for Japanese Americans to return to the West Coast and not until July 1945, that the California State Attorney General, Robert W. Kenny, notified all California State law enforcement agencies to see that Japanese Americans were afforded full protection under the law. Although this would seem obvious, there had been too many cases where law enforcement had turned their backs on the returning Japanese Americans. Just as their departure had been, their return to the West Coast would be another mountain to climb. By that time, Japanese Americans must have been wondering if they were ever to be accepted in this country. Some of the thousands at Tule Lake had given up hope of this completely, as they had truly been labeled "traitor," but not the Manzanar group who had always been loyal to the USA, for many were determined to return to their homes, and the only homes they knew were in California.

The public's attitude might have been different towards the Japanese Americans had they returned to the West Coast after the bombing of Hiroshima and Nagasaki. The ghastly result of the US Air Force dropping two atomic bombs on civilians decidedly changed the average American citizen's attitudes about the Japanese people. The press and newsreels were now showing the devastation and human suffering that our country caused from not one but two atomic bombs. People were, for the first time, able to see the innocent civilians of Japan, previously hidden behind their military who had orchestrated all the iniquities against non-Japanese troops and civilians. I have never forgotten the image of the little Japanese girl with all of her clothes burned off her body, standing in shock and crying in an area leveled by the bomb, or the pictures of Japanese civilians with massive areas of their skin burned by radiation, or the miles-long lines of people infected with radiation waiting to see a doctor. We were witnessing the pain and suffering of a new weapon that we had released upon the innocent bystanders of war—a weapon we knew little about—and the result was frightening. Where the press had previously focused on the atrocities perpetrated by Japanese military leaders, now we were seeing the horrors we had committed against an innocent Japanese public, and anybody not appalled, should have been. Showing the suffering we had caused should have changed our attitudes about the Japanese people there and here. After the unconditional surrender of Japan, it seems would have been a more appropriate time for the Japanese Americans to return home to the West Coast. Maybe then loyal Japanese Americans would have been received with the respect they deserved.

During this time, when some citizens were treating returning Japanese Americans badly, there were others offering them the opportunity of employment. Their reputation for hard work had not been forgotten and their knowledge of landscaping, gardening, and farming was still unequalled. The *Manzanar Free Press* carried numerous listings for jobs during early 1945. Two interesting requests for employment of Japanese Americans came from then famous movie stars. Victor McLaglen, ex-boxer and star of movies such as *Gunga Din* and *The Informer*, requested help on his farm in Clovis, California. Another request came from Franchot Tone, Oscar nominee for his role in *Mutiny on the Bounty*, looking for a couple to work at his home in Southern California. Although the returning Japanese Americans' struggle was far from over, some people were reaching out to them with acceptance.

CLOSING CAMP

After the evacuees that claimed loyalty to Japan had been moved to Tule Lake, the government accepted that they had nine camps filled with Japanese Americans who had pledged to support the USA. It was at this point that the war in the Pacific was beginning to turn in our favor and camp closures became a consideration. The

WRA's first step towards closure was to accelerate the relocation process that had been ongoing throughout the war. Although all Japanese Americans in Manzanar by this time had declared their loyalty to the USA, the army set in place a further screening process before evacuees could return to the West Coast. This screening process was in effect from January to July 1945. Ralph Merritt, in his final report, had this to say about the process, "It was the most extraordinary and unprecedented procedure I have ever witnessed and in my opinion entirely without legal precedent or authority." He went on to say he did not see one justified case for denial of rights to return to the West Coast. He felt the process itself was flawed and unnecessary. It was just another of the many ridiculous government decisions the evacuees would be forced to endure.

It is not hard to understand that there were thousands of evacuees who did not want to leave their camp. The reasons were ones you might expect: age, health, lack of finances, no job or home to go to, and fear of attack from the public. In the case of those first arrivals to Manzanar from Terminal Island, the Navy had leveled the island while they were in camp. Their fishing community and homes had disappeared.

It was announced that the Manzanar schools would be closed at the end of the 1945 spring semester. The WRA also notified all evacuee parents in camp it was their responsibility to see their children were entered in another school by September. Some evacuees in camp requested permission to send their children to school in the two nearby towns of Independence and Lone Pine for the fall semester. This request was denied by Ralph Merritt. His reason was that the two schools were small and at capacity.

Nancy Zischank driving evacuees to the train for relocation

This photo shows the Ford Woody driven by WRA Sr. Evacuee Escort, Nancy Zischank exiting camp for a trip to Reno, Nevada. Three times each week Nancy made this trip to take evacuees to the train in Reno for relocation to the East. In total, Nancy logged about 60,000 miles each year.

At the time the evacuees were being pushed to leave the camps, the WRA staff realized that they too needed to find employment and move on. By June 1945, after the Manzanar schools were closed, 128 WRA employees, mostly teachers in Manzanar who represented more than half of the total WRA staff, left camp. There were a few who stayed to fill positions vacated in administration, for they had lost personnel too. By June 1945, there were only 4,115 Japanese Americans in Manzanar. In all nine camps, excluding Tule Lake, the total camp population had dropped to 46,400. By that time, 49,244 had already relocated. Other than those trying times when the camp first opened, it was this final hour in the camp's life in which providing services to the evacuees was the most challenging. Most evacuees capable of working had relocated, leaving a preponderance of very old and very young. In addition, the WRA experienced a loss of some key staff members, including the head of the hospital, Dr. Little, assistant project directors, Lucy Adams and Robert Brown, as well as other experienced staff members. Despite these losses, the evacuees continued to be fed, the hospital stayed open and all basic services continued. It was a time of consolidation, for half the camp was empty. It was also a time of deep concern for those evacuees remaining in camp, for they were the ones most anxious about being accepted back into West Coast society. They wanted to go home and move on with their lives, yet had every reason to worry about how they would be treated once they arrived.

On July 12, 1945, WRA National Director Dillon Myer announced that all camps except Tule Lake would be closed by the end of the year. On September 4, 1945, after VJ (Victory in Japan) Day, the Western Defense Command withdrew from all of their activities and opened the West Coast to all persons of Japanese ancestry. Ninety percent of the remaining Manzanar population headed to Los Angeles. This should not be too surprising, for most of Manzanar's original population came from that area. On November 21, 1945, the last evacuee, a four year old boy, left Manzanar. That month, Civil Service interviewed all WRA employees for job placement in other government agencies. On March 9, 1946, all capital assets passed over to the General Land Office for liquidation and all consumer goods were transferred to the War Assets Corporation for immediate sale. The last WRA Manzanar staff meeting was held on February 15, 1946, however, there was a skeleton crew that remained until March 1946. The last WRA employee to turn off the power and leave the camp was Malcolm Inman, electrical/refrigeration supervisor. Ralph Merritt would report to work for the Federal War Assets Administration and oversee the bid, sale, and removal of all tarpaper covered wooden structures and most of the staff housing.

Ralph Merritt, in the closing statement of his final WRA report, had this to say, "Manzanar will return to the desert and be forgotten, but the spirit and

171

achievements of staff and evacuees who here worked together will not die or be forgotten, for the people of Manzanar, of many national and racial origins, learned by practice the way of tolerance, understanding, and peace." Ralph Merritt was right about many things, but Manzanar will now not be forgotten for it has been the successful determination of those who lived there to keep it alive, and of the NPS Historic Society to carry the torch.

DISMANTLING THE CAMP

Former evacuees dismantling a Manzanar barrack for lumber

Much of Manzanar camp was dismantled in the same way it was assembled—piece by piece. The first structures taken apart were done so by evacuees to provide the lumber which was then used to box their belongings for shipment back to the West Coast. In July 1945, three buildings were dismantled for this purpose.

In the original agreement between the federal government and the Los Angeles Department of Water and Power, LADWP negotiated to retain any or all structures on site after the closure of the camp. They decided to only keep some staff housing. All tarpaper structures were to be sold by bid by the federal government and removed from the site by the end of 1946. Most of the buildings were bought for the lumber and dismantled on site. It actually took longer to dismantle the tarpaper buildings then it had to build them. A few were removed intact to local towns. There were a few blocks of twenty structures acquired by San Joaquin Valley farmers. A big farm in Laton, California bid on three entire blocks of twenty builds each. It is believed the buildings were to be occupied by migrate labor.

The Manzanar hospital had built a wonderful reputation in the Owens Valley, and therefore it was given serious consideration for continued use. The first to show interest in the hospital was Inyo County. Next there was talk of it being used as a veterans' hospital. Both suggestions were dropped and the once finest hospital within 200 miles met the same fate as all the other tarpaper buildings—bid, sold, dismantled, and removed. Before the building was destroyed, the community hospital in Bishop was able to acquire most of its medical equipment.

The auditorium also met with special consideration. The Federal War Assets Administration sold it in 1947 to Inyo County for $6,500 to be used in situ for local community activities. Before this, the nearby Independence High School had had no indoor basketball court, instead using an undersized court in the American Legion Hall. The Manzanar Auditorium was used by Independence High and other local town teams to replace the Independence American Legion Hall. It was also once the site of a game by the Harlem Hobos, a team similar to the more famous Harlem Globetrotters. It also served as the VFW Lodge Hall until 1951 when it became the Inyo County heavy equipment maintenance garage. Finally, Mr. Ross Hopkins, the first National Park Service Superintendent, recognized the value of the building to the National Park Service as a Manzanar Historic Site center. The building was in pitiful condition when the Department of the Interior, National Park Service bought it in 1996 for one million dollars, the estimated cost of building a replacement Inyo County maintenance facility. It has now been beautifully restored by the NPS and serves them well as a historic site center. It has the distinction of being the only original wooden building to have never been removed from the Manzanar site.

The NPS acquired 804 acres in a land swap with the LADWP who, in exchange, received 2,500 acres from the Bureau of Land Management. The NPS currently holds rights to all the Manzanar land previously used for housing Japanese Americans during WWII. It would be a wonderful addition if they could also acquire the rights to the Manzanar airport, for it plays an interesting part in the WWII history of the area and is conveniently located next to the camp.

Director Ralph Merritt, while employed by the WRA, recommended staff housing be retained by the LADWP for employees' families and returning veterans. He correctly anticipated a post WWII housing shortage. The LADWP subsequently retained eight buildings (K, L, M, N, O, P, Q plus a dormitory) to this end, while all other staff housing, the staff mess hall, administration building, post office, town hall, and the project director's apartment were removed by the end of 1946. The Inyo County Housing Commission leased the eight staff housing units from the LADWP for five years and rented out apartments to relieve the housing shortage until their lease ran out in 1952. Inyo County hired a crew of eight men headed by George Gillespie to cover building maintenance, landscape upkeep, and trash removal, and to maintain electrical, water, and sewer systems. Some of those to be the last to live in Manzanar WRA housing were Bill and Louise White, Jack and Barbara Collins, Frank and Lucille Lockridge and family, Bob and Lavern

Whiting, and Walt Phillips. Immediately after the lease expired, the LADWP sold and removed all remaining onsite housing. The staff mess hall, arguably my favorite building in camp, was purchased in 1946 by bid, disassembled in eight by twenty foot panels and moved to Rosamond, south of Mojave. It was resurrected there to make two separate residences.

Housing unit "O" now in Lone Pine

Information found on another of the bids revealed that Mr. Herbert E. Miller paid $610 on March 15, 1952, for WRA, four unit housing structure "O," which had previously been occupied in WWII Manzanar by Clyde and Ruth Simpson and family, Herbert E. Norton, Ralph P. Merritt, Jr., and Oliver and Alice Atwood and their son John. The building was moved to Hay St. in Lone Pine, California. There are now a number of the original housing units scattered around the town of Lone Pine, and with that, what was once a busy, populous camp and home for 10,000 Japanese Americans and over 400 staff and family members simply disappeared.

DECLINE OF NEARBY TOWNS

With the death of Manzanar and the end of WWII, came another financial blow to both Independence and Lone Pine. Throughout the war, Independence, along with other Owens Valley towns, had trained aviation cadets. The Ross Aeronautical Flight School flew out of the Independence and Manzanar airports. The cadets would take flying lessons early in the morning before the wind came up, later do calisthenics at Independence High School, and finally have classroom instruction. The classrooms were available to the cadets in the late afternoon and evenings after the regular students had left for the day. After a couple of years the program changed from training men to fly, to training women to fly. At any one time there were thirty or more pilots in a class living in local hotels and motels, and eating their meals in the local cafes. Between the flight program, the Manzanar Military Police, and over 400 employees and their family members living in Manzanar, local businesses were experiencing a bonanza. Along with the booming hotels, motels, and cafes, there was a grocery store, hardware store, feed store, telegraph office, barber shop, a very small ladies' shop, and a dentist. Doc Baxter, the dentist, had an office behind the drug store and was in what one might call semiretirement. If anybody had a dental problem, Doc Baxter would come down to his office and do what he could. In his earlier days he had followed the gold camps with his dental equipment on a horse drawn wagon. I went to him one time and he made a choirboy out of me. It was the most pain I had ever experienced. Doc Baxter passed away years ago, and none of the businesses mentioned exist today. Between the cadets, pilots, and aviation mechanics, Manzanar staff and their families, the military police, and the businesses that supported the camp, these two small towns received a financial boost that has never been felt since. After their WWII heyday, they suddenly changed from the family towns they were during the war, to the largely retirement communities they remain today. And the WRA employees? What happened to them? They scattered to the four winds. Of those hired from Southern California, most returned to that area. A surprising number of the employees in top positions went to work for UNRRA overseas. Of the locals hired, most stayed in the Owens Valley.

ATTEMPT AT RETRIBUTION

The evacuation of US citizens has been challenged, reaching all the way to the Supreme Court, with the decision to incarcerate Japanese-American citizens during WWII upheld by that court. Recently a group of legal scholars listed it as one of the poorest decisions made by the Supreme Court, although it is doubtful any of these same scholars were living at the time the Supreme Court made their decision. The question is, did we violate one of our most basic constitutional rights? The answer is, yes. We took US citizens, removed them from their homes and placed them in camps without a trial. So we have to ask, what were the factors the Supreme Court used to support their decision. Was it the holding of dual citizenship? Could it have been the possibility of a Japanese invasion, or that the West Coast had been declared a theater of war? The question remains, what drove our nation to violate the basic human right of freedom? One thing we do know is that this was no ordinary time. It appears the Supreme Court agreed with the other branches of government, giving them tremendous latitude in allowing the injustice. If their excuse at the time was the potential for a Japanese invasion, then the survival of the West Coast became much more important than individual liberties during this time of war.

Through the Japanese American Evacuation Claims Act of July 2, 1948, the US government attempted to compensate the Japanese-American evacuees for the indignities and hardships they suffered during their incarceration. The act was the right thing to do and it came about at the right time, but it simply didn't go far enough. It was designed to cover the losses the Japanese Americans suffered as a direct result of the evacuation, however it only compensated for verifiable losses of real property. Administered by the Justice Department, it had a set limit of $100 million which could be paid out. Although over $140 million in claims were made, less than $37 million was actually distributed. Japanese-Americans faced real financial hardship before, during, and after the war. They not only lost their homes, stores, boats, farms with crops ready to harvest, and the inventory from their businesses, they lost unverifiable wages while in camps, their savings in order to support their families while there, proceeds from business ventures that would have occurred had they not been interned, as well as the less tangible dignity, health, pets, personal possessions, and much more. In my view, this was the time for the government to step up and make real restitution for the damages they had caused, but they didn't go nearly far enough in doing so. Although many in government had begun to feel the guilt of their actions, popular public opinion was still resistant to accepting anybody of Japanese descent as worthy of compensation. It would have gone a long way had the government set a tone of forgiveness for the country. Japanese aliens as well as their American-born descendants faced further hardship as they attempted to find their new place in society after the war. Many were completely homeless, with no more savings, and no job prospects, competing for employment with returning WWII veterans as well as Caucasian civilians laid-off from the slowdown of defense work. It was reported shortly after the war that 67% of Japanese Americans were living below the poverty line—a legacy of the fear and prejudice felt by a nation surrounding them.

Forty years after the Japanese American Evacuation Claims Act, pushed by members of congress, the government went further with the 1988 Civil Liberties Act which sent official apology letters for the internment and gave $20,000 tax free to each eligible person of Japanese ancestry. The legislation stated the government's actions were based on "race prejudice, war hysteria, and a failure of the political leadership" and not legitimately necessary to protect the country. Eligibility criteria included being evacuated, relocated, interned, or otherwise deprived of liberty or property during the internment period, based solely on Japanese heritage. On the surface, the Civil Liberties Act appeared to be a positive step, but it was poorly thought out and executed. President Ronald Reagan did not fully understand the consequences of what he was signing. Certainly many people of Japanese descent lost and deserved to be compensated more than the $20,000. On the other hand, there were many that received the apology and compensation and should not have: five thousand people who were considered disloyal to the United States and who returned to Japan after the war; people born in the camp or who were very small children there who really experienced no personal financial losses; Japanese-American soldiers who fought in the war; and the over four thousand

Japanese-American students who relocated to the east and spent the duration of the war in college, some never seeing the inside of an internment camp. The total cost to the American taxpayer for the program was over $1.25 billion. Despite the intent of the act, there were numerous complaints about it, often from those who received no compensation. Many Japanese Americans who suffered and lost the most had passed away by the time the act came to be and therefore received nothing. Italian and German Americans who were also interned during the war were never compensated, nor were any soldiers of non-Japanese descent who fought and died in Europe alongside of those of Japanese ancestry. The Veterans of Foreign Wars wanted to know why Japanese Americans in uniform were the only ones fighting overseas who received compensation. Only those who had personally experienced financial losses as a result of the evacuation should have been compensated.

Surprisingly, some of the criticism for the compensation came from the very people eligible to receive the money. Former California Senator Samuel Ichiye Hayakawa, who passed away in 1992 and whom many respected as an intellectual man of integrity, disapproved of the Japanese-American Evacuation Claims Act. He was one of a number of Japanese Americans who refused to take the money for very sound reasons. He not only refused his own payment, but rallied against the act altogether. Another man, the proud Hank (Henry) Shozo Umemoto wrote this to the U.S. Department of Justice on refusing to take the $20,000, "Instead of being considered a victim of injustice, I would rather have the Japanese Americans go down in history as a patient, proud, and courageous group who endured that wartime incident peacefully with pride, courage, and determination and hope that someday there will be peace all around us." It is a difficult thing to stand up for your beliefs when a substantial sum of money is at stake, but having had the pleasure of talking to Hank Umemoto a couple of times, his actions do not surprise me. The world needs more upstanding people like Mr. Umemoto.

The inequities displayed by both pieces of legislation aimed at compensating the Japanese Americans for their losses show one thing about the people running our government—they are so focused on politics and on looking like they are doing the right thing, that they often do not take the time or put in the effort to ensure they are really DOING the right thing. The official apology proffered in the 1988 act could certainly be supported, but not the carte blanche offer of taxpayer money based almost solely on ethnicity with no regard to how much, or how little, each person was affected, especially forty years after the fact. The time for compensation was in 1948 when the Japanese Americans really needed it—as they were attempting to rebuild a life from the financial and emotional ruins they were left in. In the meantime, this once maligned ethnic group in our society has managed to rise up and set an example for the rest of us. Their strong work ethic, professionalism, and commitment to education has served them well.

CHAPTER XIV
NEGLECT AND REBIRTH

HISTORICAL EVIDENCE

From 1952 until 1992, Manzanar was left to return to its natural state—a high desert landscape covered in sagebrush, rabbit brush, tamarisk, tumbleweeds, and a few drought tolerant trees. The only signs of previous habitation were the ramshackle auditorium, the rock sentry gates, the cemetery obelisk, and a couple of nearly hidden rock walls. Except for the auditorium, all remaining signs of the previous camp can be attributed to one talented, renowned stonemason, Japanese American Ryozo Kado (1890 - 1982). While interned at Manzanar he built the two sentry posts at the main gate, the two rock walls at the first and second project director's residence, and the cemetery monument that is probably the most photographed and best recognized icon of Manzanar. While passing the main gate on my way to school I remember seeing Mr. Kado working at the main sentry post. At the time, I didn't realize I was witnessing the creation of a piece of work that would withstand time, and in all probability, outlive me. While seeing him sculpt two cement tree stumps at the main gate, I was in awe witnessing him turning cement into something that really did look like wood. I remember stopping and watching him and thinking that I had never seen anything like it before. Time has faded the appearance of the cement sculptures, but when I was a kid, they really did look like tree stumps. Mr. Ryozo Kado was a genius with stone and mortar. Neither forty years of neglect, nor harsh weather, nor vandalism have succeeded in erasing what Kado created out of stone, cement, hardship, and desert. In the section to follow and throughout the book you can find proof of his handiwork.

A second Japanese-American evacuee who left an indelible mark on preserving Manzanar's history is Toyo Miyatake, a professional photographer before, during, and after the war. There were other professional photographers who took pictures of WWII Manzanar, most notably, Ansel Adams and Dorothea Lange, but none took as many photographs or covered as wide a range of the camp's life as Miyatake.

Photographer Toyo Miyatake

He stated to his son, "It is my destiny to preserve in pictures what has happened here so that it will never happen again." Because it was illegal for anyone of Japanese origin to possess a camera, Miyatake smuggled a lens and shutter into the camp and built a camera enclosed in a wooden box. With permission from Director Ralph Merritt, Miyatake was officially allowed to set up his camera for the shot, but a non-evacuee had to trip the shutter. Later on, Merritt allowed Miyatake the freedom to take his pictures at will. Miyatake had the vision to catalog his negatives for history, and with his son and grandson following in his footsteps, the Miyatake Studio is still in operation today with its full collection of Manzanar photos.

MANZANAR REBORN

Today the National Park Service is changing the face of the Manzanar site by uncovering and identifying the camp's landmarks and documenting events that took place on those sites. They have made solid progress since 1992, yet Manzanar will never look as it did during WWII. To the visitor, it

Rebuilt guard tower

takes imagination to visualize that this one square mile once confined thousands of Japanese Americans and housed hundreds of staff members—that people were visible everywhere, walking, moving about, standing in lines, and generally going about their day. The park service could replace every building, yet it would remain a ghost town compared to the vibrant, tarpaper city of its busiest days, and that is as it should be. It is to be hoped that Manzanar's continued existence will remind us of a past we never want to repeat.

In the interest of documenting a painful, yet unforgettable blemish in our history, the National Park Service has begun replacing and refurbishing features of the Manzanar camp site. So far, the park service has made a replica of a guard tower and the unique entrance sign. They have big plans for Block 14 where they have completed a replica of a mess hall and two barracks, and intend to continue on until they have also finished block 14 latrines, wash room, and ironing room. This section of camp will provide one of the very best opportunities to get a feeling for life in WWII Manzanar. The NPS has also begun installing wayside panels located throughout the camp area, designating with pictures and text, what transpired at each location. The goal is to eventually have thirty panels in place so visitors can walk or drive through the compound, getting a more accurate feel for the hardships placed upon the evacuees, as well as for the facilities and activities available in the camp.

Obelisk marking the Manzanar Cemetery

Besides the replicated, unpartitioned latrines where one can visualize the lack of basic human privacy allowed, visitors will also be able to see signs for one of the three Buddhist temples, the outdoor movie theater, the baseball fields, golf course with sand greens, and hospital gardens which created an unexpected Eden, contrasting sharply with the barbed wire surrounding the camp. In the staff area of the camp, the NPS has uncovered foundations and walkways, has restored the iconic traffic circle, and is working on installing wayside panels. Ultimately there will be three panels in the staff area recognizing the existence of over 400 non-evacuees who once lived out the war in the Manzanar camp. NPS plans also include building a replica of a staff four-unit apartment. The most important location today to visit when touring Manzanar is the completely rebuilt auditorium, which now houses the interpretive center. Inside you will find an impressive array of old videos, photos, and historical documents that will enlighten even the most well informed Manzanar historian.

CHAPTER XV
WRA MANZANAR REUNION

Original camp residents attending the WRA staff reunion: Front row, from left: Thomas Williams, Fredrick Causey, Martha Shoaf (the only WRA employee), Ann Causey Zahn, Joan DaValle Beyers, David Inman, Don Inman. Back row from left: Shirley DaValle Meeder, Cecile Miller Gordon, David Oille, Robert Stengel, Dr. Harold Dennis, Art Williams, John Atwood

For over sixty years, each spring, the Japanese Americans have made an annual pilgrimage back to Manzanar. In all the years since the closing of the camp, never once did the Manzanar WRA staff ever organize a return of their own to the site where they had once worked and most had lived. Several Manzanar school teachers got together a few times in Southern California, but for the remaining staff and families, Manzanar had become nothing more than a distant memory. Once the National Park Service (NPS) acquired the Manzanar property and began plans to open it up as a historic site, the interest level that had lain dormant for decades was rejuvenated. In my case, it occurred even before the NPS began working out of a double car garage in Independence. It was this simple beginning that led to the historic, 2004 Manzanar Camp Staff Reunion.

MY RETURN TO MANZANAR VIA
A MODEL TUNA BOAT

My first involvement with the NPS was not to organize or attend a reunion—that would come much later—but to answer an NPS request for memorabilia to display at an onsite center which, at the time, was in the early planning stages. I had been returning to the valley annually for a few years to visit with high school classmates and friends, Robert Gracey, Dorothy Bonnifin, and Jack Hunter. It was at one of our luncheon get-togethers where we began discussing the way in which so many of the facts about Manzanar had become lost or distorted. It was suggested that, since I had lived in the camp, I should contact the National Park Service Superintendent recently assigned to Manzanar, Mr. Ross Hopkins. The very next morning, Gracey, friend and Inyo County Supervisor at the time, introduced me to Mr. Hopkins. I immediately liked this man who was full of excitement about his new position and quick to present his vision for a Manzanar historic center. My first observation, though, was that his plan covered only the history of the plight of the Japanese-American evacuees. Where certainly I felt they should be the main focus of the story, I believed strongly that completely ignoring the fact that there were others there living and helping to manage the daily functioning of the camp, was to present an extremely biased and incomplete presentation of the history of Manzanar. Mr. Hopkins seemed genuinely surprised to hear that there were staff members and their families living inside the Manzanar camp. I might feasibly have been the first Caucasian he had talked to who had lived inside the fenced camp. Early on in our discussions, Hopkins pointed out that memorabilia was needed for display, and asked if I had anything that I would be willing to donate. I rather reluctantly offered the future museum a model tuna boat that had been in my family for over fifty years. It was lovingly hand carved by Mr. Bunkichi Hayashi, a member of the camp's Internal Security Police force and a dear friend of my father's.

This boat, which is now on permanent display in the historic center's museum, is remarkable in the detail that Mr. Hayashi was able to evoke with nothing more than a pocket knife, a file, and a few other simple tools allowed him as a Manzanar evacuee.

Hand carved replica tuna boat

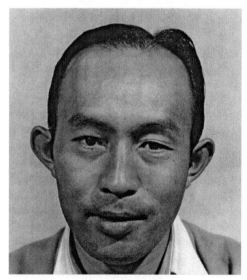

Bunkichi Hayashi

He obviously had amazing talent as well as detailed knowledge of tuna boats, as this model boat was fashioned after Mr. Hayashi's own boat that he had sailed out of Terminal Island. He had taken his boat as far away as Central America in his search for tuna. On his model he had carved out bunks in the sleeping quarters, woven mattresses out of string, made port and starboard lights, carved a miniature radio complete with copper wire running to the mast, and included functioning rigging. The agreement that Mr. Hopkins and I worked out was for my brother Thomas Williams and I to donate the model boat to the NPS, at which point they would have it restored to its former glory and locate the Hayashi family. At the grand opening of the Manzanar Historic Site, my brother and I were to present the boat to the Hayashi's, and they would present it back to the museum for permanent display there. In reality, the agreement and the boat were disconcertingly lost as Hopkins retired and his replacement did nothing more than send the boat to storage in Death Valley where it sat for years. Luckily, the next superintendent, Frank Hayes, who had never heard of the boat or the agreement until I met with him, liked the original plan and quickly assigned park ranger Richard Potashin to follow through with the restoration of the boat and the search for the Hayashi family. By the opening of the museum, a decade after the boat originally landed in the hands of the NPS, this beautiful piece of history had been magnificently restored and put on display, but the Hayashi's had not yet been located. Later, I came across the Hayashi's wedding photo which had been presented to my father when he attended their wedding in camp, in my parent's personal effects, and suggested it too be displayed at the museum. After more than a year, Mr. Potashin called me to say that Mrs. Hayashi and her daughter had come into the center and identified the photo as that of her own wedding. Sadly, Mr. Hayashi had passed away. The story would have had a truly remarkable ending if only Bunkichi himself had lived to see his boat on prominent display after sixty long years.

THE REUNION COMES TOGETHER

While working to get the WRA acknowledged by the NPS, I recognized the potential interest and opportunity for a staff reunion. The situation appeared ideal, for it would be the first time we had gathered since the end of WWII, and we were to be allowed to do so on the very site where we had all lived. It was exciting just to think about it. Getting approval from the NPS proved to be easy; finding people proved to be the hard part. I had, it seems forever, had an interest in finding out what happened to those I knew while living in the camp. I wondered about them on numerous occasions, for in leaving Manzanar, I had lost some very close friends. Where had they gone and what had they done with their lives? I was now retired, and for the first time, had the time and opportunity to try to find them. Amazingly, I was able to locate Shirley (DaValle) Meeder in my own home town, nearly 250 miles from where we had passed our Manzanar years together. It was a surprise to discover we shared the same dentist and country club, yet in our adult years, had never recognized each other. Shirley put me in touch with her sister Joan (DaValle) Beyers and the three of us former Manzanar kids set out to find the other long lost kids of the WRA. Joan turned out to possess a remarkable quality. She was an avid chronicler who had collected the names of all the WRA kids in camp. Before realizing she had made her own list, I had made a list of twenty-two Manzanar kids from memory. When she told me she had a list of ninety-eight names covering all the WRA kids in camp, I had an extraordinary mental flashback of not only her request for my first, middle, and last name and the spelling of each, but also of me questioning her why she wanted such information. She was requesting information I could only imagine the government asking for. I still find it remarkable that I would remember her asking. It must have been the unusual nature of the request. I had no idea why she wanted it or that she would keep it safely tucked away for decades. She actually had the full names of all the WRA staff children including the babies, but that was not all, for she also had a remarkable collection of photos, camp passes, and other items which would impress any collector of Manzanar memorabilia. The DaValle sisters and I worked off of Joan's list of names for over a year trying to locate the kids we had once known. At the time, we did not have a list of the WRA employees nor did we know anyone from that generation who could undertake the creation of such a list, so we focused our efforts on the children. After a year of searching, we decided to take who we had located from Joan's list and organize our reunion. It was the metamorphosis of the old WRA Manzanar auditorium into the new NPS Visitor Center that provided the location for our gathering.

To those of us who lived in that little southeast corner of the camp, Manzanar was never a city or town; it was always just a camp. Our connections to a town were six miles away in Independence where we went to school and maintained local friendships. Therefore, this reunion would have been only partially fulfilling had we neglected to invite our old friends from Independence to our once-in-a-lifetime get together. They had at one time been an important part of our lives. There are friends that I made in Independence that I still consider close: Jack Hunter, Bob Gracey, Dorothy (Wilson) Bonnifin, Gladys (Mitchell) Coulter, and Betty (White) Jewett, to name a few. Dorothy, Gladys, and Betty not only went to school with me, but were also the soda jerks at the local drug store. With a love of milkshakes like the one I possess, I couldn't possibly forget the three soda jerks who made the greatest, thickest milkshakes I have ever known. At the time of the reunion, some of the Independence locals we had known had moved, yet still made the effort to join us, along with those still living in Independence, for the reunion. We also wanted to include all of those children, like Wayne Lawing, who lived outside of the camp, and yet whose parents worked alongside of our own on the inside. The line determining who to invite to the reunion did not stop at the barbed wire fence that many of us lived behind.

On May 22, 2004, shortly after the grand opening of the Manzanar National Historic Site and the annual Japanese-American pilgrimage, the surviving staff and families of Manzanar held their one and only reunion. This day was to become an extremely happy, exciting, emotional one for each of us, in the shadows of which, we knew that it might likely be the last time we would ever see each other. Sixty years had passed and we had already experienced the loss of several of our friends. In our passing years many of us live a life where one day is often not much different from the one preceding or the one upcoming. For those of us who attended the WRA reunion, May 22, 2004, was not just another ho-hum day. We had not only lost the entire community where we were raised—people and buildings all vanished—but many of us had also lost contact with every teenage friend we had ever known. For sixty years these people had existed only in our thoughts. The day finally arrived when we could see these old friends again and discover where they had been and what they had been doing. The DaValle sisters, Joan and Shirley, had previously asked each of us for pictures of both our time in camp and present day to attach to a wall board for display in the reception center. It was the first thing we saw as we entered and proved to be a great orientation tool. Sixty years can play havoc with one's overall appearance and facial features. As a reunion coordinator, I had seen a present day picture of Fred Causey, but he had not seen one of me. I ran into Fred the evening before the reunion and said, "Fred Causey, how are you?"

He replied, "David Oille."

I said, "No, Art Williams."

Fred had been one of my closest friends in camp, we went to school together and even worked baling hay during part of the summers together, yet not surprisingly, some sixty years later, he could not distinguish who I was. With the marvelous display board of the DaValle sisters, much of this embarrassment and confusion was eliminated.

Joan and Shirley DaValle

Joan and Shirley greeted each person as they walked into the Manzanar Visitor Center and guided them through the collection of pictures, past and present. Their year of searching for the kids of the WRA prepared them to answer questions about those who had passed away or were unable to attend. Some people's lives after camp we knew essentially nothing about, only that they had passed away. Their lives since Manzanar remain a mystery to us. Bill Boczkiewicz, Bill Hayes, Don Nail, and Dan Cox are four such lost friends. Bill Boczkiewicz was one of the first to move into the camp and one of the last to leave. He and I were the first two teens with parents working in Manzanar to attend school in Independence. There were others missed at the reunion who could not make the trip for various reasons: Richard Collins, Lynne (Hayes) Sutherland, LaPriel (Strong) Bush, Bud Gilkey, and Pat Nail were a few of those missed. There were some people who we knew had dated while living in camp and it was particularly interesting to see them meet again, after losing track of each other for most of their lives. It was a happy time recalling the past, telling stories, joking, and laughing. It was not long before a couple of hours had been spent visiting, and it was time for lunch. Getting something to eat could not stop our eager chatter.

One of the most interesting discoveries was made when Cecile (Miller) Gordon approached Dr. Harold Dennis, asking him what he was doing at the Manzanar reunion. He informed her that he was one of the former WRA camp kids. She reminded him, "Dr. Dennis, you delivered my first baby."

Keith and Cecile (Miller) Gordon with Judy and Dr. Harold Dennis

Years before, they had had a doctor-patient relationship some 400 miles from Manzanar, and neither ever knew that the other had once lived in the camp. The subject of living in Manzanar never came up. This is not surprising to me, for I do not recall ever opening a conversation with casual acquaintances to discuss the fact that I had lived in Manzanar during WWII. It was not a subject I particularly cared to dwell upon. Another factor is that, at the time both lived there, Cecile was only five years old, while Harold Dennis was a young teenager.

Cecile Miller with her parents

With the nearly one hundred WRA employees' children in camp and the difference in their age, it is not too surprising that they did not know each other previously. Finally, Cecile and her mother were not in camp very long. The two left the camp after a tragic accident that took the life of Cecile's father while he was in flight training at the Manzanar airport. The entire WRA staff and their families were shaken by the tragedy, for her young father, as principal of the Manzanar camp school was very popular both with the evacuees and the WRA families.

Our reunion needed someone to fill in the gaps and entertain while lunch was being served. Fred Causey, who spent-twenty two years flying jets off of US carriers before retiring as a Lt. Commander, and has since donated his time as a docent each year to the NPS at Manzanar, took over the job by doing tricks and playing the harmonica, and yes, he did find the real David Oille, who had been one of his camp friends. One could say we were a very close group of friends. It was fun to see so many friendships take off where we had left them so many decades earlier.

Next on our reunion program was to revisit the staff housing area where we had once lived. All the actual housing had disappeared long ago, the white apartments, green lawns, and white painted stone borders, replaced by sand and sagebrush and a few surviving traces of what was once an immaculately kept staff housing area. This bleak transformation led to a interesting challenge—for each attendee to plant a sign at the location in which they thought they had once lived. Upon returning to the staff area with a map, I was surprised to find most signs were remarkably close to the actual former locations of the designated apartments—in fact, in many cases, very close to the location of their actual front door.

Martha Shoaf, former Manzanar school teacher

Martha Shoaf, a former Manzanar school teacher and the only former WRA employee in attendance, had difficulty pushing her walker in the sand and around the bushes, but she persevered, finding the entrance to the site of Dormitory H where she had once lived. Martha had an adventurous life, starting with graduating from UCLA and taking her first job at Manzanar. She followed it with many years of teaching school in Trona, California, interspersed with traveling to foreign countries. She retired from teaching at Trona and donated time as a docent to the NPS at Manzanar. Martha was a free spirit and adventurist who was very popular with the other young teachers at Manzanar. She passed away in 2012. She once said she loved living and teaching at the camp and hated to leave. Martha's sister Susan also worked in camp.

Following group pictures, the NPS took over the rest of the afternoon with interesting walking tours of the camp. Jane Wehrey took us to the Sheppard Ranch site and covered the early history of Manzanar during the period in which Manzanar was inhabited by Native Americans. This was followed by her presentation of the period in which Manzanar was a thriving farming community, ending with the takeover of the valley's water rights by the City of Los Angeles. Our next stop on the NPS tour took us to the site of the WRA hospital. Here, Alisa Lynch covered camp medical issues up to and including the period in which the WRA ultimately developed the finest hospital facility within two hundred miles in either direction. Richard Potashin, who is arguably the most knowledgeable source on WWII Manzanar, presented information at our final stop—the camp cemetery.

Jane Wehrey with Richard Potashin sharing historical information with reunion attendees

The finale of the reunion was a delicious, western-style barbecue hosted by the Eastern California Museum in Independence. This museum has been around for over eighty years and has captured the history of not just Manzanar, but all of Owens Valley. For decades they were the only one in the valley to collect photos and additional historic material from WWII Manzanar. We were privileged to receive a tour of their coverage of Owens Valley history, including that of Manzanar. After finishing our wonderful meal and completing our tour of the Eastern California Museum, many were thinking the day's activities had ended.

In fact, the final agenda item was a request by the NPS for everyone who had lived in the camp to attend a private, round table discussion concerning their experiences and feelings about living in camp. What was most revealing during this discussion was how different individuals living in the same place, at the same time, experiencing the same things each day, could have such diverse views and opinions about it some sixty years later. To be expected, Martha Shoaf, the oldest attendee, talked the most about her feelings and experiences, and seemed to recall the most. As nighttime fell and old eyelids drooped, the reunion ended where it had begun. It was a long and wonderful day of laughter, fulfillment, and closure for many of us with previously unanswered questions. In the final count, where twelve out of ninety-eight former WRA children, and only one actual WRA employee out of 228 may not seem like a very impressive turnout for a reunion, when one considers the nearly sixty years that had passed since the camp had closed, that no WRA employee list existed prior to this, and that many of the people involved had passed away or moved out of California and could not travel that far, one might conclude that thirteen original WWII, WRA inhabitants of Manzanar was a rich and worthy group of attendees.

Reunion Barbecue hosted by the Eastern California Museum

Attendees of Manzanar Staff and Families Reunion

1944 — MEMORIES OF MANZANAR — 2004
SIXTY YEARS LATER

...beautiful mountains, stars at night, wonderful friends, first inklings of gardening, exploring the desert and Alabama Hills, shopping in Lone Pine for Levis, school in Independence.
— *Ann (Causey) Zahn*

...aspects of barracks living, barbed wire fencing and guard towers, a sandstorm, a loving Japanese woman, Grace, who took care of me, and, unfortunately, my father's death in a light plane accident.
— *Cecile (Miller) Gordon*

...playing with Japanese friends outside our home, going to social functions at Manzanar with my parents, traveling in a bus to school in Independence. All of my memories are positive ones.
— *Ruth (Strong) Jones*

...good food, windstorms, close friends, Saturday night movies in Lone Pine, swimming in aqueduct, riding wild donkeys in the desert.
— *Fred Causey*

...waiting for the school bus in the wind and bitter cold, terrible hot summer nights trying to sleep, fantastic breakfasts in the mess hall, swimming in the aqueduct, playing pool at the Army Camp, victory garden, duck hunting, the beauty of the mountains, and finding lasting friends.
— *Art Williams*

... fun times, attending school in Independence with my brother Don, St. Bernard dog, "Bing."
— *Mary Alice Inman in memory of Bruce Inman*

... beauty of the Sierra Mountains in our backyard and the Whitney Portals, riding the bus to school, pride in the appointed personnel who left their homes to make Manzanar a functioning "city."
— *Lynne (Hayes) Sutherland*

… the first year in tarpaper barracks and latrines, later finding close friends and enjoying activities with them, playing hide and seek, hiking, swimming, baseball, dances, movies, jeep rides with soldiers, warming ourselves by the guard house heater waiting for the school bus.

> — *Joan (DaValle) Beyers*

…hot, cold, victory garden, attending the Japanese school, camp farm and Japanese Gardens, hunting and fishing with my father and older brother.

> — *Tom Williams*

…doing insane things at night with David Oille and Art Williams—breaking into the auditorium and fooling around, playing tag while driving the farm tractors across the desert, and then hiding under buildings from the Japanese Police as they looked for us with their flashlights.

> — *Pat Nail*

…the fun we had playing kick the can. I remember enjoying Manzanar very much.

> — *LaPriel (Strong) Bush*

…the mountains, friends, the school bus ride, and the school in Independence.

> — *David Oille*

…passing out from the heat, blistering my feet wearing sandals while walking between classrooms, seeing the thermometer in mother's typing classroom reach 129° F and the typing machines being too hot to touch, watching the movie "Tender Comrade" in the starlight ten nights in a row when it was too hot inside our apartment.

> — *Sue (Nail) Hanson*

MANZANAR MEMORIES

Soldiers in towers, guardhouses, barbed wire,
Manzanar riot, mess halls and latrines.
What to expect—what would it require?
Showers, communal, like nothing we'd seen.

Tarpaper barracks with sand drifting through,
Summertime gardens and wintertime snow.
No running water—we had to make do.
Breathtaking scenery and friends we still know.
None of our parents showed their dismay.
Manzanar memories all become one,
Is it possible that work became play?
Preparing for life and what was to come.

— *Shirley (DaValle) Meeder*

APPENDICES

APPENDIX #1
CAMP STRUCTURES

Evacuee Structures, Warehouses, and Garages

Structure Use	Size (feet)	Number
Barracks	20 × 100	504
Mess Halls	40 × 100	36
Baths and Latrines	20 × 30	72
Recreation Halls	20 × 100	36
Ironing Rooms	20 × 28	36
Laundry Rooms	20 × 50	36
Warehouses	20 × 100	40
Vehicle Garages	20 × 100	4
Total structures		**764**

Hospital and Children's Village Structures

Structure Use	Size (feet)	Number
Administration (for hospital and Children's Village)	255 × 147	1
Obstetrical Ward	25 × 150	1
General Wards	25 × 150	4
Isolation Wards	25 × 150	2
Mess Hall	40 × 60	1

Structure Use	Size (feet)	Number
Doctors' Quarters (5 doctors)	20 × 100	1
Nurses' Quarters (23 nurses)	20 × 100	1
Hospital Laundry	20 × 100	1
Hospital Morgue	23 × 33	1
Heating Plant	40 × 38	1
Warehouse	20 × 100	2
Children's Village	25 × 150	3
Total Structures		**19**

Staff Area Structures

Structure Use	Size (feet)	Number
Administration Buildings	40 × 100	2
Administration Storage	20 × 30	1
Town Hall	20 × 50	1
Police and Reception Station	20 × 100	1
Post Office	40 × 100	1
Staff Mess Hall	20 × 100	1
Family Apartment Buildings	20 × 100	2 (4 apartments in each)
Men's Dormitories	20 × 100	2 (6 apartments in each)
Women's Dormitories	20 × 100	2 (6 apartments in each)
Dormitories H, I, J	24 × 140	3
Housing Units G, K through W	20 × 94	14 (4 apartments in each)
Total structures		**30 in staff area + 1 at the hospital**

Military Police Camp

Structure Use	Size (feet)	Number
Barracks	20 × 100	4
Officers' Quarters	20 × 100	1

Structure Use	Size (feet)	Number
Administration and Storeroom	20 × 100	1
Recreation Building	20 × 100	1
Mess Hall	20 × 100	1
Guardhouse	20 × 50	1
First Aid Station	20 × 28	1
Bath and Latrines	20 × 30	1
Motor Repair Building	31 × 39	1

APPENDIX #2
WCCA MANZANAR PERSONNEL

Below is a list of employees who worked for the Wartime Civil Control Administration (WCCA) at Manzanar. Based more on politics than qualifications or job performance, very few of these employees were offered jobs after the transition to WRA. The WCCA listed two Japanese-American evacuees on their personnel roster. Both were professionals who proved invaluable to the startup of the camp. These men were offered similar jobs with the WRA but were never included on the staff personnel list.

Adkins, ? - Head of Construction Division
Banks, Stanley M. - Assist. to Works Division. Before Manzanar, Stan worked for the Works Progress Administration (WPA), San Bernardino, Ca. He was the engineer for the first Ontario Airport runway.
Barton, Roger - Lodging and Mess Division
Benedict, L. M. - Public Relations Chief
Black, Harry L. - Assist. Camp Manager. He ran the day to day operations at Manzanar and was the one people went to with their problems. I have heard he was the Major Black of Black Fox Military Academy in Los Angeles.
Black, Warden - Requisition Clerk
Brander, Charles E. - Assist. Chief Clerk
Brooks, Ralph S. - Head of Public Works and Maintenance
Brown, Robert L. - Public Relations Director. Stayed on to become WRA Assist. Project Director of Operations. More on Robert L. Brown in Chapter V: Selecting a Site
Burns, Thomas - Chief of Commissary in Dept. of Mess and Lodging
Butcher, John D. - Steward in Mess and Lodging
Chuman, Frank - Medical Administrator. Frank, a Nisei Japanese-American, worked for the WCCA and the WRA from March 21, 1942, until September 21, 1943. He was the first Manzanar medical administrator. He left Manzanar, attended law school, and practiced law in Southern California. He is the author

of *The Bamboo People* covering 112 years of Japanese-American life in the United States now used by Universities, Law Schools, and Asian study groups.

Cunningham, Harry E. - PBX operator?

Day, Lloyd F. - Assist. Chief, Police Dept.

Dillard, Ella W. - Secretary in Clayton Triggs's office

Donovan, W. E. - Lodging and Mess Division

Dougherty, Barbara - Secretary in Clayton Triggs's office

Engstrom, Emil - Lodging and Mess Division

Erskine, Samuel T. - Warehouse Section

Feil, Ralph D. - Electrical Engineer. Stayed with WRA

Flugstad, Wilson D. - Service Division

Frazer, Lewis J. - Personnel Section

Goto, Dr. James - Surgeon in Charge of Hospital. Evacuee.

Hale, Earle E. - Fire Department Captain

Harrington, ? - PBX?

Harrison, John R. - Supt. of Production Division. Graduate of Stanford in Social Science and Cal Berkeley in Forestry. Worked in forestry and then as a supervisor with the WPA. At one point had up to 2,000 men from the CCC building various public facilities in the San Bernardino/Riverside area. He was recruited to take a job of setting up and supervising farming activities at Manzanar. He left Manzanar and took a commission in the Navy where he served in the Pacific. He said his annualized salary while at Manzanar was $3,600 per year plus $6.00 per diem. He stayed at the Dow Hotel in Lone Pine for $2.50 per night.

Henderson, M. - PBX

Hicks, Louis - ?

Hooper, E.H. - Principal Fiscal Accountant. Stayed with WRA to become Assist. Project Director Administration

Horton, Kenneth L. - Chief of Police. He was head of the Bishop police and fire departments. He returned to the Bishop Police Department when the WRA took over operations inside the camp.

Hunt, Dorman C. - PBX Operator

Kidwell, Mervyn J. - Community Service Division

Kincheloe, Frederic H. - Chief Personnel Accountant

King, John R. - Head of a Warehouse Section

Lander, W. J. - Finance and Records Division

McDowell, Harvey D. - Steward in Lodging and Mess Division

Miller, Arthur H. - Medical Section Chief. Stayed with WRA as Assist. Personnel Chief

Mills, William B. - Chief Property Accountant

Montijo, Raymond - Maintenance Division

Myers, George G. - Fire Captain

Nelson, Harold A. - Supplies Section

Newton, Edward C. - Police Captain

Nielsen Aksel G. - Head of Recreation

O'Conner, ? - Construction and Maintenance

Pullion, Ellis - Possible predecessor to Harry Black, Assist. Camp Manager

Reddinger, Norman V. - Chief of Communications

Starr, William S. - Steward in Mess and Lodging Division

Sturdevant, Frank - Police Dept. He was a career policeman, beginning his career with the Redondo Beach Police Department. His love of the mountains, wildlife, and fishing attracted him to Owens Valley and accepting a job with the WCCA. In a couple of months he felt training Japanese Americans to be internal security policemen was not job fulfilling and returned to conventional police work with the Redondo Beach Police Department where he finished out his law enforcement career.

Summer, Charlie - Worked in farming. A local hire.

Thorne, Herbert F. - Camp Maintenance

Togasaki, Dr. Yoshiye - Public Health Administrator. Evacuee.

Triggs, Clayton E. - Camp Manager of the Owens Valley Reception Center. He was the man in charge and there could not have been a better pick. He gained valuable experience in working for the WPA organizing and setting up camps and dealing with local communities. He had served on the Owens Valley Coordinating Committee and recognized there were going to be deep concerns within the local communities upon having a camp built for Japanese Americans in Owens Valley. He encouraged hiring locals. He was an excellent organizer, a delegator, and a fine communicator. He kept the local communities informed as the camp was being built. He also knew from experience he was going to need considerable help from the evacuees. He recognized it would be good for them to be busy and take an active role in the day to day operations. He had five top priorities: see the arriving evacuees were given accommodations and three meals per day, provide medical care, ensure a healthy, sanitary camp, start up a farm operation, and minimize outside staff while maximizing the evacuee work force. He would be in charge of the "Owens Valley Reception Center" during the initial startup until the WRA took over.

Walkonis, Joseph G. - Historian from the War Dept. sent to record the history of the reception center. Left camp May 1, 1942.

White, Frank J. - Steward in Mess and Lodging

White, Lowell - Finance and Records Office

Winchester, Joseph - Supervisor, Mess and Warehousing

Williams, Arthur Loren - Police Dept. Captain. Came from Redondo Beach Police Dept. Stayed on as WRA Assist. Chief of Internal Security. See more information in WRA staff section.

APPENDIX #3
WRA EMPLOYEES: FAMILIES, JOB TITLES, HOUSING ASSIGNMENTS

STAFF ORGANIZATION

The staff organization progressed through several changes and ultimately increased from two to three divisions, each division headed by an assistant project director ultimately reporting to the project director. Note that some job titles changed with the organization changes. All the pictures I could find of WRA employees were turned over to the NPS at Manzanar and are available for viewing at their front desk.

Office of Project Director Divisions

Community Management	Operations	Administrative Management
Internal Security	Agriculture Section	Supply Section
Health Section	Industry Section	Postal Service Unit
Education Section	Engineering Section	Finance Section
Welfare Section	Construction and Maintenance	Budget and Accounting
Community Analysis	Fire Protection	Cost Account. & Property Control
Business Enterprises	Motor Transport and Maintenance	

EMPLOYEE INFORMATION

At any given time the WRA employees numbered up to 229. Include into that figure their spouses and children and you find there were quite a large number of non-evacuee residents in Manzanar. The following is the most complete list ever before developed of the WRA employees and their families, although the post 1945 data is less complete. When known, family associations are noted with husband listed first, then wife, and children. Included in the information is a list of all known WRA housing assignments. Housing with three digit numbers, such as (1-1-1), refers to tarpaper barracks. The numbers refer to block number-building number-unit. Housing within the staff area is noted with a letter and then a number, such as (A-1). Additional information pertaining to the staff is included below as well. This is an ongoing list that I have turned over to the Manzanar Historic Society and any verifiable proof of additions or changes submitted to the NPS, Manzanar would be greatly appreciated.

Abel, Leland - Secondary Teacher. Wife: **Doris** - Secondary Teacher. Child: **George Alan**. Res: 1-12-1, K-1. Leland and Doris left Manzanar to fill teaching positions in Laton, California.

Adams, Lucy Wilcox - Assist. Project Director, Community Management. Children: **Ernest** and **William**. Res: D-4, G-4. Lucy was born in California, raised near Elk Hills, California and attended Stanford University where her liberal thinking was nurtured. Married, had two sons, Ernest and William, and shortly thereafter found herself a widow. Took a job with the Bureau of Indian Affairs working with the poor in education. In 1941 she was promoted to a position in Washington D.C. and shortly thereafter recruited by the WRA. If you were to select the toughest job in the camp, hers would certainly be a finalist. In January 1945, she was recruited by UNRRA and worked in Hungary, Korea, and finally Washington D.C. After retirement she taught at the University of California at Berkeley for five years. She lived to be 98.

Alch, Mathile - Counselor. Res: Dorm I-9. Born in Korno province Russia and came to the USA as a child. Graduated from St. Louis University, served in the US Navy during WWI and later spent many years both in this country and in Europe doing welfare work. Before Manzanar, she worked as a social services supervisor with the city and county in Dallas, Texas. In April 1944, she accepted a position with the WRA at Manzanar. She passed away in Manzanar in January 1945.

Allen, Joseph S. - Assoc. Design Engineer.

Anderson, Ann S. - Personnel Officer. Res: L-2

Anderson, Edna M. - Senior Staff Nurse. Res: Hospital

Anderson, Jesse - (unknown - labor). Res: 1-13-1

Anderson, Victor - (unknown - labor). Res: 1-13-3

Anderson, Violet - Elementary Teacher. Res: 7-11-1

Anderson, Zelda - Jr. Counselor

Archuleta, Bennie - (unknown - labor)

Armstrong, Fred T. - Carpenter. Res: 1-13-2

Arnold, Vorus L. - (unknown - labor). Res: Lone Pine

Atwood, Oliver J. - Evacuee Escort. Wife: **Alice (Brown)** - Elementary Teacher. Child: **John** born 10/22/27, in Manzanar 1943-1945. Res: 1-11-2, O-4. After Manzanar, Alice took an elementary school teaching position in Independence in 1945.

Backhoff, Iva - Elementary Teacher. Res: 7-9-4

Bailey, Dixie M. - Sr. Elementary Teacher. Res: 7-1-4, H-3

Bailey, William - (unknown – labor)

Baird, Genevieve - Elementary Teacher. Res: 7-9-3, Lone Pine

Balker, ? - (unknown). Children: **Jay** and **Paul**

Banks, Franklin E. - Foreman Labor

Bartlett, Agnes, Dr. - Principal Medical Officer. Res: Hospital. Replaced Dr. Little in July 1945 and stayed until camp closure in November the same year. Raised in Japan, spoke perfect Japanese. This was extremely useful for those patients who could not speak English.

Barton, Earl W. - Evacuee Property Officer. Res: Lone Pine

Barton, Roy - Foreman Plumbing

Basson, Nathan H. - Sanitarian

Batavia, Nenette - Assist. Counselor

Beall, Ruby D. - Elementary Teacher. Res: Dorm J-20

Beckwith, Ruth E. - Sr. Elementary Teacher. Res: 7-8-5

Beekman, Eva Mary - Elementary Teacher. Res: 7-2-3

Belanger, Agnes F. - Elementary Teacher. Res: Dorm J-6

Belanger, M.K. - Teacher

Bell, Agnes O. - Secondary Teacher. Res: 7-11-1

Bengs, Margaret - Telephone Operator. Res: Independence.

Bennett, Neal A. - Assoc. Design Engineer. Res: Independence

Bermaye, Ione - Teacher

Berriman, Clyde R. - Jr. Cost Account. Children: **Mildred Lenore (McCallister)** and **Wilma Clydene** in Manzanar 1943 - 1945. Res: Independence, L- 1

Best, Ray - Supply Officer and Head of Transportation. At Manzanar briefly during 1942 and the camp's start up under the WRA. Promoted to Project Director at Tule Lake.

Beven, Frances M. - Secondary Teacher

Blamey, Joseph - Business Mgr. Free Press

Boczkiewicz, Ransom - Principal Fiscal Account. Wife: **Mary** - Telephone Operator in the administration building. Child: **William Fredrick** born 3/11/27, in Manzanar 1942-1945. Res: 1-6-2, 1-11-1, N-1. Ransom and Mary were two of the first to work for the WRA in Manzanar and two of the last to leave. Prior to Manzanar Ransom was chief clerk of the Concho Indian Agency, Oklahoma. It is believed the family moved to Seattle after Manzanar, for the son, Bill Boczkiewicz, was found in our search to have passed away there.

Boericke, Ethelwyn - (unknown)

Bonner, Elvis F. - (unknown). Res: Lone Pine

Born, Theodore G. - Internal Security Officer. Res: P-3

Bouche, Brieuc L. - Head Teacher. Res: 7-10-3

Bouche, Lucille L. - Elementary Teacher

Bowker, Kenneth - Chief Construction Foreman. Wife: **Martha K.** - Senior Staff Nurse. Res: Lone Pine

Boyer, Archie M. - (unknown). Res: Lone Pine

Bradshaw, Clyde - Chief Construction Foreman. Res: Lone Pine

Brander, Charles E. - Personnel Officer

Branson, Donald H. - Foreman Plumbing

Bright, Joe T. - Internal Security Officer. Res: Reward Mine. A local from Independence, his father operated the Reward Mine across the valley from Manzanar in the Inyo Mountains.

Brill, Helen W. - High School English Instructor. She was instrumental in getting many students relocated to colleges through the Student Relocation Program.

Brimley, Russell - Art student from Bishop. Res: 1-8-?. Russell was not an employee, but resided in the camp.

Britten, Patricia - Heavy Duty Truck Driver turned Evacuee Escort. Res: W-4. The daughter of **Oliver Sisler**, Patricia drove relocating evacuees to Reno. Married a University of California at Berkeley graduate before coming to Manzanar. He was a B-17 pilot, shot down and captured by the Germans. He was in a concentration camp while Patricia worked at Manzanar. She took the job at Manzanar to stay busy and to reduce worrying about her husband. She and her husband would have a child, **Julie Britten** after the war. They settled in the Visalia area.

Bromley, David S. - Evacuee Property Officer. Res: D-3. Returned to Bishop, California. In 1945 published his poetry in a book titled, "These bitter years"

Brooks, Lloyd W. - (unknown)

Brown, Charles W. - (unknown). Res: Lone Pine

Brown, Harriett H. - Elementary Teacher. Res: Dorm I-8

Brown, Harvey, Jr. - Senior Engineer Public Works. Res: C-3. Born October 10, 1896, at North Wilkes-Barr, North Carolina. He came from a long line of English stock. He attended University of South Carolina, University of Mississippi, and received a civil engineering degree from Penn State University, class of 1917. He was married and had a daughter. Prior to Manzanar he spent 25 years in design and construction in various parts of the world. At Manzanar he was head of public works. He started in June 1942, and one year later would leave to work in the war industry in San Francisco.

Brown, Melba de la Motte - Secondary Teacher. Res: 7-9-4

Brown, Robert L. - Assist. Proj. Director Operations. Res: D-3

Brown, Mayne A. - Typist

Bruce, William J. PhD. - Community Enterprise Supt. Children: **James, Susan,** and **William**. William was in Manzanar 1942 - 1944. Res: 7-8-4. William came from Portland, Oregon. In December 1943, he accepted a position in Washington D.C. Was married and had three children.

Bruttig, Leland J. - Personnel Technician. Res: P-4

Budd, Ruth C. - Librarian. Res: Dorm J-1. Resigned from WRA and accepted a job in Honolulu, Hawaii.

Burkhardt, Jack E. - Internal Security Officer. A local hire.

Burnam, Everett E. - Internal Security Officer. Res: 1-9-4

Buzzetti, Ray F. - Placement Officer. Res: Lone Pine. A college graduate, Ray had been with the WPA and Montana State Welfare Farm Credit Administration, and had at one time been a semiprofessional basketball player. Drafted from his job with the WRA at Manzanar into the U.S. Army.

Campbell, Alan - Project Attorney. Children thought to be Alan's: **Colin Joseph, Paula Sue, Robert Alan,** and **Sonja Dale**. Res: L-1

Campbell, Ned - Assist. Project Director. He was born in Texas in 1905. Graduated from Texas Christian University and received a law degree from the University of Colorado. One of his early jobs was with the Bureau of Indian Affairs in Arizona. He was recognized as a young, ambitious employee who got things done. When his boss, Si Freyer was asked by Milton Eisenhower to work for the WRA he took Ned Campbell with him. He became one of the very first employees with the WRA and would land the job of Assist. Project Director at Manzanar under Roy Nash and later for Ralph Merritt. He became the man in the hot seat dealing directly with an often angry Japanese-American community. He had to carry out orders from Washington D.C. which many times were based on poor decisions. As a result he became unpopular with the Japanese Americans in camp. His involvement with Harry Ueno's arrest intensified the Japanese Americans' dislike for him. He left Manzanar in 1943 to work for UNRRA in North Africa during the rest of the war. He retired in Monterey California.

Cannedy, Ida B. - Grad. Nurse Sr. Staff. Res: Hospital

Cantua, Louis - Carpenter. Res: Independence

Carnes, Virginia R. - Medical Social Worker. Res: Hospital

Carney, Joseph W. - Auditor. Wife: **Lucille** - Senior Staff Nurse. Children: **Joy Anne, Mary Evelyn, William Joseph**. Res: E-3 & 4

Carpenter, Ira L. - Assoc. Fire Protection Officer. Res: 1-9-2

Carrasco, Relles A. - Carpenter Foreman

Carroll, Frank - Truck Driver. Res: Lone Pine

Carter, Genevieve W., PhD. - Superintendent of Education. Child: **Virginia Ann**. Res: C-1. Born in Illinois in 1907, and educated in New Mexico. After receiving a degree in psychology at the University of New Mexico, she received a doctorate from the University of California at Berkeley. As a staff member at the University of California she was sent to Manzanar on May 19, 1942, to document the impact and progress of the relocation for the university's sociology department. Reported back to Manzanar on June 15, 1942, as superintendent, a position she would hold until the schools closed in 1945. She met the challenge of establishing a complete school system from ground zero. The grammar and high schools were staffed and operational in just three months. The first summer she contacted all sixty-five schools which the Japanese-American students had come from. In the rush of relocation, they had not been allowed to complete their spring semester of school. Dr. Carter acquired their records and the first summer conducted classes completing their spring semester's work so the students were ready once the fall semester began. After Manzanar she would return to working in social welfare research in Los Angeles and Washington D.C. She is honored with a plaque in the Washington

D.C. headquarters of the National Association of Social Workers as an "outstanding pioneer." She passed away in 1998, in Albuquerque, New Mexico.

Carter, MD - Medical Officer

Carter, Perve - Heavy Duty Truck Driver, Evacuee Escort. Res: Lone Pine

Cashion, William J. - (unknown). Res: 1-13-2

Causey, Frederick P. - Office Engineer. Wife: **Mildred E.** - Property Clerk. Children: **Ann Elizabeth Theresa (Zahn),** born 6/7/23, in Manzanar 1944-1945, and **Fredrick George Polk, Jr.,** born 12/27/28, in Manzanar 1944-1945. Res: R-4. Fredrick Causey, Sr. was a graduate civil engineer. One of his first jobs was with the federal government laying out and surveying in streets in Washington D.C., more specifically around the Jefferson memorial. The outbreak of the war found him designing military defense installations on Trinidad Island for the protection of their oil fields and refinery. The completion of the assignment next took him to Manzanar. He worked in engineering for the WRA until the camp closed. After Manzanar, he was assigned to work in Sacramento. He passed away in 1948.

Ceballos, Manuel - (unknown)

Chamberlain, Bertis - Manufacturing Superintendent. Res: Lone Pine. Had previously worked for the WPA in California.

Chandra, Vidya - Secondary Teacher. Res: E-?

Chasen, Arthur - (unknown)

Chavira, Rudolph - (unknown)

Chester, Edward G. - Secondary Teacher, Assist. Procurement Officer. Wife: **Blanche J.** - Secondary Teacher. Res: F-1

Choate, Helen F. - File Clerk

Christensen, Anita L. - Secondary Teacher. Res: H-10. Married a Manzanar MP who was killed during the war. She never remarried.

Chuman, Frank - Medical Administrator. Frank, a Japanese-American, worked for the WCCA and the WRA from March 21, 1942, to September 21, 1943. He was the first Manzanar medical administrator. He left Manzanar, to attend law school and practice law in Southern California. He is the author of *The Bamboo People,* covering 112 years of Japanese-American life in the United States. His book is used in universities, law schools, and by Asian study groups.

Clark, Richard A. - Guard. Res: Lone Pine. Left Manzanar for a position in security with the Navy at Inyo-Kern.

Clary, Elaine E. - Secondary P.E. Teacher. Res: Dorm H-10. Elaine played on UCLA's girls basketball team. Hired right out of college in 1943, first as a preschool teacher for staff children, followed by a PE teacher for Japanese-American children. Roomed with Arlin Hooper in Dorm H. Loved the mountains and hiking and hiked Mr. Whitney. Never taught after Manzanar. Married 60 years had seven children. Retired to Big Bear, California.

Cline, Wilfred - Foreman Agriculture. Res: Lone Pine

Collins, Henry P. - Internal Security Officer. Wife: **Pauline** - Head of local Office of Price Administration (OPA), a federal agency established during WWII to prevent wartime price inflation. Child: **Richard Duncan,** born 9/4/29, in Manzanar 1943-1945. Res: Independence, P-4, F-1. Born in 1899 in Fresno, California,

Henry was the son of a judge. In his early years he played banjo and guitar and sang in a traveling band. He met Pauline Duncan in Fresno. They married and had their son, Richard. Henry left the band and went to work for Pennzoil. A gifted salesman, he was soon promoted to sales manager for Pennzoil in Bakersfield, California and moved to Santa Barbara. Henry and Pauline's love for the San Joaquin Valley took them back to Fresno. He worked for the WCCA at the Fresno Fairgrounds in Internal Security and took a similar position with the WRA at Manzanar. Pauline headed up the local OPA. She and her son Richard lived in the camp only a year before returning to Fresno to sell real estate. Henry worked until the camp closed. He and Pauline are buried in their family plot at the Academy Cemetery in the foothills of the Sierras outside of Fresno.

Conn, Lyle - Internal Security Officer. Retired from the San Diego Police Dept. before employment with the WRA at Manzanar. A late hire, he started in April 1945.

Cooper, Ralph W. - Storekeeper. Wife: **Ann P.** - Elementary Teacher. Res: Lone Pine

Cooper, Valerie - Teacher

Coppin, Earl - (unknown)

Coverley, Harvey - Acting Project Director

Cowart, Douglas T. - Assist. Cost Accountant. Wife: **Alice R.** - Gate Clerk/ Main Gate, Mail and Files Department. Res: S-1. Son of Alice: **David Dale Oille**, born 6/20/29, in Manzanar 1944-1945. Douglas was born in Scotland, raised in Texas. Worked for the WRA at Fresno prior to Manzanar.

Cox, Clarence W. - Internal Security Officer. Res: E-4

Cox, Daniel H. - Personnel Transactions Officer. Wife: **Helen C.** - Fiscal Accounting Clerk. Children: **Daniel Douglas**, born 6/16/29, in Manzanar 1944-1945, and **Nancy Lee**. Res: T-1. Daniel was originally from Baltimore Maryland where he had worked for a printing business. Lost his lower arm in an industrial accident. First worked for the WRA at Tule Lake, transferred to Manzanar in 1943 and worked there until camp closure.

Cox, Edith M. - Elementary Teacher. Res: 7-1-4, Dorm I

Cox, Robert O. - Assist. Storekeeper. Res: Lone Pine

Cramer, Marjorie C. - Elementary Teacher. Res: 7-3-4

Crilly, Frank C. - Assist. Supt. Equipment. Wife: **Ann.** Child: **Marion Jean.** Res: Independence, W-1

Crites, Marvin A. - Secondary Teacher. Wife: **Beulah E.** - Social Worker

Cushion, Ruth M. - Leave Officer. Res: Hospital, D-4, L-3

Dahl, Axel - Internal Security Officer. Came from Minnesota.

Dales, Janice - Elementary Teacher. Res: 7-2-3

DaValle, Marjorie - Secondary Algebra and Geometry Teacher. Children: **Joan Marjorie (Beyers)**, born 3/26/30, in Manzanar 1942-1945 and **Shirley Lucile (Meeder)**, born 11/14/31, in Manzanar 1942-1945. Res: 7-2-4, M-1. A single parent with two teenage daughters. She was born September 22, 1900, in San Dimas, California. Her father was a civil engineer, noted surveyor and orange grower. Her mother would pass away early in life leaving her father to raise four children. Marjorie learned to cope with adversity and do things for herself. She graduated from the University of Southern California in 1922. She taught high school Spanish and mathematics, married, and stopped teaching to raise her two daughters. Her husband was a graduate pharmacist who owned his own pharmacy, but lost it during the depression. They divorced in 1942. Needing to go back to work, she accepted a teaching position at Manzanar for $2,000 per year. She saw Manzanar as a safe place to raise her two daughters and save for their college educations. She succeeded in putting both through college after the war on a teacher's salary. Although the living conditions were primitive, she never complained and tried to make the experience enjoyable for her daughters. She returned to southern California after the war and taught until retirement. She passed away August 15, 1963. Marjorie was frugal, an adventurist, enjoyed teaching, and loved her daughters.

Davenport, George N. - Guard. Res: 7-3-3

Davenport, Dorothy - Secondary Teacher

Davis, Arch W. - Reports Officer, Manzanar Free Press. Res: E-6

Davis, Martha Belle - (unknown)

Day, Henry P. - Carpenter Foreman. Children: **David** and **William**. Res: 1-13-4

Day, Lloyd F. - Assist. Chief of Internal Security. Filled this position first with the WCCA. Left the WRA in September 1942.

Dean, Charles - (unknown)

DeForest, Charlotte - Junior Counselor. Res: Dorm I-9

Deniston, William T. - Carpenter. Res: 1-13-1

(Dennis), Oma Spivy Umhey - Secondary Teacher of 11th/12th grade English. Child: **Harold Spivy**, born 10/8/30, in Manzanar 1943-1944. Res: 1-12-4, P-3

Denny, Charlie - (unknown). Res: 1-13-1

d'Ille, Margaret Matthew - Supervisor of Community Welfare. Res: 7-2-1. Margaret was born November 20, 1879, in Springfield, Illinois. Her father was the dean of University of Southern California and served both before and after as minister in a number of different Christian churches. Margaret graduated from the University of California, Berkeley. While at the university she met Ralph Merritt and many years later they reunited at Manzanar. For ten years she worked in Japan with the YWCA where she learned the Japanese language. Her knowledge of Japanese culture would serve her well at Manzanar. She married twice, both times late in life. She passed away in Los Angeles, California, March 28, 1954, at age 75.

Dittmar, Jessie E. - Clerk / Stenographer. Child: **James**. Res: K-4

Dolan, Claude - (unknown). Res: 1-13-3

Dombrowski, Felix A. - Blacksmith. Wife: **Mary L.** - Elementary Teacher. Res: 1-12-3

Dougherty, Barbara A. - Secretary to Assist. Proj. Director. Res: A-2

Drake, Lone - Elementary Teacher. Res: Dorm H

Dudley, Eppie - Graduate Nurse Sr. Staff

Dunkin, Leroy - (unknown)

Dunn, Drew H. - Guard, Truck Driver. Res: Keeler

Durante, Carl E. - Draftsman

Dykes, Eldredge B. - Elementary Principal. Wife: **Mary Alice** - Secondary Teacher. Res: S-2. Eldredge replaced Clyde Simpson.

Eades, Elsie M. - Assistant Personnel Officer. Res: Lone Pine, Dow Hotel. Had worked at the Dow Hotel in Lone Pine.

Earle, Mary B. - Cost Accountant. Res: Independence

Earll, Elliott G. - Operations Analyst. Wife: **Mary Alice** - Elementary Teacher. Child: **Diane**. Res: Q-4

Ecklund, Clifford A. - Carpenter

Elder, Jean K. - Junior Staff Nurse

Ely, Helen W. - Secondary Teacher. Res: 7-2-2

Emus, Miriam - Elementary Teacher

Estaves, Edward - (unknown). Res: Lone Pine

Evans, Jeanette - Elementary Teacher

Everson, Joseph - Internal Security Officer. Retired from Los Angeles Police Dept. before employment with WRA at Manzanar. A late hire, he started in April 1945.

Fairfield, Louise - Assistant Supervisor of Student Teachers. Res: Independence

Fashbaugh, Clarence W. - Carpenter Foreman. Res: Lone Pine

Feil, Ralph D. - Electrical Engineer. Child: **Nancy Ruth**. Res: Lone Pine, G-4

Ferguson, Arthur - (unknown)

Ferguson, Charles K. - Adult Education Director. Wife: **Lois** - Elementary Teacher and Teacher Training Instructor. Res: 7-9-1. After completing his master's thesis focusing on Los Angeles Asian-American Communities, he witnessed the incarceration of those with whom he had worked. As a result, he and his wife Lois applied for work at Manzanar where he directed the adult education program until Dr. Strong arrived. Charles and Lois spent decades in supporting the lives and memories of those incarcerated in the Japanese internment camps.

Fickert, Babette - Secondary Teacher. Res: 7-2-2. Born in Red Bluff, California in 1920, Babette became an accomplished artist at a very young age. Her art career was interrupted when she went to teach at Manzanar. After the war, she continued her painting and eventually got a job making army shaded relief maps. She married Arthur E. Dowell in 1956 with whom she had one daughter, Barbara. Babette died of brain cancer in 2001.

Fien, Joseph M. - Fire Chief. Retired from Los Angeles Fire Department. Replaced Fire Chief Hon in January of 1945, and worked until camp closure.

Fietus, ? - (unknown). Children: **Rosemary** and **Peter**.

Figliola, Edward - Art Student from Bishop. Res: 1-8-? Not an employee of WRA but resided in Manzanar.

Folk, Anna C. - Supervising Nurse

Forester, Annabelle - Clerk

Forester, Kenneth J. - Mechanic

Forrest, Albert E. - Truck Driver

Forsyth, Marjorie - (unknown)

Fowler, Robert - Sr. Teacher Agriculture. Child: **Bobette**. Res: 7-10-1

Fox, Rollin C., PhD. - Junior/Senior High School Principal. Children: **Jonathan Atwell**, **Ronald Clay**, and **Virginia Lenette**. Res: N-4. B.A. from University of

Alabama, M.A. from Columbia University, Rollin was working on a PhD from UCLA when he was hired to replace Leon High as the Junior/Senior High School Principal. He had been principal at Delhi Central in New York for 15 years. Married with three children. After the high school was closed and Aksel Nielson went to Germany with UNRRA, Rollin Fox took over as the supervisor of community services until the camp closed.

Frizzell, Louis F. - Secondary Music and Drama Teacher. Res: 7-10-2, 1-9-2. Came from Eagle Rock in Southern California. Dedicated, talented, and caring teacher.

Gale, Vernard T. - Garage Mechanic. Res: 1-13-4

Garner, Pete J. - Truck Driver

Gavigan, Irene V. - Supervising Nurse. Res: Hospital

Gewehr, Richard - Butcher. Wife: **Harriett** - Clerk Stenographer. Res: 1-6-1, 1-11-4

Gilkey, John W. - Chief of Internal Security. Wife: **Mabel A.** - Telephone Operator. Child: **Robert,** born 1927, in Manzanar 1942-1945. Res: 1-11-3, T-4. Born in Idaho. Educated at San Jose State College in criminology. Worked ten years in records and night detail for the Palo Alto City Police Department. After Manzanar, worked in security for the Saudi Arabian government.

Godfrey, Albert - Art Student from Bishop. Res: 1-8-?. Not a WRA employee but lived in camp.

Goldberg, Janet - Secondary Journalism and Social Studies Teacher. Res: E-6

Golden, Margaret, L. - Secondary Science Teacher

Goodman, Howard W. - (unknown). Res: Keeler

Gratch, Libby - Elementary Teacher. Res: 7-1-3

Greenlee, Clive - Secondary English and Speech Teacher. Res: 7-10-2, E-3. A blind instructor with a seeing eye dog. I remember him well as I'm sure everyone in camp that had ever met him did. He lived alone in a tarpaper barrack, and took all of his meals at the staff mess hall. His seeing eye dog led him everywhere in camp. I used to wonder how his dog could take him to where he wanted to go when every building looked alike.

Grimsley, Ray E. - Assist. Storekeeper. Res: 1-9-4

Groth, Martha F. - Secondary Teacher. Res: 7-1-3

Groves, Lauren - (unknown)

Gunn, Helen - Parcel Post Supervisor. Res: Independence

Haberle, Henry R. - Manufacturing Superintendent. Wife: **Emmy** - Secretary of Assistant Project Director of Operations. Res: Lone Pine

Hagen, Edwin N. - Truck Driver. Res: Lone Pine

Hagen, Ernest M. - (unknown)

Haglin, Andrew - Carpenter. Res: 1-13-4

Hale, John J. - Heavy Duty Truck Driver, Assist. Storekeeper. Res: Lone Pine

Hall, William L. - Chief Steward Mess Division. Native of Kansas, raised in Livingston Montana. Prior to Manzanar spent 20 years working in camps in the Northwest and California.

Hanson, Logan - (unknown). Res: Lone Pine

Harbach, Maurice L. - Project Steward. Res: Lone Pine

218

Harbey, Charles T. - Plumber. Res: Independence

Hardick, Mathilde D. - Laboratory Technician. Res: Hospital

Harding, Florine - Elementary Teacher. Res: 7-9-3

Hardy, Bernice - Secondary Teacher

Harris, Elliott - (unknown)

Harris, Leealta L. - Jr. Clerk Typist. Res: Manzanar Airport. With housing in short supply, Leealta placed a trailer at the Manzanar Airport where she lived while employed in Manzanar.

Harrison, Lena M. - Secondary Teacher. Res: 7-1-4, Dorm I

Harth, Dorothy - Assistant Counselor of Community Welfare. Child: **Erica**. Res: Q-2. Prior to Manzanar was Director of National Travelers Aid Association in Riverside, California. Had Erica living with her in Manzanar. Left camp in 1945 for employment in San Francisco.

Hawes, Lillian Josephine - Chief Nurse. Res: Hospital. She came from the Northwest.

Hayes, Virginia A. - Secondary Social Studies and English Teacher. Children: **Lynne Ellen (Sutherland)**, born 8/13/29, in Manzanar 1942-1945 and **William Trent**, born 7/6/28, in Manzanar 1942-1945. Res: 7-11-2, L-4. A Southern California native, Virginia was married with two children. Her geologist/pilot husband was killed in a flying accident. Her first teaching job after the accident was at Manzanar. Mrs. Hayes was one of the long-term employees who stayed until the school closed. She took a teaching job at McFarland in the San Joaquin Valley to put both of her children through college. She was a dedicated teacher and mother.

Haysworkth, Bill - (unknown)

Head, Edith O. - Head Nurse Supervisor. Res: Hospital

Heath, Walter A. - Relocation Placement Officer. Wife: **Mrs. Tommie** - Statistician. Res: D-1, K-2. Walter was drafted into the army.

Henderson, Mitchell - Supv. Telephone Operator

Hesse, Myron A. - Curriculum Advisor. Res: Independence, ?

Hetzel, Illiene H. - Payroll Clerk. Res: Lone Pine

Heyer, Vern - Postal Employee. Res: I-15-?

Hicks, Lewis - First Assist. Project Director. Worked at Manzanar briefly before having a nervous breakdown.

Hill, Henry A. - Assist. Farm Superintendent. Wife: **Helen A.** - Elementary Teacher. Res: K-3

Hines, Marie - Elementary Teacher. Res: 7-1-3

High Leon C. - Secondary Teacher, Junior/Senior High School Principal. Child: **Raymond Owen.** Res: D-2. After being promoted from teacher to principal, Leon left Manzanar to take the Principal's position in the high school at Lone Pine in 1943.

Hogan, Fred - (unknown)

Hon, Frank G. - Fire Protection Officer. Res: 1-9-1, N-2. Prior to Manzanar, Hon had retired after 27 years with the Los Angeles City Fire Department. He replaced Joseph Fien in August 1942. Transferred to WRA camp at Poston,

Arizona in January 1945. After the war returned to Orange County, California. Had one daughter.

Honda, Rosio - Warehouse #28

Hooper, Arlin - Elementary Teacher. Res: 7-11-1, Dorm H

Hooper, Edwin H. - Assist. Project Dir. Administration. Wife: **Mae C.** - Secretary to Project Director. Res: A-1. Edwin was originally from Tennessee. The couple had a home in Sacramento.

Hoppers, Robert - Assist. Storekeeper. Res: 1-9-4

Horton, Kenneth - First Chief of Internal Security. Born November 2, 1909, in Bishop, California. Attended University of Nevada School of Engineering, married and had a home in Bishop. While working at Manzanar was on a leave of absence from the Bishop Police Department. Returned to Bishop in 1942.

Hosford, Lois D. - Assist. Elementary Principal. Res: 7-8-2

Howard, Chester Merle - Internal Security Officer. Res: Independence. Worked for the Border Patrol before working at Manzanar. Only worked for the WRA for about a year. Ran for Inyo County Sheriff and was elected for several terms. A man of varied interests, Howard was also a beekeeper.

Howard, Douglas - (unknown). Wife: **Alice**

Hulen, Otho - Assist. Storekeeper. Res: F-6

Humpage, Helen R. - Elementary Teacher. Res: Independence

Hunualt, Fred - Guard. Res: 7-?-?

Hunt, Frances A. - Acting Medical Social Worker

Hunter, Marion Pauline - Jr. Clerk Typist. Res: Independence. An early hire, Pauline lived with her parents in Independence. Saved enough money to put herself through nurses training. As a registered nurse, she first worked for Dr. Schultz in Lone Pine. Married Ted White, a local boy, and they lived in Morro Bay. She was the public health nurse while her husband was the mayor of Morro Bay.

Hutchison, Walter G. - Motor Pool Supervisor. Wife: **Avis F.** - Supv. Telephone Operator. Res: Independence

Ingalls, Gretchen I. - Secondary Teacher. Res: 7-3-4

Inman, Malcolm - Trades Instructor for Electrical and Refrigeration. Wife: **Harriett** - (unknown). Children: **Bruce**, born 7/11/31, in Manzanar 1945, **David**, born 11/18/36, in Manzanar 1945, and **Donald**, born 6/12/29, in Manzanar 1945. Res: Q-1. Malcolm was born near New Bedford, Massachusetts in 1906. Graduated from high school and studied electricity in a vocational school. Prior to Manzanar he worked many years in his professional field for the navy. He took a position with the WRA to train and supervise Japanese Americans in both electricity and refrigeration. Following WWII, he continued in government employment with the Bureau of Reclamation on Davis Dam in Arizona, followed by employment at the Miramar Naval Air Station in San Diego. He passed away in 1961.

James, Hazel - Secondary Teacher

Jenkins, James F. - Mechanic

Jewett, William A. - Head Guard. Res: Independence

Job, Martha J. - Elementary Teacher. Res: E-2

Johnson, Herman J. - (unknown). Res: Lone Pine

Jones, Eleanor F. - Elementary Teacher. Res: 7-2-2

Jones, George - (unknown)

Jones, Kenny M. - (unknown)

Jullien, Leon C. - Assist. Storekeeper. Res: Lone Pine

Kane, Walter E. - (unknown)

Kellesvig, Thelma M. - Secondary Teacher, Assist. Relocation Advisor. Res: R-2

Kendall, Murray - Internal Security Officer. Had been a Sec. Lt. in the Military Police prior to employment with WRA at Manzanar.

Kennedy, Geraldine L. - Telephone Operator

Kennedy, Henry P. - Carpenter. Res: 1-13-4

Kess, Bernard - Secondary Teacher. Res: 7-10-3

Killian, Don - Art Student from Bishop. Res: 1-8-?. Not a WRA employee, but resided in Manzanar.

Kincaid, Mary S. - Elementary Teacher. Children: **Beth, Mary Maude**, and **Wayne**. Res: 7-8-6

King, Herbert F. - (unknown)

Kinney, Betty - Jr. Clerk Typist. Res: Lone Pine

Kirrer, Alma M. - Jr. Clerk Typist. Res: Independence

Knipp, Carrie V. - Sr. Elementary Teacher. Res: Dorm J-4

Koelker, John - (unknown). Res: 1-13-3

Kramer, Mary Jean - Secondary Latin Teacher. Res: Independence, J-18. Mary Jean was the youngest teacher at Manzanar High School.

Krueger, Robert B. - Relocation Advisor. Res: D-1. While employed by the WRA, Robert married Martha Davis in Reno, Nevada on April 28, 1945.

Lamphere, Arthur R. - Secondary Teacher. Res: 7-10-3

Lane, ? - (unknown). Children: **Dorothy Linda** and **Martha Carolyn**

Lankow, Arnold Andrew - Secondary Teacher. Res: 7-3-2

Lawing, Jewel W. - Chief Construction Foreman. Wife: **Ann Janette** - Teletype Operator. Res: Independence. A contractor in Little Rock Arkansas, Lawing moved to California at the beginning of the war. He worked for Hughes Aircraft in laminations on the wooden flying boat. The Corp of Engineers asked him to work for the WRA constructing the auditorium. He had construction experience building large buildings.

Leach, Elva M. - Jr. Clerk Typist. Res: Independence

Lee, James J. - (unknown). Res: 1-13-2

Leibovitz, Margaret - Assist. Auditor. Res: Dorm J-10

Lewis, Lucile W. - Elementary Teacher. Res: 7-9-3

Lipsom, Ralph A. - Senior Storekeeper. Child: one son, name unknown.

Little, William Morse, MD - Principal Medical Officer. Wife: **Christine G.** - Senior Staff Nurse. Children: **Richard** and **Raymond**. Res: Hospital. Dr. Morse and his wife, a registered nurse, arrived from the Reno, Nevada area in October 1942. He replaced Dr. Goto as head of the hospital in early 1943. Stayed on until July 1945, when he and his wife and two children returned to Nevada.

Lockridge, Frank - Internal Security Officer. Children: Three school age children, names unknown. Res: Manzanar staff area. Came to work late in the camp's life. Married.

Logan, Max C. - Guard. Res: E-5

Lorenzino, Paul - Sr. Adm. Assistant. Res: Lone Pine

Lowry, John E. - Property Officer. Wife: **Leonore A.** - Junior Staff Nurse. Res: V-2

Lucey, Ed - (unknown)

Lutton, Mary L. - Elementary Teacher

Lutzow, Van C. - Concrete Pipe Layer. Res: Independence

Lutzow, Wilbur F. - Head Guard, Internal Security. Children: Two daughters, names unknown. Res: Independence. A local hire from Independence. Married. Drafted by the army during the early part of the war.

MacKey, Ernest - (unknown)

MacNair, James L. - Mileage Administrator, Supt. Equipment & Maintenance. Res: E-1, C-3

MacPherson, Harold J. - Mechanic Helper

Madrid, Jesus C. - Mechanic Helper

Maier, Paul K. - Medical Officer. Wife: **Sylvia F.** - Statistical Clerk. Res: M-3

Maillet, Arthur J. - Truck Driver. Res: Lone Pine

Mann, Howard - Procurement Officer

Marsh, Maule W. - Truck Driver. Res: Lone Pine

Mason, Fred L. - Plumber. Res: Independence

McCallum, Lester R. - Property & Warehouse Officer. Res: Lone Pine

McConnell, Horace R. - Chief of Agriculture. Wife: **Helena** - File Clerk. Res: A-4. They left Manzanar for Simi Valley, California.

McCullough, Frank - Truck Driver. Res: Lone Pine

McFarland, Ellen - Elementary Teacher. Res: 7-9-3

McGavern, Sanford - Apprentice Teacher. Wife: **Wilhelmina** - Secondary Teacher. Child: **Joanne Carol**. Res: 7-9-6

McLaughlin, John D. - Truck Driver. Wife: **Florence** - Clerk Stenographer. Res: D-?. Prior to WWII, Florence spent a year in Japan. With the help of a private tutor, she became fluent in Japanese.

McMurray, ? - Art Student from Bishop. Res: 1-8-? Not a WRA employee but resided in camp.

McPhee, G.B. - Post Master, (USPS–not WRA)

Meacham, Charles H. - Art Student from Bishop. Res: 1-8-? Not a WRA employee but resided in camp.

Merritt, C. - Senior Staff Nurse.

Merritt, Ralph P., Jr. - Audit Clerk. Res: O-3

Merritt, Ralph P., Sr. - Project Director. Res: D-5, G-1 & 2

Mertens, George - Guard

Miller, Arthur H. - Assist. Personnel Officer

Miller, Arthur M. - Sr. Employment Officer. Res: Lone Pine. A native of Vermont, educated at Union College 1909, Columbia University 1911 followed by Army service where he rose to the rank of major and spent two years on the War Planning

Board. He next served in public relations with the New York Edison Co. He was an author of two books. *Leadership* published in 1920 was adopted officially by the War Department and a copy placed in every ship's library by the navy. His second book was titled *Management and Men*. Before Manzanar he supervised the building of several hospitals. He was married and had one son, Anthony. His home was in Pasadena, California. He was an extremely popular WRA employee with the Japanese Americans

Miller, Bernice E. - Secondary Teacher

Miller, Harriett A. - Elementary Teacher. Res: Dorm I-6

Miller, Marshall M. - Elementary Principal. Child: **Cecile (Gordon),** born 11/9/37, in Manzanar 8/42 to 10/42. Born in Sevastopol, California in 1911. Graduate of Chico State, attended University of California. One of the very first to brave public pressure and take a teaching job in the camp. Was soon recognized as principal material and promoted. Took flying lessons from the Ross Aeronautical School at Manzanar. Was killed on takeoff along with his flight instructor James Brennan at the Bishop Airport. In observance of the loss, the elementary school was closed for three days. He was very popular with both internees and staff in camp. His wife and young daughter left the camp soon after the accident.

Milligan, Clarence C. - (unknown). Res: Lone Pine

Milligan, Clarence W. - (unknown). Res: Lone Pine

Mitschke, William J. - Junior Counselor. Res: D-4

Mizner, Delbert L. - Evacuee Escort. Res: U-2

Moen, Gladys R. - Secondary Teacher. Res: 7-2-3

Moon, Laurabelle - Under Mail Clerk. Res: Lone Pine

Moore, Adele L. - Assistant Superintendent Children's Village. Res: C.V.2

Morgan, Alfred D. - Guard. Res: Lone Pine

Morgan, Charles - (unknown). Came from Oregon.

Morgan, Virgil M. - Supervising Teacher, Assist. Procurement Officer. Wife: **Janey.** Children: Three children names unknown. Res: R-1

Morgan, (unsure who the parents of these Morgan children are) **Benjamin Mac, Catherine Elice, Enid, Roberta,** and **Yvonne**

Morhardt, Joseph E. - Relocation Interviewer (temporary)

Most, Lillian R. - Secondary Teacher. Res: 7-9-4

Moxley, Elizabeth M. - Head Teacher. Res: 7-8-5, H-20

Muir, Arthur J. - Cost Accountant

Munier, Lester - Postal Employee. Res: I-15-?

Murphy, Clifford H. - Assist. Relocation Advisor. Wife: **Elizabeth H.** - Junior Counselor. Child: **Susan.** Res: S-4

Murray, Dee - (unknown)

Nail, Donald H. - Res: Commander of MPs at Manzanar—not WRA. Wife: **Elizabeth C. N.** - Secondary School Typing Teacher. Children: **Sue (Hansen)** - Student Education Assistant, Auditor, born 4/11/26, **Donald Horace,** born 2/8/30, **Pat Carle.** All Nail children were in Manzanar 1944-1945. Res: V-1. Capt. Donald Nail was the highest ranking officer of the Military Police in Manzanar. Elizabeth earned her M.A. from the University of Texas. She assumed head librarian position after school closed.

Neal, Edson - Truck Driver

Nettles Beatrice - Office Services Manager. Res: R-2

Newhouse, Wren - Carpenter. Res: Lone Pine

Nicolaus, Anita L. - Sr. Elementary Teacher. Res: 7-1-3, C-2

Nielsen, Aksel G. - Community Activities Supervisor. Wife: **Melva** - Music Teacher. Res: C-2. Started work April 8, 1942, with the WCCA as head of recreation. One of the few to be hired by the WRA during their takeover. He worked until June 1945 when the school closed. Took a job with UNRRA in Germany as assistant director.

Norton, Herbert E. - Cost Accountant. Res: O-2

Nowell, Willis L. - Assist. Fire Protection Officer. Res: N-3. While working at Manzanar, Willis's two sons were in the military, one fighting in the Pacific.

O'Brien Marjorie P. - Cost Accounting Clerk

Oliver, Dan R. - Foreman Agriculture. Res: Lone Pine

Oliver, Wanda RN - Chief Nurse. Res: Hospital

Olson, Gustave - (unknown)

Olson, Leslie - Assist. Sanitation Engineer. Res: 7-8-?

Oltmans, Sarah C. - Head Teacher. Res: 1-7-?, Dorm I-7. Before WWII it was unheard of to find a Caucasian who was fluent in Japanese, but Sarah had taught in Japan and was fluent. One of the stories told by Hank Umemoto in his book *Manzanar War Relocation* tells that Sarah taught English at Manzanar High School, and was both demanding and strict. A couple of the boys in class were calling her a "Baa-san (old hag) and making other nasty remarks in Japanese. Without a response, Sarah shifted immediately to giving the class instructions in fluent Japanese. You could hear a pin drop. Sarah later would take a position with UNRRA in Syria.

Opler, Catherine H. - Assist. Clerk Steno. Statistics

Opler, Morris E. Dr. - Community Social Science Analyst. Res: 1-12-2. A graduate anthropologist from Cornell University who came to Manzanar from the University of California at Berkeley to conduct social science studies on the impact of the evacuation on the Japanese American. He became the best source of information on prewar/wartime Japanese-American communities and evacuation experiences covering those at Manzanar. He routinely reported his finding to both the University of California at Berkeley and to the WRA office in Washington D.C. His ability to work with the project director and some Japanese Americans fell short of his research. He would leave Manzanar on November 16, 1944, to report to Washington D.C. and the Office of War Information.

Palisano, Dolores - Jr. Clerk Typist. Res: Lone Pine

Paulson, Albert - (unknown). Res: Lone Pine

Pearlson, Gladys - Assist. Personnel Officer. Res: Dorm I-4

Peters, J.B. - Finance Chief

Pierson, Elizabeth - Elementary Teacher. Child: **William Raymond**

Plumb, Vanche - Elementary Teacher. Res: Dorm J-2

Polson, Clarence E. - Carpenter. Res: 1-13-4

Poole, Lee C. - Business Enterprise Superintendent. Child: **Gary Dean.** Res: F-3 & 4. I remember Lee for he lived in a bachelor's apartment and had a football. It was the only football available to the staff boys. If he saw us he would come out to play catch. When we were invited to play against a much larger, older group of evacuee boys, we called on him to play for us teenage boys. He was the team. Built like a football player he carried the ball on almost every play. Lee was a native of Arkansas, born March 15, 1914, and a graduate of the University of California at Berkeley in the class of 1938 with a degree in economics. His job was head of community enterprises, the "enterprise" in question being the commissary owned by the evacuees. He reported directly to Project Director Roy Nash and to Larry Collins who directed enterprises in all ten camps. He took a job with UNRRA in the Balkans.

Potts, Marion - Head Teacher, Assist. High School Principal. Res: 7-1-4, 7-8-3. Marion spoke fluent Japanese.

Prentice, Earl A. - Project Steward. Res: Lone Pine

Price, Glenn - Truck Driver

Price, Marcia - Elementary Teacher

Prichett, Cecil F. - Junior Counselor. Child: **John.** Res: V-4

Proff, Joseph F. - Procurement Officer. Children: **Charles, Diane,** and **Joseph.** Res: F-5 & 6

Proff, Melville - Sr. Telephone Operator

Pusey, Harriett C. - Guidance Counselor. Res: 7-1-2. Graduate of Brea College in Kentucky.

Quarnstrom, Dagmar K. - Supervising Nurse. Res: Hospital

Racely, Wilbur A. - Utility Oper. Superintendent. Res: E-1

Ramberg, Jean M. - Ass't Counselor. Res: Independence

Raper, Frank C. - Mechanic

Rasmus, Evelyn M. - Elementary Teacher. Res: 7-1-2

Rasmussen Harry E. - Chief Garage Foreman. Child: **William**

Rau, Dorothy F. - Secondary Teacher. Res: 7-3-4

Reynolds, Chester C. - Mechanic

Riggs, Buck D. - Foreman Mechanic. Res: M-2

Riley, Goldie M. - Telephone Operator. Res: Independence

Ritch Mary P. - Typist

Ritch Russell R. - Typist

Ritchie, J. Lincoln - Acting Relocation Advisor. Res: Q-3. Had managed the Dow Hotel in Lone Pine prior to working for the WRA at Manzanar. Left Manzanar to manage a resort at Lake Tahoe.

Robbins, Eva M. - Superintendent of Children's Village. Res: C V 1

Robinson, Margaret D. - Jr. Clerk Typist

Rock, Jesse J. - Electrician. Res: E-2

Roe, Harry C. - (unknown)

Rogers, Harold - Secondary Teacher. Res: D-2. Taught French and Spanish in his mid-twenties and had served in the U.S. Navy. A gifted person who could speak twenty different languages including Japanese. After the camp closed, he went to Japan, married a Japanese girl, had a family and never returned to the USA.

Ronnquist, John A. - Carpenter. Res: 1-13-3

Rude, Bertha M. - Secondary Teacher. Res: Dorm H-7. Married a student pilot while he was training at the Manzanar airport.

Saks, Jay Benson - Attorney. Earned his AB PhD from John Hopkins, and his LLB from University of Maryland. Replaced Throckmorton. Had formally worked for the Department of Justice.

Salsbury, Albert E. - Personnel Transactions Officer

Sampson, ? - (unknown). Child: **Harold**

Sandridge, Arthur M. - Senior Engineer. Wife: **Violet**. Child: **Arthur Milton**. Res: A-2, C-4

Sandridge, Gladys R. - Elementary Teacher. Extremely effective third grade teacher. Each year students were tested and several students from her class were able to skip a grade.

Sanger, Roland J. - Assist. Fiscal Accountant. Children: **Nina Elizabeth** and **Roland Wayne.** Res: 1-10-1, P-1

Schaffer, Meyer - (unknown)

Schauland, Mary Ann - Supv. Student Teachers. Res: Lone Pine

Schmidt, Willard - Chief Internal Security. Res: D-?. Employed for eighteen years active duty with the Berkeley City Police Department where he worked his way up to sergeant. Moved to Assistant Director Training School in San Jose where he met John Gilkey. He headed the Sacramento City College criminology department. Moved to Manzanar where he worked for a few months before being promoted to position in charge of internal security for all camps. His office was in Washington D.C. Later, he took over the police chief's position at Tule Lake following all the violence there.

Schwartz, Joseph - Assist. Storekeeper. Res: 1-9-4

Schweisinger, Gladys C. - Adult Education Supervisor. Res: Dorm I-2

Scroggins, Helen M. - Jr. Clerk Typist. Res: Independence

Shellenberg, Eva M. - Jr. Steno Clerk. Res: Independence

Shelton, ? - (unknown) Children: **Betsy,** and **Joseph**

Shepherdson, Justus F. - Sr. Foreman Carpenter. Res: 1-9-3

Shilber, Bernice - Medical Social Worker. Bernice retired from Manzanar to take care of her husband who was wounded in action.

Shoaf, Martha Lee - Fourth Grade Teacher. Res: 7-3-4, Dorm H. Born June 28, 1919, in Los Angeles, California. Graduated from Eagle Rock High School and in 1942 got her BA from UCLA. A friend was going to Manzanar to teach, so Martha went back to UCLA and got her teaching credential. She arrived at Manzanar February 3, 1943. She was paid $1,620 per year to work twelve months out of the year. One day while hitchhiking (she had no car and there were no buses) she was picked up by the Supt. of Schools in Trona, California and offered a job at $2,300 for only nine months of work per year. She loved Manzanar, but said goodbye in August 1944 and taught at Trona until 1948. She spent years teaching in foreign countries including Austria, Germany, France, and Japan. She returned to

Trona and taught until her retirement in 1983. She later became a docent for the Ridgecrest museum and Manzanar. She passed away in 2012.

Shoaf, Susan - Secretary. Res: Dorm H

Showalter, Charles G. - Carpenter Foreman. Res:

Shultz, Fred T. - (unknown). Res: Independence

Silber, Bernice G. - Medical Social Supervisor. Res: Hospital

Silverthorne, Kent - Act. Proj. Attorney. Res:

Simpson, Clyde Lindsay - Elementary Principal. Wife: **Ruth D.** - Senior Staff Nurse. Children: **Enid, Mamelle** and **James L.** Res: 7-10-4, Independence, and O-1. Clyde left camp for a job with UNRRA.

Sisler, Oliver E. - Construction & Maintenance Superintendent. Res: W-4. Born December 19, 1891, in California. Grew up in the Fresno area. Built homes in the Three Rivers area of the San Joaquin Valley. Worked for the National Park Service supervising construction of CCC camps in Sequoia National Park. In October 1942, accepted employment with the WRA. Supervised the construction of the auditorium and all staff housing following Phase I. Left Manzanar February 15, 1946, and returned to employment with the National Park Service. Passed away November 5, 1973. Daughter Patricia Britten worked at Manzanar also, driving relocating evacuees to Reno.

Sleath, Jack C., MD Acting Medical Director. Res: Hospital

Smeltzer, Ralph E. - Secondary Math Teacher. Wife: **Mary E.** - Secondary Teacher. Res: 19-14-?. He was a conscientious objector. He and his wife Mary went to Chicago and set up a hostel for relocating Japanese Americans.

Smith, Anna Lucile - Secondary Teacher. Res: 7-1-3, J-8

Smith, James H. - Secondary Teacher. Res: W-2

Smith, Marion H. - Sr. Clerk. Res: Lone Pine

Smith, Phyllis - Elementary Teacher

Soloman, Roberta - (unknown – education)

Solomon, Robert B. - Junior Counselor. Child: **Arthur**. Res: Q-1

Soltwedell, Margaret G. - Secondary Teacher. Res: Dorm H-8. Margaret's husband was an MIA with the army.

Southey, Bill - (unknown). Res: Independence

Southey, Louise - Postal employee (USPS – not WRA). Res: Independence. Married to WWII pilot.

Steele, Tillie - Jr. Clerk Typist. Res: Independence

Stengel, Robert - Postal employee (USPS – not WRA).

Stevens, Walter - (unknown). Res: 1-13-2

Stiegelmeir, Fred A. - Buildings & Grounds Supt.

Stingley, David D. - Hospital Administrator. Res: R-3

Stokes, Elmer - (unknown)

Strong, Dr. W. Melvin - School Curriculum Advisor. Children: **LaPriel (Bush)**, born 3/22/30, **Norma Marie (Larsen)**, born 7/15/42, **Ralph LaVal**, and **Ruth Juanita (Jones)**, born 11/1/35. All Strong children were in Manzanar 1943-1944, except for Ralph who visited Manzanar in the summers. Res: 7-9-1, K-1

Stump, Mabelle L. - Secondary Teacher. Res: Independence

Sullivan, James C. - Unknown

Summers, Charles F. - Truck Driver, Labor Foreman. Res: 1-9-3

Tatum, Louise - Jr. Clerk Typist (summer hire). Res: Independence

Taylor, Rita - Elementary Teacher

Temple, Thomas M. - Chief of Community Services. Born November 3, 1890, in Toledo, Ohio. His educational background included University of Chicago graduate school, Oxford, and the Sorbonne. His Quaker background, long experience in working with others, and a personality that refused to be ruffled served him well.

Templet, Edith C. - Elementary Teacher

Thomas, Eleanor P. - Sr. Secondary Teacher. Res: 7-9-4, Lone Pine

Thompson, Burr N. - Foreman Plumbing. Children: **Mary Louise** and **Nancy Barbara**. Res: U-1

Thompson, George - Carpenter Foreman. Res: Lone Pine

Thorne, Herbert - Assist. Construction Supt. Res: A-3

Throckmorton, Robert - Project Attorney. Wife: **Frances** - Senior File Clerk. Cal Berkeley grad. Child: Bobbie Gail, born 4/1/43 in Manzanar hospital. Res: C-4. He left Manzanar and took a commission as ensign in the U.S. Navy on 8/1/43.

Theusen, Lewis K. - Sr. Admin. Assistant. Child: Name unknown. Res: E-5

Umhey , Oma Spivy - Secondary English Teacher. Child: **Harold Spivy Dennis**, born 10/8/30, in Manzanar 1943-1944. Res: 1-12-4, P-3

Vanderjagt, Peter - Secondary Teacher. Res: 7-10-3

Van Dussen, Leonard E. - Guard

Van Zandt, Marion L. - Elementary Teacher. Res: V-3

Vaughn, Irene - Children's Village. Res: C V 1

Vaughn, Irene B. - Elementary Teacher. Res: Dorm I-3

Vierra, Glen - Truck Driver. Res: Independence

Waggoner, Oscar F. - Art Teacher. Res: Dorm I-3

Warren, Henry S. - Engineer. Res: Independence. In a shocking incident, Henry was killed in an automobile accident near Taft, California, in 1945.

Weber, George R. - Fiscal Accountant. Res: Cartago

Weil, Esther L. - Secretary. Res: H-4

Wellck, Florance L. - Secretary

Wells, Harry B. - Secondary Teacher. Wife: **Shirley** - Head Nurse Supervisor. Res: 7-9-5

Wentner, Lyle - Assist. Project Director. Replaced Lucy Adams and worked until the camp was closed.

Wentworth, K.L. Dr. - Director of Adult Education. Wife: **Dolores**. Prior to Manzanar, Wentworth was Elementary Principal in Albuquerque New Mexico.

Wetzel, Gertrude - Chief Nurse. Res: Hospital. Transferred to Washington D.C.

Wheeler, Helen Winifred - Dir. Adult Education. Res: 7-11-1

Whitaker, Mildred C. - Elementary Teacher. Res: Dorm H-9

White, Beatrice H. - Head Teacher. Husband: **Dennis**. Res: 7-1-4, Independence

White, Thomas C. - Property & Warehouse Officer. Child: **Dennis**. Res: F-4

Williams, Arthur Loren - Assist. Chief Internal Security. Wife: **Mary M.** - Chief Dietitian. Children: **Arthur Loren Jr.**, born 9/8/28, **Thomas Dana**, born

10/8/38, both in Manzanar 1943-1945. Res: Independence, D-5. Born in Whittier, California, Arthur served in the marines in Asia. Educated in criminology at UCLA. Worked thirteen years for the Redondo Beach Police Department. Was that city's first traffic control officer. Worked for both WCCA and WRA. He left the WRA at Manzanar in early 1945, bought the Independence Hotel and managed it for just over a year. He sold the business and worked for the California State Liquor Quality Control Board in Santa Barbara. In 1950, he was promoted to the head of the State Liquor Quality Control Board for Ventura County. He worked there until his retirement. Mary was born in Cripple Creek, Colorado. Her father had a saw mill and supplied lumber to the city and the mines. She graduated from Central High School in Pueblo, Colorado followed by the finest dietetics college in the country at the time, in Battle Creek, Michigan. She worked at the veteran's hospital in Santa Monica prior to Manzanar. After Manzanar she was one of three food administrators for the State of California. She went into private practice serving as the state registered dietitian for several medical institutions.
Williams, Lillian R. - Elementary Teacher. Res: 7-2-2
Williamson, Marion F. - Secondary Teacher. Res: Dorm H-1
Willis, Nowell L. - Assist. Fire Protection Officer
Willson, Wally - (unknown). Res: Lone Pine
Wilson, Burney O. - Sr. Procurement Officer. Res: Lone Pine. Born in 1895, he worked before Manzanar for the Klamath Indian Reservation.
Wilson, Ella S. - Telephone Operator
Wilson, Herbert E. - Carpenter. Res: 1-13-1
Wilson, Joe A. - Carpenter. Res: Lone Pine
Winchester, Joseph - Chief Project Steward. Wife: **Nova** - Steno Clerk. Child: **Martin Rudd**. Res: Lone Pine. Joseph was one of the very first arrivals with the WCCA. One of the few offered a job with the WRA after the switch, he stayed until the camp closed in 1945. Joe and Nova married in Lone Pine. Leaving the wedding, they jumped in his car with tin cans dragging and everyone cheering. Shortly, they came back into town. Nova's dress was covered in blood and she had a broken nose. It seems wild horses ran out in front of the car and to save his brand new bride, Joseph threw himself across her to protect her but broke her nose in the process. He recovered control of the car, missed the horses, and returned with his bride. On July 4, 1945, Mrs. Winchester gave birth to a son, Martin. We know the family moved after the camp closed to Fresno for we found their son had graduated from McLane High School in 1963.
Wodeage, Bertha - Instructor: Junior College English 1a, 1b
Wood, W. Reginald U. - Internal Security Officer. Wife: **Mary P.** - Assist. Clerk Steno. Statistics. Children: **Joan** and two whose names are unknown. Res: Historic Commodores House, Independence. Reginald was born in Baltimore Maryland January 13, 1910. Attended John Hopkins University studying pre law. Went to work for the FBI. Moved to California working as a special investigator for the Los Angeles district attorney. Went to work for the WRA at Manzanar June 1, 1942. Lived in the historic Commodores House in Independence. About the time of the segregation, he transferred to Tule Lake Internal Security where he and

his family lived in camp housing until fire destroyed their apartment. The family escaped without injuries. At the same time he was working for the WRA, he opened a grocery store in Tule Lake. He worked at several different jobs in San Diego and Orange County after the war, one of which was travel agent for the navy and marines in the San Diego area. Mary, born in England, had a PhD in English. Daughter Joan was born in Manzanar Hospital.

Woodall, Blanche K. - Assist. Chief Nurse. Res: Hospital

Woods, Velma - Secondary Music Teacher. Children: **Karen** and **John**. Res: E-2

Woods, Velma E., Dr. - Assist. Statistician. Res: Dorm J-9. Velma came directly from the University of California, Berkeley where she had received a Doctorate degree in Education. She spent many years training and teaching as a psychologist including two years at the University of Hawaii. She was the secretary in the education department.

Yandell, Elsie L. - Typist Clerk

Yarbrough, Frank W. - (unknown). Res: 1-13-1

Yeager, Helen - Jr. Clerk Typist. Res: Lone Pine

Zimmerman, Chloe A. - Secondary Teacher. Res: 7-9-2, 7-8-7

Zischank, Nancy C. - Sr. Evacuee Escort. Res: Hospital, D-4, L-3. Nancy lived in the camp and was our neighbor for a few years. She was married working for the WRA while her husband was in the service. They owned a cabin at McGee Creek where they planned to open a ski resort after the war. She drove evacuees from Manzanar to Reno, Nevada to put them on a train going east for relocation. She did this for years. After the war she and her husband resided in the Bishop area.

APPENDIX #4
WRA SALARIES

Project Director	6,500
Statistician	3,200
Assist. Project Director	5,600
Sanitation Engineer	3,200
Principal Medical Officer	5,600
Design Engineer	3,200
Attorney	4,600
Equipment Maintenance Superv.	3,200
Relocation Program Officer	4,600
Assist. Procurement Officer	3,200
Senior Medical Officer	4,600
Assist. Fiscal Accountant	3,200
Supt. of Education	4,600
Auditor	3,200
Senior Engineer	4,600
Leave Officer	2,600
Finance Officer	4,600
Assist. Auditor	2,600
Personnel Officer	4,600
Internal Security Officer	2,600
Assist. Relocation Program Officer	3,800
Medical Social Worker	2,600
Chief of Internal Security	3,800

Dietitian	2,600
Medical Officer	3,800
Chief Nurse	2,600
Jr. Sr. High School Principal	3,800
Vocational Advisor	2,600
Counselor	3,800
Supervisor Student Teachers	2,600
Community Analyst	3,800
Head Teacher	2,600
Farm Superintendent	3,800
Chief Construction Foreman	2,600
Const. & Maintenance Supt.	3,800
Motor Pool Supervisor	2,600
Fire Protection Officer	3,800
Jr. Cost Accountant	2,600
Procurement Officer	3,800
Carpenter Foreman	2,200
Chief Project Steward (mess halls)	3,800
Assist. Storekeeper	2,000
Fiscal Accountant	3,800
Acting Leave Officer	2,000
Assist. Personnel Officer	3,800
Supervising Nurse	2,000
Evacuee Property Officer	3,800
Secondary School Teacher	2,000
Electrical Engineer	3,300
Sr. Elementary School Teacher	2,000
Relocation Advisor	3,200
Sr. Clerk	2,000
Assist. Chief Internal Security	3,200
Fiscal Accounting Clerk	2,000
Hospital Administrator	3,200
File Clerk	1,800
Night School Director	3,200

Senior Staff Nurse	1,800
Assist. Jr. Sr. High School Principal	3,200
Security Guard	1,680
Assist. Counselor	3,200
Secretaries	1,620 to 2,100
Elementary School Principal	3,200
Elementary School Teacher	1,620

APPENDIX # 5
ORIGINAL RIOT REPORT OF
ARTHUR L. WILLIAMS, SR.

The following is the complete, word for word police report as it was typed up following the Manzanar Riot. This report was submitted by my father, Assistant Chief Arthur L. Williams, Sr., Internal Security for Manzanar. My father had been in the marines and had served in the Far East, experiencing mobs several times in China. He stated after the Manzanar riot that these earlier experiences were invaluable for what was to come the night of December 6, 1942. This report of the riot as it occurred that night has been in our family files for over seventy years now.

MANZANAR, CALIFORNIA

> *December 6, 1942*
> *SUBJECT: Riot*
> *The following is a brief outline of the rioting which occurred on my shift, the night of December 6, 1942.*
> *6:20 p.m; Received a telephone call from Dr. Goto at the hospital, stating that a mob was marching on the hospital from block #22. The doctor said there were approximately two thousand men in this gang, so the doctor's informant told him. He said they were coming after Fred Tayama. He asked for protection, adding that Fred Tayama was in Ward number 3.*
> *6:25 p.m; I called Mr. Merritt and explained the situation. He asked me to telephone the M.P. barracks*
> *and ask them for an escort to meet the hospital ambulance at the rear of the hospital. He requested that they take a a circuitous route.*
> *6:28 p.m; I immediately advised Mr. Merritt of the results of my call to Lt. Kunkler.*
> *6:30 p.m; Dr. Goto called and said the gang was approaching; help was badly needed. I told him the army ambulance would pick Tayama up at the back of the hospital.*

6:31 p.m; I again called and was told by the sergeant answering the telephone at the army barracks that the ambulance was leaving.
I immediately called the hospital and gave a nurse this information.
6:35 p.m; Dr. Little telephoned and requested help; he stated the mob was there. I told him the army should arrive any minute.
6:40 p.m; I called Mr. Merritt.
6:45 p.m; Jack Shimatsu, 14-6-2, a Japanese policeman in the station he stated, that his father had attended the meeting in block #22. He said that a mob of about two thousand was coming to the station to kill all the police. He said they blamed all the police for the arrests which have been made.
6:47 p.m; I called Capt. Hall and requested him to send a guard to protect the police station. He stated that he would do so immediately.
6:50 p.m; The mob could be heard approaching; they were cheering and shouting in Japanese as they reached the police station. They came in the side door and front door at almost the same instant that they came in the Chief's office where I was. I went to the front office of the station and when I returned, someone had given them the keys to the jail. It also was filled with men. The sentry on the main gate fired three shots, evidently for help. I met the same men who had served on the committee representing the mob earlier in the day; with them I walked to the front office. They darted this way and that, speaking in Japanese to the rioters who were in the police station. They cleared the interior of the station of nearly everyone but the committee. However, the hallway leading from the side door into the jail was filled with men. I could see them in the jail and hear them loudly talking. They demanded that I release Harry Ueno, 22-3-4, who was being held in jail on a charge of attack with a deadly weapon. I told them I had no authority to do so, but it looked as though they had taken matters into their own hands. The spokesman of the committee then told me that they didn't intend to take Ueno that way. If I couldn't do it, they wanted to see Mr. Merritt; in fact, they wanted to see him anyway. I tried to explain to them the magnitude of the action they had taken. I pointed out to them that someone probably would be killed, or at least wounded, unless they disbanded and returned to their homes.. He replied, "We don't care if we are killed; we are ready to die:. I reminded him that he had promised Mr. Merritt, Capt. Hall and Chief Gilkey in the afternoon that there would not be another illegal demonstration like the one which had occurred earlier that afternoon. He said that during the meeting held in block #22 he and the others had talked to the crowds which had gathered, and the crowd had insisted on coming to the police station and securing the release of Ueno. He said, "I no longer have any control over them." Two or three times he walked out the front door and said something to the mass of people assembled; he spoke in Japanese. About five or ten minutes after

the sentry had fired the first three shots, he fired the same number of shots again. The committee insisted that I call Mr. Merritt, which I did. He asked what they wanted. I explained that they demanded the release of Ueno, and that they wanted to see him. He asked, "How does it look?" I replied, "Very bad". Mr. Merritt said, "Call Capt. Hall and ask him to take command; if necessary declare martial law. The committee will have to do their negotiating with Capt. Hall; they have failed to keep their promise to me." I turned from the telephone and told the group that Mr. Merritt was not at home and that we would have to wait a short while. I called Capt. Hall and explained Mr. Merritt's request to him. I attempted to return from the front office to the adjoining rear office, but was prevented from doing so; I found the door had been locked from the opposite side. How many people had entered this rear office through the side door I had no way of telling. After the riot, we learned that all of the criminal fingerprint cards had been stolen. Also my gloves and pipe were gone.

Shortly thereafter, the first detachment of soldiers arrived, under command of Lieut. Zwaik. They immediately cleared the front of the station, but upon my request they permitted the committee to remain in the front office with five of my Japanese policemen. Three of the policemen had come for protection; the other two had remained on duty in the office. Lieut. Zwaik and his men had considerable difficulty in forcing the mob back even with the west side of the police station. However, this was done without any bloodshed.

Mr. Campbell called at about the same time the soldiers arrived. I explained the exigency to Mr. Campbell, the Asst. Project Director.

Capt. Hall arrived soon after; more soldiers came on the scene. Capt. Hall entered the police station and immediately went into conference with the mob's committee. They talked for approximately thirty minutes. The Captain made an honest effort to come to a peaceful understanding. When all efforts in this direction apparently failed with the committee, the Captain went outside, walked past the first line of his soldiers, and while between his men and the gang of Japanese rioters, he asked them in a clear, calm voice, so that all could hear, to return to their homes. His talk was met by several Japanese throwing large stones. I don't know who their target was, but the stones narrowly missed Capt. Hall and fell among his soldiers.

The command was given to use the tear gas, but the rioters still stood their ground. I heard the command, "Gas", but I didn't see any Japanese walk away. Shortly after this command about four or five tear gas bombs were shot into the crowd. The wind was blowing from the north to the south, and since most of the rioters were assembled north of where the gas bombs fell, the majority of them could have suffered no ill effects. Because of the smoke it was difficult to see for a few moments what the reaction was. However, as it blew away I saw three men lying on the ground. They quickly got up, though, and ran with everyone else either to the west or north.

I must go back far enough in my report to state that before Capt. Hall and the rioters' representatives had completed their conference, the mob sang many Japanese songs and shoutly [sic] loudly in Japanese.

I walked back about halfway to the sentry box which is on the main gate. From this point I heard a crash and saw a car strike the northeast corner of the police station. A moment later I heard a machine gun fire approximately seven or eight times. This machine gun seemed to be located very near where the automobile had struck the building. The automobile, after striking the police station, seemed to gain speed again and travelled the entire length of the police station on the east side and struck an army truck lent to the W.R.A., which was parked on the southeast side of said building.

The Japanese rioters were in the dark or disappearing into the interior of the Center, but I could clearly hear them cursing the soldiers. They were still loudly shouting in Japanese, too. I entered the sentry box at the main gate to get warm. I remained at this point for approximately forty-five minutes, then left for home.

Respectfully submitted;

Arthur L. Williams

Asst. Chief, Internal Security,

War Relocation Authority,

Manzanar, California.

In my father's riot report there is no mention of casualties. I find this to be an unusual omission for my father had years of experience in investigative reporting. I can only speculate why he did not report on this aspect of the riot. He also stated at the beginning of his report that it was a "brief outline" and that also is unusual for him, for he had a tendency to be extremely thorough.

I have no way to verify the cause of the omissions in his report, but I have some speculations.

Since the Army MPs had shot into the rioters there was going to be an investigation and Capt. Hall probably preferred there be only one report covering injuries and deaths.

Ralph Merritt, Project Director was also sensitive to casualties and might have asked my father to leave that portion of the riot out until there was more detailed information from the hospital.

Immediately following the shooting, my father was behind the MPs and he probably did not want to step between the MPs and rioters to check casualties.

The rioters were fleeing the scene during and after the shooting and it was no doubt not a safe time to try to follow them into the darkness to check casualties.

APPENDIX #6
MILITARY PERSONNEL AT MANZANAR

Although incomplete, this list may yet offer information to some searching for a particular MP.

Ackerson, Edward - 319th Escort Guard Co.

Adams, Corp. E.D. - 747th. On the staff of the Manzanar Sentry.

Anspaugh, Pvt. Theodore R. - 747th. On the staff of the Manzanar Sentry.

Archer, Capt. - 747th. Transferred to the 322nd.

Armstrong, Mess Sgt. W.F. - 747th. Former cavalry.

Ashworth, Major - In charge of Manzanar WCCA Internal Security Police up to June 1, 1942. Was not stationed at Manzanar but did visit.

Bean, Supply Sgt. W.E. - 747th. His wife, Helen, would join him in Owens Valley.

Becker, Pfc. Sam - 747th. Arrived from Poland at age 3.

Beckermeyer, Pvt. William - 747th. From Kinsey, Mo. Was in 140th Infantry.

Belluomini, Corp. R.V. - 747th.

Bogard, Lt. Eugene - Regular Army. Commanding Officer of registration of evacuees age 18 to 36 for the draft.

Bozovich, Pvt. Stanley Stanton - Editor in chief of the Manzanar Sentry.

Brafman, Pvt. John - 747th.

Buckner, Lt

Bugg, S/Sgt - 319th Escort Guard Co.

Burch, Lt. - Commanding Officer of the Manzanar military detachment, spring 1945.

Canfield, Wade - 319th Escort Guard Co.

Carruso, Gordon - 319th Escort Guard Co.

Cherubini, Pvt. Ramon - 322nd. On the night of the riot he fired into evacuee crowd.

Christensen, Calvin - 319th Escort Guard Co.

Dodd, Lt. Col. H.S. - 747th Headquarters Company, stationed at Santa Anita Race Track Assembly Center. Visited Manzanar in May 1942.

Demo, Russell - 319th Escort Guard Company

Durbin, Lt. C.L. - 747th. In charge of athletics, addressed Inyo County PTA on military discipline and courtesy.

Fackler, Capt. Ed, Jr. - In charge at time that 319th MP Guard Company was redesignated "Service Command Unit #1999" on April 26, 1944. Not all servicemen in SCU #1999 were MPs.

Farrington, Capt. Wayne - Replaced Capt. Martyn Hall as commander of MPs in May 1943.

Fox, Neil - 319th Escort Guard Co.

Fraser, Jim - 319th Escort Guard Co.

Gallagher, Pvt. - 747th. From Boston, Massachusetts.

Gardner, Pvt. H.J. - 747th.

Gassman, Corp. - 319th Escort Guard Co.

Gallardo, Cpl. - 319th Escort Guard Co. cook.

Goddard, Lt. R.J. - 747th.

Graham, Sgt.

Green, Maj. - Accompanied Col. Mueller from Fort Douglas to Manzanar in December 1942. Probable reason for visit to assess the MP's strength and competence following the riot.

Hall, Capt. Martyn L. - 322nd Commanding Officer (CO). Was CO during the riot.

Hash, 2nd Lt. - 319th Escort Guard Company.

Havilla, Pvt. Robert - 319th Escort Guard Company. Born Aug. 24, 1924 in San Francisco, Ca. Drafted into the army after graduation from high school. First reported to Fort Ord, Monterey, Ca. Completed six weeks basic training in Florence, Arizona. His first guard duty was at Manzanar. After a B 24 Liberator bomber overshot the Manzanar runway one night, he was assigned guard duty at the plane.

Henderson, Maj. - CO of a detachment of California State Guard, located in Bishop, which was called in to support the MPs during the riot. He and his unit were there briefly.

Horton, Pfc. William

Jones, Elmer - 319th Escort Guard Co.

Jones, Leon - 319th Escort Guard Co.

Kee, Capt. John Wesley - 747th. Arrived May 7, 1942 as a newly assigned officer of B Company.

Kiner, Claude Gale - 319th Escort Guard Company. At age 31 was killed by accidental gunshot on October 3, 1943 when he and another MP were practicing fast draw.

Knapp, Richard - 319th Escort Guard Co.

Kraft, Sgt. - 319th Escort Guard Co. He was regular army.

Krouse, Benjamin - 319th Escort Guard Co.

Kunkler, Lt. Ferdinand J. - 322nd. Officer at time of the riot, reporting to Capt. Hall.

Lemons, Wesley - 319th Escort Guard Co.

Macedo, Ernest - 319th Escort Guard Co.

Maggi, Joseph - 319th Escort Guard Co.

Mahoney, Lester - 319th Escort Guard Co.

Martin, Bernard - 319th Escort Guard Co.

Mayfield, Andrew - 747th. At age 22, on March 30, 1942, was shot and killed by another MP at Manzanar. It was reported as an accident, but racial prejudice is suspected.

McCullough, Raymond - 319th Escort Guard Co.

McCushion, Capt. - Mentioned in connection with the search and seizure from evacuees in spring 1942.

McLean, M - 319th Escort Guard Co.

Melzer, Capt. - 319th Escort Guard Company, Medical Officer.

Millen, Pvt. John - 747th.

Moore, Pvt. Tobe - 322nd. One of the MPs who fired into the rioters on December 6, 1942.

Mueller, Col. Harry S. - Arrived at Manzanar from Ninth Service Command at Fort Douglas on December 7, 1942, to take command following the riot the previous day.

Nail, Capt. Donald - CO of 319th Escort Guard Company which replaced 322nd MP Escort Company in June 1943. Relieved of command on February 7, 1944.

Nilsen, Amandus - 319th Escort Guard Co.

Osborn, Pvt. F.D. - 747th.

Otter, Robert - 319th Escort Guard Co.

Otto, Keith - 319th Escort Guard Co.

Payne, Pvt. Harry - 747th.

Peavey, 1st Sgt. Donald - 319th Escort Guard Company.

Peterson, Walter - 319th Escort Guard Co.

Phillips, Pvt. Edward - 747th. MP who shot an evacuee who strayed outside the Manzanar fence line. WRA project director Nash was told by the Manzanar MP Commanding Officer that Phillips would stand trial.

Receputo, Corp. - 747th. His wife Ann joined him from their home in Boston, Mass.

Reed, Sgt. George - 322nd. A sergeant who received burns from a gas tank explosion.

Repp, Pvt. George - 747th. Starred in movies.

Resta, Tony - 319th Escort Guard Co.

Richmond, First Sgt. Elbert - 747th. Born Jan. 1, 1896 in Hinton, W. Virginia. In WWI he served with the 57th Infantry stationed at Camp Logan, Texas.

Rios, Pvt. Julian - 747th.

Route, Medical Sgt. - 747th. From Wisconsin.

Ruggiero, Pvt. - 322nd. Was sentry at main gate at time of the riot on Dec. 6, 1942. He fired two volleys of three shots each into the air to call out the MPs.

Sayler, Edward - 319th Escort Guard Co.

Severson, Lt. Harvey - Commanding Officer of 747th Battalion of Military Police when it arrived on March 19, 1942, from Fort Ord, Monterey, California. Took part in investigation of MP who shot evacuee on May 16, 1942.

Schneider, Gordon - 319th Escort Guard Co.
Schwab, Allan - 319th Escort Guard Co.
Singer, 1st Lt. - 319th Escort Guard Company.
Smith, F.A. - 319th Escort Guard Co.
Smith, George - 319th Escort Guard Co.
Smith, Lt. Henry W. - 747th.
Smith, Pvt.
Thomas, Robert - 319th Escort Guard Co.
Tierman, Sgt Victor - Regular Army. Explained registration procedures to those evacuees age 18 to 36 eligible for the draft.
Urban, Sgt. J.A.
Walker, Robert - 319th Escort Guard Co.
Wallace, Larry - 319th Escort Guard Co.
Whitaker, Edward - 319th Escort Guard Co.
Williams, Pvt. J.R.
Zamora, Jesus - 319th Escort Guard Co.
Zwaik, 2nd Lt. Stanley N.

APPENDIX #7
MILITARY POLICE DATES AND
EVENTS OF INTEREST

The majority of the information on Military Police who served at Manzanar, was taken from the WRA files in the UCLA archive with the assistance of Dick Mansfield, docent for the National Park Service at Manzanar. This is in no way a complete list of events or personnel.

March 19, 1942 -
Escort Guard Company (company B) of the 747 Battalion of MPs arrives at Manzanar from Fort Ord, California two days before the arrival of the first evacuees. Lt. Harvey Severson, is their commanding officer. There are 135 men in total. Some of the states represented are Massachusetts, Missouri, Kansas, Tennessee, New Jersey, Illinois, Washington, Oregon, and California.

March 30, 1942 -
One of the MPs in the 747th shoots and kills another MP. The victim is Andrew Mayfield, a black man, age 22.

April 1, 1942 -
Construction starts on MP camp.

May 16, 1942 -
Hikoji Takeuchi is shot by pvt. Edward Phillips in the 747th using a shotgun with buckshot. Wounds are to the abdomen, arm, and hand. The injury is serious, but fortunately Takeuchi survives. Edward Phillips is reported bragging in a local town bar that he has shot a "Jap."

May 31, 1942 -
J.A. Strickland, Assist. Chief, Internal Security conducts investigation of the Manzanar MP for the Western Defense Command.

June 1, 1942 -

Internal security employees had been working for the army under Major Ashworth. Effective this date, the internal security staff become employees of the War Relocation Authority.

June 19, 1942 -

General DeWitt reports to Colonel Bendetson, "There seems to be a distinct attitude of camaraderie and brothership [sic] between the WRA camp management and the evacuees. In other words, there is an overly friendly attitude in the opinion of the MP officers on duty at Manzanar."

June 30, 1942 -

The 322nd MP Escort Guard Company, trained at San Luis Obispo, California, replaces the 747th with Capt. Martyn Hall as Commanding Officer and Capt. Archer and Lt. Buckner as assistants. Most of these men are from New York and New Jersey.

July 8, 1942 -

Sgt. George Reed of the 322nd suffers severe burns on his right arm and leg in a gas tank explosion in the military compound. He receives treatment at the Manzanar hospital staffed with WRA employees and Japanese-American evacuees.

Dec 6, 1942 -

The notorious Manzanar Riot breaks out. Capt. Hall testified in subsequent investigations that the weapons issued to the MP company that night include four light machine guns, two heavies, eight to nine shot guns, twenty-one Enfield rifles, and twenty-one Tommie guns. During the night following the riot, the 322nd is reinforced by fifty officers and men from a National Guard unit stationed in Bishop.

Dec. 7, 1942 -

National Guard troops from Bishop are withdrawn and replaced by members of A Company, 753rd MP Battalion (three officers and 104 men). Total MP complement is increased to 239 men and officers.

Dec. 31st, 1942 -

Reinforcement units are withdrawn leaving the 322nd as the sole MP unit at Manzanar. Total complement, 135 men and officers.

MP Russell Demo (top left) with fellow soldiers of the 319th EGC

June 1, 1943 -

322nd MP Escort is replaced by 319th Escort Guard under the command of Capt. Donald Nail. They had been performing guard duty at a nearby prisoner of war camp.

July 3, 1943 -

Capt. Nail issues instructions to all residents in the camp not to cross the fence for any purpose. All residents, staff, their families, and evacuees must enter and exit the camp through the gates, and they must have the approval of the MP sentry on duty.

Oct. 2, 1943 -

MP Claude Gale Kiner, age 31, is killed by accidental gunshot. He and another MP are playing fast draw when the accident occurs.

Dec. 11, 1943 -

MPs agree to withdraw sentries at west gate located above Block 12 and the hospital, thus permitting evacuee travel to and from the fenced camp to the cemetery without MP intervention. The gate is to be open from 9 a.m. to 5 p.m. All other hours it remains locked.

Dec. 25, 1943 -

Capt. Nail advises Ralph Merritt, Project Director, starting on this day security is to be significantly reduced as the MPs will no longer patrol the camp perimeter or man the gates and guard towers between 8 a.m. and 6 p.m. except for the rock sentry station at the main gate.

March 28, 1944 -

War Department submits to Western Defense Command for reduction of MPs at relocation centers. Manzanar is to have only two officers and one half of an MP Escort Guard Company—64 men.

April 17, 1944 -

Ninth Service Command implements changes proposed by the War Department.

April 20, 1944 -

MPs' inspection of incoming baggage and packages for contraband at the Manzanar Camp Post Office stops. 319th Escort Guard Company redesignated as Service Command Unit #1999. Commander before and after the redesignation is Capt. Ed Fackler, Jr.

May 11, 1944 -

Capt. Fackler deems sixty-four military personnel are insufficient to man the eight guard towers at any time. At the request of Project Director Ralph Merritt, Capt. Fackler agrees to keep the lights on at night in all eight guard towers. They do so to give the impression that the towers are actually manned in order to comfort the local townspeople.

Nov. 11, 1944 -

Ninth Service Command issues instructions to reduce military personnel at Manzanar to two officers and forty enlisted men. Total MP complement is now down to only 30% of the original 135 men. Service Command Unit #1999's newest designation becomes the Ninth Service Command Detachment.

Nov. 13, 1944 -

Ralph Merritt telegraphs Gen. Meyer that Capt. Fickler has requested the military be relieved of responsibility for the guard towers as the towers are no longer staffed, and that the WRA will remove all lights and windows from the towers to protect government property. Merritt further requests Gen. Meyer's approval to remove the towers. Not mentioned in the telegraph is that the evacuees had been throwing rocks at the towers and breaking out the windows.

Nov. 14, 1944 -

Gen. Meyers approves removing the lights and windows, but the towers are to remain in place.

Dec. 17, 1944 -

Western Defense Command issues Public Proclamation No. 21 lifting, with reservations, the exclusion of persons of Japanese ancestry from the West Coast, effective January 2, 1945. All persons of Japanese ancestry (with a "potential danger" exception) can return to the West Coast effective January 20, 1945. Later, the Western Defense Command will take a hard line, saying release of Japanese Americans from centers is within military review and no one can leave unless the army says so. MPs will be charged with enforcing the order.

November 1945 -

Last MP detachment leaves Manzanar.

ACKNOWLEDGEMENTS

I spent over ten years in the writing of this book before I recognized I needed a thorough edit—something much more than just checking for proper spelling, punctuation, and grammar. I found an editor in Terri Williams, who just happens to be my daughter. She had written two science books and was working on a third when I persuaded her to take on the edit of this book. She took my stories, research, and photos to condense, arrange, and rewrite for clarity. Throughout these major changes, she was able to convey the information as well as the flavor and spirit which I had originally set out to share. We both shared a very strong feeling that our first and utmost priority was that this book be as historically honest as we could make it. To meet this goal, she questioned, challenged, and checked my research for accuracy, which turned out to be extremely time consuming. She was the perfect person for this kind of detailed investigative research. Thank you, Terri, for devoting over two years of your life to this project. Also, thank you to my grandchildren, Kayla and Kris, for sharing their mother's valuable time with me. Bob Lowe graciously offered his time to give his input on the book as well. His eye for details and knowledge of grammatical structure were greatly appreciated.

It would have been impossible to write this book had it not been for War Relocation Authority staff and family members providing first hand experiences of life in WWII Manzanar. Their generosity in providing interviews, pictures, and profiles has been invaluable. Books like this cannot be written without the accumulation of information from countless sources. Joan (DaValle) Beyers and Shirley (DaValle) Meeder were treasures of information and help. John Oliver Atwood, LaPriel (Strong) Bush, Ann (Causey) Zahn, Fred Causey, Dr. Harold Dennis, Bud Gilkey, Don, Bruce, and David Inman, Pat Nail, Sue Nail Hansen, David Oille, Lynne (Hayes) Sutherland, and Thomas Williams, all WWII Manzanar children, Robert Stengel, Manzanar postal employee and Martha Schoaf, Manzanar teacher, recalled experiences and provided pictures. Pat Tortorello, Russell Demo, Robert Havilla, MPs at Manzanar, and Dick Mansfield, a docent for the NPS, made significant contributions to the Military Police section in the book. My most sincere gratitude goes to historian Richard Potashin whose vision it was to add this story about the WRA and its staff to those earlier books written about Japanese-American evacuees to provide readers with a broader view of Manzanar's camp life. His encouragement, support, and knowledge cannot be understated. Special thanks also go out to the Eastern California Museum. A very special thanks to Susanne LaFaver for clarifying the source, place, and time of the Christmas story, 1942, and for her support, to the Manzanar National Historic Site for providing me with a copy of Margaret d'Ille's biography and for the use of Frank Chuman's interview, and many WRA reports. To each and every one who has worked at Manzanar over the past twenty years for their support and help in providing material for this book on the WRA. A very special thank you.

Manzanar War Relocation Center and Mt. Williamson

PHOTO CREDITS

The individuals, groups, and organizations listed below have given the author their permission to use the photos included in this book. This courtesy is deeply appreciated.

Cover photo—Manzanar's front gate guard station with Mt. Williamson in the background taken by Arthur L. Williams

Ann (Causey) Zahn—p.8 (Town of Independence)

Ansel Adams Library of Congress Prints and Photographs Division—p.48 (interior improved tarpaper barrack), p.89 (evacuee created garden), p.104 (Manzanar camp 1943), p.126 (poultry farm), p.180 (Toyo Miyataki), p.187 (Bunkichi Hayashi)

Arthur L. Williams (author)—p.1 (site of Manzanar War Relocation Center), p.2 (California map), p.6 (author and his cousin at Manzanar farm), p.24 (Art Williams on fishing barge Kohala 1934 Redondo Beach), p.27 (gun tub Ventura River), p.32 (WWII war bonds), p.47 (unimproved tarpaper barrack), p.49 (typical block layout), p.52 (staff housing area layout), p.57 (D-5 site with rock wall), p.59 (Manzanar Auditorium), p.98 (heads of internal security), p.109 (mess hall pass), p.141 (diagram of riot scene), p.152 (Tule Lake I.D.), p.161 (inner and outer sentry posts), p.174 (relocated staff housing, Lone Pine), p.181 (NPS built guard tower), p.182 (obelisk at cemetery), p.185 (reunion and those that lived in camp), p.187 (tuna boat model), p.190 (Joan and Shirley DaValle), p.191 (Gordons and Dennises at reunion), p.193 (Martha Shoaf), p.194 (Jane Wehrey and Richard Potashin), p.195 (Eastern California Museum barbeque), p.195 (all attendees of reunion)

Arthur and Thomas Williams—p.112 (Nail and Williams kids), p.162 (MP escort)

Cecile (Miller) Gordon—p.192 (young Cecile Miller with parents)

Clem Albers, National Archives—p.46 (building barracks), p.156 (marching MP's), p.164 (MP helping child), p.165 (MP helping blind man)

County of Inyo, Eastern California Museum—p.5 (Manzanar Town Hall), p.38 (Owens Valley Coordinating Committee), p.56 (evacuee built staff housing), p.56 (project director's house), p.58 (WRA teachers and secretaries in snow), p.99 (Ralph Merritt), p.119 (staff bachelor quarters), p.170 (Zischank escorting evacuees)

Joan (DaValle) Beyers—p.122 (camp movie ticket), p.129 (gate pass)

Joan and Shirley DaValle—p.118 (Girls Club DaValles and Lynne Hayes), p.144 (Joan and Shirley DaValle, tarpaper barrack)

Julie Bruns—p.10 (town of Lone Pine)

National Park Service, Manzanar National Historic Site—title page (camp map layout). p.35 (war relocation centers), p.36.37 Assembly and Relocation Centers, p.54 (administration building), p.60 (construction crew), p.86 (hospital outhouses), p.120 (Manzanar in winter snow), p.125 (Bair's Creek), p.157 (off duty MP), p.158 (MP on duty look), p.166 (319 Escort Guard Company), p.245 (group of MPs by jeep)

The Toyo Miyataki Manzanar Collection—p.44 (Manzanar church services), p.51 (Children's Village), p.89 (WRA top management), p.94 (Manzanar Elementary School class), p.97 (hospital kitchen personnel), p. 101 Hooper, Brown, Adams and Throckmorton, p.102 (Dr. Goto), p.102 (Manzanar Hospital nurses), p. 102 Three doctors sitting, p.105 (Dr. Genevieve Carter), p.107 (Manzanar barracks, 1945), p.172 (dismantling barrack), p.250 (Manzanar camp and Mt. Williamson)

Warren McLeod—p.26 (Lockheed in peace time), p.26 (Lockheed under camo)

Photo source unknown—p.29 (WWII poster)

BIBLIOGRAPHY

BOOKS:

Baker, Lillian. *The Japanning of America: Redress & Reparations Demands by Japanese-Americans.* Medford, OR: Webb Research Group, 1991.

Bromley, David S. *These Bitter Years.* Batavia, NY: Verservice, 1945.

Chalfant, W. A. *The Story of Inyo.* [Los Angeles, California]: Chalfant, 1933.

Collins, Donald E. *Native American Aliens: Disloyalty and the Renunciation of Citizenship by Japanese Americans during World War II.* Westport, CT: Greenwood, 1985.

Conrat, Maisie. *Executive Order 9066: The Interment of 110,000 Japanese Americans.* [S.l.]: Univ Of California La, 1992.

Daniels, Roger, and Eric Foner. *Prisoners without Trial: Japanese Americans in World War II.* New York: Hill and Wang, 1993.

Daniels, Roger. *The Politics of Prejudice: The Anti-Japanese Movement in California and the Struggle for Japanese Exclusion.* Berkeley: University of California, 1977.

Eisenhower, Milton Stover. *The President Is Calling.* Garden City, NY: Doubleday, 1974.

Fukuyama, Yoshio, Helen Yamamoto, and Mary Johnston. *Citizens Apart: A History of the Japanese in Ventura County.* [Ventura, Calif.]: Ventura County Historical Society, 1994.

Garrett, Jessie A., and Ronald C. Larson. *Camp and Community: Manzanar and the Owens Valley.* Fullerton: California State University, Japanese American Oral History Project, 1977.

Hersey, John, Ansel Adams, and John Armor. *Manzanar.* [New York]: Times, 1988.

Houston, Jeanne Wakatsuki., and James D. Houston. *Farewell to Manzanar.* Austin: Holt, Rinehart and Winston, 2000.

Inyo County, California, Anno Domini, *1912: Beautiful Owens Valley.* [Bishop, Calif.]: Bishop Chamber of Commerce in Cooperation with Chalfant, 1983.

Irwin, Sue. *California's Eastern Sierra: A Visitor's Guide.* Los Olivos, CA: Cachuma, 1991.

Konigsmark, Ted. *Geologic Trips Sierra Nevada.* Gualala, CA: GeoPress, 2002.

Krammer, Arnold. *Undue Process: The Untold Story of America's German Alien Internees.* London: Rowman & Littlefield, 1997.

Lange, Dorothea, Linda Gordon, and Gary Y. Okihiro. *Impounded: Dorothea Lange and the Censored Images of Japanese American Internment.* New York: W.W. Norton, 2006.

Lindquist, Heather C. *Children of Manzanar.* Berkeley, CA: Heyday, 2012.

Lowman, David D. *Magic: The Untold Story of U.S. Intelligence and the Evacuation of Japanese Residents from the West Coast during WW II.* [Utah]: Athena, 2001.

Lowman, David D. *The Mother Lode.* Los Angeles, CA: Automobile Club of Southern California, 1979.

Napolitano, Andrew P. *Lies the Government Told You: Myth, Power, and Deception in American History.* Nashville: Thomas Nelson, 2010.

—*Personal Justice Denied: Report of the Commission on Wartime Relocation and Internment of Civilians.* Washington, D.C.: Commission, 1983.

Pryor, Alton. *Historic California: Its Colorful Names and How It Got Them.* Roseville, CA.: Stagecoach Pub., 2002.

—*Reflections in Three Self-guided Tours of Manzanar.* [Los Angeles, Calif.]: Manzanar Committee, 1998.

Shirley, Craig. *December 1941: 31 Days That Changed America and Saved the World.* Nashville, TN: Thomas Nelson, 2011.

Sowaal, Marguerite. *Naming the Eastern Sierra: Dirty Sock to Bloody Canyon.* Bishop, CA: Chalfant, 1985.

Unrau, Harlan D. *Manzanar National Historic Site, California: The Evacuation and Relocation of Persons of Japanese Ancestry during World War II : A Historical Study of the Manzanar War Relocation Center.* [Denver, Colo.?]: U.S. Dept. of the Interior, National Park Service, 1996.

Wehrey, Jane. *Manzanar.* Charleston, SC: Arcadia Pub., 2008.

—*Voices from This Long Brown Land: Oral Recollections of Owens Valley Lives and Manzanar Pasts.* New York: Palgrave Macmillan, 2006.

LIBRARIES AND MUSEUMS:

Dwight D. Eisenhower Library and Museum
Franklin D. Roosevelt Library
FDR-53, April 1943
Library of Congress
National Archive
The Virtual Museum of the City of San Francisco
Final Report: Japanese Evacuation from the West Coast 1942
County of Inyo, Eastern California Museum

MAGAZINES:

Reader's Digest, March 1943
World War II, May 1997

NEWSPAPERS:

Inyo Independent. October 13, 1877, March 6, 20, 1942, January 1, 1943, May 20, 2004
Los Angeles Times.
    "A Life Long Lesson in Justice" by Teresa Watanabe.
    "Harry Ueno, 97, Hero to Japanese Americans in Internment Camps" by Myrna Oliver.

FBI REPORTS:

Nanka Tei Koku Gunyu-Dan, Declassified by 9145-CI-JC
Lt. Commander Itaru Tachibana, Declassified 9145-CI-JC

WAR RELOCATION CENTER REPORTS:

Documentary Reports No. 22 thru 33 June and July 1942.
War Relocation Center Final Reports
    Finance Section- R.C. Boczkiewicz September, 1942 - March, 1946
    Supply Section-Edwin H. Hooper, June, 1942 - March, 1946
    Maintenance and Construction Section - Arthur
    M. Sandridge and Oliver E. Sisler
        October 12, 1942 - February 15, 1946

Project Directors Report-Robert L. Brown and Ralph
P. Merritt, March 15, 1942 - February, 1946
War Relocation Community Analysis Report - January 28, 1944
Manzanar War Relocation Files - UCLA Archive, Military Police
Final Report: Japanese Evacuation from the West Coast 1942
General Management Plan, August, 1996

INTERVIEWS:

The following persons provided material for this book that was either acquired
through interviews taken from the Manzanar National Historic Site, The University
of California at Fullerton, or by the author:

William Adams, Dr. William Asano, John Atwood, Joan (DaValle) Beyers, Julie
Brun, LaPriel (Strong) Bush, Ned Campbell, Fred Causey, Kevan Collins, Richard
Collins, Diana Bush Deluca, Dr. Harold Dennis, Robert "Bud" Gilkey, Cecile
(Miller) Gordon, Art Hansen and the Manzanar Exhibit Staff, Dr. William Hart,
Robert Havilla, Jack Hunter, Don Inman, Wayne Lawing, Alisa Lynch, Richard
Mansfield, Rose Masters, Mildred (Berriman) McCallister, Charles McConica,
Shirley (DaValle) Meeder, Allan Miyatake, Archie Miyatake, Pat Carle Nail, David
Ollie, Kirk Peterson, Beth (Sennett) Porter, Richard Potashin, Art Sakioka, Martha
Lee Shoaf, Elaine (Clary) Stanley, Robert Stengel, Lynne (Hayes) Sutherland,
Miyoko Tabata, Henry Shozo Umemoto, Jane Wehrey, Thomas Dana Williams,
and Ann (Causey) Zahn.

CPSIA information can be obtained at www.ICGtesting.com
Printed in the USA
BVOW05s1436100514

352936BV00002B/8/P